Skepticism and Fallibilism

Skepticism and Fallibilism

JONATHAN L. KVANVIG

Great Clarendon Street, Oxford, OX2 6DP,
United Kingdom

Oxford University Press is a department of the University of Oxford.
It furthers the University's objective of excellence in research, scholarship,
and education by publishing worldwide. Oxford is a registered trade mark of
Oxford University Press in the UK and in certain other countries

© Jonathan L. Kvanvig 2025

The moral rights of the author have been asserted

All rights reserved. No part of this publication may be reproduced, stored in a retrieval system,
transmitted, used for text and data mining, or used for training artificial intelligence, in any form or
by any means, without the prior permission in writing of Oxford University Press, or as expressly
permitted by law, by licence or under terms agreed with the appropriate reprographics rights organization.
Enquiries concerning reproduction outside the scope of the above should be sent
to the Rights Department, Oxford University Press, at the address above

You must not circulate this work in any other form
and you must impose this same condition on any acquirer

Published in the United States of America by Oxford University Press
198 Madison Avenue, New York, NY 10016, United States of America

British Library Cataloguing in Publication Data

Data available

Library of Congress Control Number: 2024947191

ISBN 9780198924791

DOI: 10.1093/9780198924821.001.0001

Printed and bound by
CPI Group (UK) Ltd, Croydon, CR0 4YY

Links to third party websites are provided by Oxford in good faith and
for information only. Oxford disclaims any responsibility for the materials
contained in any third party website referenced in this work.

The manufacturer's authorised representative in the EU for product safety is Oxford University
Press España S.A. of el Parque Empresarial San Fernando de Henares, Avenida de Castilla, 2 –
28830 Madrid (www.oup.es/en).

Contents

1. Introduction	1
1.1 The Project	1
1.2 A Preview in Outline	7
2. Skepticism and the Commonsense Tradition	11
2.1 The Skeptical Task	11
2.2 Pragmatism and The Problem of Paralysis	14
2.3 Commonsense Epistemology and Its Implications	22
2.4 Alethic and Epistemic Stories	27
2.5 Conclusion	41
3. Versions of Fallibilism	43
3.1 Introduction	43
3.2 Generic Fallibilism	45
3.3 Fallibilism's Central Issue	48
3.4 Sensitive and Complacent Fallibilisms	52
3.4.1 Alternatives to the Standard Account and Their Weaknesses	60
3.4.2 Infelicity and Varieties of Complacency	69
3.5 A Way Forward	78
3.6 Conclusion	84
4. Infallibilism and Idealizations about Knowledge	86
4.1 Introduction	86
4.2 Skepticism and High Standards for Knowledge	86
4.3 Acceptable Idealizations	96
4.4 Logic and Reasoning	104
4.5 Why An Appeal To Determinism Must Fail	109
5. Infallibility Through Non-Demonstrative Reasoning	113
5.1 Introduction	113
5.2 Beginning Assumptions	114
5.3 Basic Elements	127
5.4 Beyond Simple Beginnings	131
5.5 From Fallible to Infallible	138
5.6 Conclusion	142
6. Close Approximations	144
6.1 Introduction	144
6.2 A Positive Account	149

vi CONTENTS

6.3 On the Relation to Assumptionalism		163
6.4 Conclusion		166
7. Conclusion		168
7.1 Introduction		168
7.2 Sensitive Fallibilism, Virtue Epistemology, and Living Well		169
7.3 Summing Up		174
Bibliography		177
Index		185

Chapter 1
Introduction

1.1 The Project

There are two common responses to skepticism, the epistemological claim that knowledge is at least non-existent and perhaps also unachievable, and both are to be avoided. So I argue here. The first response is to succumb to it, trying then to find some adequate basis for life that foregoes presumptions of knowledge. The second response is dismissive, viewing it as an overwrought, hyperbolic response to human limitations, so wrongheaded that nothing beyond a laconic response is needed before returning to important philosophical tasks.

Here I will contend that the first response is much too often premature, and the second response is much too often cavalier. The path toward skepticism begins with bare argumentation for a skeptical conclusion, but, as the role of role of antinomies in the history of philosophy shows, the proper response to such argumentation is theory development, not full and immediate endorsement of the conclusion. As I will argue, there is a burden of theory development that is needed before embracing such a skeptical position. Equally problematic, though, is dismissive hand-waving, of the sort most often associated with the common sense tradition tracing to G.E. Moore (as well as the much earlier version of it in Thomas Reid), viewing consideration of the position being argued for as something not worthy of serious attention. While there may be some truth to the idea that philosophical reflection in general, and epistemological reflection in particular, are optional aspects of the good life, once such reflection begins, the things worth attending to range from the ones to be taken most seriously and the ones deserving short shrift. Attitudes differ as to what falls into each of these categories, and when disagreement arises about where a given claim or position falls, such disagreement gives grounds for meta-reflection on how and where to start the relevant reflective project. My own stance on epistemology worth doing gives short shrift to ideas such as the universal embracing of contradictions as well as the nihilistic idea that there is no such thing as truth. Others may view things differently, and investigating such disagreements would lead to a project of its own. For this project, however, I start from the assumption that it is a mistake to look at skepticism and the arguments for it in a way similar to my own attitude toward nihilism about truth.

Such an attitude presumes, however, that development of a skeptical position beyond bare argument and conclusion can occur, for if skepticism is nothing more

Skepticism and Fallibilism. Jonathan L. Kvanvig, Oxford University Press. © Jonathan L. Kvanvig (2025).
DOI: 10.1093/9780198924821.003.0001

2 INTRODUCTION

than a bare argument for a skeptical conclusion, it supports simple and superficial efforts to tinker with the premises so as to reveal why they might seem true even though false. Once viewed in this way, skepticism is not really so much a serious epistemological position as it is a piece of misleading data to be explained away. The process involved can simply be that of Rawlsian reflective equilibrium,[1] or Chisholmian particularism,[2] or some alternative methodology, but the goal is simply that of finding the right way to dismiss the view.

It will take some effort to substantiate this approach, for it is easy to think that that the standing of skepticism has already been established by the quality of the arguments developed by skeptics throughout the history of epistemology. It is true that impressive argumentation is a good benchmark of serious philosophy, for speculation undisciplined by the demands of reason might be fine for conversations over happy hour but not in one of the central disciplines of any decent institution of higher learning. Yet, serious argumentation by itself isn't all that is needed. One of the lessons of Chisholm's problem of the criterion, Moore's defense of common sense epistemology, and Rawls's method of reflective equilibrium is that much of our theorizing requires compromises between competing ideas that are somewhat attractive initially. One can characterize this phenomenon in terms of competing intuitions, but since I'm not quite sure what an intuition is or why we'd want to rely on them, I'll talk instead in terms of thoughts or ideas and how obvious they strike us. In such terms, a Moorean defense of common sense counsels to never give up the more obvious for the less obvious, and so in the face of skeptical argumentation against common sense affirmations of knowledge, we should always ask whether the premises of the argument are as obvious as, or more obvious than, the claim that we know many things. Serious argumentation may prompt adjustments for purposes of reflective equilibrium, but when we begin to ask about the status of a philosophical position, we need something beyond a list of arguments given against those who disagree. We need a positive account and explanation of the position itself.

The point of view from which this study begins, then, is that of distinguishing these two aspects of skeptical opposition to the presuppositions of common sense. Skeptics achieve notoriety by claiming that human knowledge isn't available and by giving arguments in support of this claim. Those who disagree can be divided into the camp of those who insist that skeptical standards can be met and those who claim that skeptical standards are overwrought. Both responses assume that there is a clear idea of how these standards can be properly characterized, but that is the point at which our scrutiny of skepticism begins. For it is easy to be overly optimistic here. What we seek is a positive account and explanation of skepticism and its standards for knowledge. Simply claiming that if you know you can't be

---

[1] See Rawls (1971).
[2] See Chisholm (1977).

wrong, or that real knowledge is infallible or incorrigible or metaphysically certain, is not explanation enough. As we will see, there are trivial ways to endorse the slogan, and ways to imitate the skeptical demand for infallibility. To show that these responses don't understand what is required for knowledge, elaboration and clarification of the skeptical standard is required.

As we will see, providing the details threatens incoherence at the heart of the skeptical position. For, once we investigate carefully the skeptical standard, we will encounter difficulties. These difficulties pose a significant challenge to skepticism, for if the high standards for knowledge that skepticism proposes can't be articulated adequately, there is no skeptical position deserving of serious consideration in a complete epistemology.

These difficulties coalesce around the topic of knowing the future, and a large part of the initial task concerns explaining why this is so. Once the problem is clearly seen, we'll also see why the threat of incoherence is real and deep. Hence, the next task will be to show that the threat can be met, and that in doing so, we find the kind of theory development on the part of skepticism that clearly makes it a serious option among the leading competitors regarding the nature and scope of knowledge.

The conclusion of this part of our study will thus be that skepticism is a serious enough position that simple appeals to Moorean methodology aren't enough by way of response. Instead, I will argue for two central claims. The first is that skepticism matters—that it is important, that it is significant. The significance of skepticism, however, doesn't arise just by looking at skeptical arguments and conclusions, but instead because it is possible to develop a skeptical theory and position that make it a serious option among competing epistemologies. By analogy, foundationalism is a serious option among competing epistemologies, not because of the regress argument for it, but rather because of further efforts prompted by that argument to clarify what it is for there to be a stopping point when it comes to the giving of reasons, a stopping point that is itself warranted, but not on the basis of further reasoning or argumentation. These efforts amount to theory development, and the position that deserves to be taken seriously arises in the process of such theory development. Something similar needs to occur for skepticism, where its significance arises in the process of theory development, yielding a position deserving of the our attention in a way similar to that of foundationalism.

In the face of the theory development we will find, we can then turn to the task of what an alternative to skepticism looks like. It will have to be a version of fallibilism, for the idea of endorsing infallibilism while trying to avoid skepticism isn't going to work.

Fallibilism comes in many varieties, and here I'll begin with a distinction between complacent and sensitive versions of the view. The complacency or sensitivity I speak of adverts to skepticism and the prospects for development of a

4   INTRODUCTION

skeptical theory of knowledge. If that project were to fail, complacency in the face of skeptical argumentation would be all that is needed. Given the development already described, however, a sensitive version of fallibilism will be needed.

So, while I will be arguing that a dismissive view of skepticism is defensible in the absence of theory development on the part of skepticism, complacency isn't adequate once we see how skeptical theory development can proceed. Once so developed, I join forces with those who take skepticism to be significant, but not with any of the typical explanations of it. To be specific, I will argue that skepticism isn't significant because it is true or likely to be true or anything along those lines, but rather in spite of, and at least partly because of, its falsity.

In addition, I will argue that the significance of skepticism is not a matter of the way in which it buttresses epistemic *angst*, though that response is widespread.[3] Instead, I'll argue for the view that skepticism is important even if, and because, it is probably false, in a way that provides a sobering, realistic, and hopeful approach to the life of the mind.

The task, then, will be to develop a version of sensitive fallibilism with these benefits. The benefit of the view I'll develop arises in virtue of the skeptical account of cognitive ideality and the role such ideality plays as a ground of intellectual humility. Moreover, this virtue and this grounding for it is not something to lament or regret, but rather something to embrace, as one aspect of what is needed or useful for a well-lived life. Skepticism is to be warmly embraced as a result, not dolefully acknowledged as a cause for anxiety, apprehension, or disquietude. It provides, instead, a kind of important reassurance about what it takes to live well, for it grounds one of the central virtues of life.

This position links epistemology with more general normative concerns, but without endorsing any pragmatism that would make practical considerations part of the nature of knowledge or a constraint on what truths we should be concerned about from a purely intellectual point of view. On these points, I remain committed to intellectualist and purist positions.[4] But it would be remarkable indeed for epistemic normativity to bear no connection to normativity conceived more broadly, and here I'll argue both for a purely epistemic significance for skepticism, but also for the link just noted to broader normative concerns.

Once we see this position clearly, it is tempting to view the concern about some purported groundlessness of our beliefs as doubly overwrought. First, there is a lot of space between having everything you want and having nothing at all, and this talk of groundless belief might be the epistemic version of a false dichotomy

---

[3] A recent expression of this view is Pritchard (2015), echoing a Wittgensteinian theme concerning the ultimate groundlessness of our beliefs. These ideas can be gleaned from Wittgenstein (1969), though caution is needed when attributing a view to an anti-theory philosopher.

[4] For intellectualism, the view that all truths are significant from a purely intellectual or theoretical point of view, see Kvanvig (2008), and for the purist position that resists pragmatic encroachment into the nature of knowledge, see Kvanvig (2011a).

of these endpoints. We might not get the grounding we want for our beliefs, but maybe what we get shouldn't be thought of in such dire terms, either. Second, there may be a kind of intellectual pride or arrogance revealed by the negative attitudes suffered at the prospect raised by a developed skeptical position. After all, if you can't run a mile in under four minutes, you are not likely to suffer shame or distress because of that limitation. So why some deep anxiety about having intellectual accomplishments that are not of the highest quality? Aspirations are, in general, good things, perhaps, but they can also reveal a sense of self that is, we might say, inflationary. I like to cycle fast for long distances, but I experience no negativity about not being able to compete in the Tour de France. So when we find an account of what the highest quality knowledge looks like and we notice that what we achieve isn't at that level, we can lament our limitations or acknowledge them. The latter can be an expression of intellectual humility while the former can be an expression of pride.

Suppose, though, that one's character were freed from such arrogance. One might still lack the virtue of humility, intellectual or otherwise, but one could see in the skeptical account a call for humility that need not and does not depress. Any successful craftsman knows this sensation, the sensation one experiences on finally seeing what skills need to be developed in order to make or create something of the highest quality, and part of this sensation involves a realization of where the limits are concerning what can be accomplished. The result can be renewed vigor for trying, and the same can be true for the bigger project of living well after seeing the significance of philosophical skepticism. Pretense about the quality of our accomplishments diminishes as a result, and the arrogance of aiming for complete God-like control over the attempt to find the truth is replaced with a humble acknowledgment that our best intellectual achievements are far from our own doing and pale shadows of what the skeptic says we need.

It needs also to be point out that humility, intellectual and otherwise, has its downside, for all virtues, considered in themselves, can lead to poor outcomes. That is the point of the idea of virtues in excess.[5] It is also the attraction of the idea of the unity of the virtues. Exaggerated ideas here claim that you can't have one of the virtues without having them all, but that claim overreaches. More circumspectly, there is the matter of balance to needs attending to, for virtues can often be associated with appropriately counterbalancing virtues, and the limit of this identification might be that the perfect combination of weights and balances requires the presence of all of the virtues. The point to focus on here, though, is about what might be needed as a balancing virtue when the concern is that too much intellectual humility leads to giving up. I've addressed this issue in Kvanvig (2018), where I argue that ordinary, mundane faith is what is needed, where faith is understood in terms of allegiance to a goal. In our context, it is the antidote to

---

[5] The best discussion I've seen on this point is Watson (1984).

6 INTRODUCTION

intellectual humility in excess, for if there is anything worth committing to from a purely intellectual point of view, it is to the project of finding the truth and figuring out which truths are the most important ones.

So the remedy for the problem of too much humility isn't to foster more self-confidence or to aim for unwarranted arrogance. Heaven knows we've seen enough false bravado to not need to see more of it when it comes to the question of what we know and what we don't know. Rather, the story about the appropriate counterbalance for too much intellectual humility is one with an outward, rather than inward, focus. It is a question of what, intellectually speaking, is worth seeking and where to devote ourselves, answered from a purely intellectual point of view. Finding such a focus for a life is another part of living well, but something to mention in passing here, because our concern is not so much to counterbalance some possible downside for seeing the significance of skepticism, but rather to understand that significance and to reveal how it arises. Thus, I return to the point that the significance of skepticism is primarily a matter of pointing us to what intellectual life can be like.

This significance doesn't require that the skeptic be right about what knowledge involves, though if the skeptic is correct, that is a clarion call for less arrogance and more humility. Yet, we need not concern ourselves with the question of whether the skeptic is correct unless the skeptic can articulate what the high standards are that are claimed to be needed for the great intellectual accomplishments of knowledge, understanding, and theoretical wisdom. So, from the present perspective, it would be a loss to discover that no such articulation could be found, for the centering role that skepticism plays in a perspective on intellectual life would be lost and the natural human tendency toward pride and arrogance can flourish. Perhaps we can see such in facile dismissals of skepticism throughout much of the twentieth century.

I note as well a qualification about focusing this problem on knowledge. I have argued for a couple of decades that knowledge isn't as important as the history of epistemology makes it out to be, and it is easy to imagine skeptical arguments and stances that would apply to whatever else is proposed to replace knowledge. We can think of this adaptability in structural terms by dividing epistemological axiology into its normative and evaluative parts. Among the normative items are properties such as justification, rationality, warrant, reliability, etc., and among the evaluative elements are the great epistemic goods of true belief, knowledge, understanding, and theoretical wisdom. It is in the evaluative domain that we typically find the items claimed to be the target or goal of inquiry, though the later Chisholm proposed making reasonability itself the goal.[6] To simplify discussion, I assume here with typical versions of skepticism that knowledge is the goal, target, *summum bonum*, or essential component of it or of any path to it. If this assumption is

---

[6] See Chisholm (1989).

mistaken, as I have maintained, the discussion would need to be transposed into a new context that first identifies the goal of inquiry and what the greatest epistemic goods are, and then addresses skeptical stances with respect to these great goods that don't involve knowledge. As I see things, the same issues that arise in the traditional target where the possibility of knowledge is under attack would also arise in any re-ordering of epistemological axiology, so clothing the discussion in traditional garb won't mislead and makes discussion simpler because of familiarity.

The project here, thus, comprises two stages. The first stage takes aim at the issue of the significance of skepticism. I argue that skepticism is significant, but for reasons quite different from typical accounts, which find the significance of skepticism in the truth of the position or in the quality of arguments for it. These approaches are inadequate, and the proper approach to the issue requires careful articulation of a skeptical position that goes beyond bare thesis and argument for it. I show how to articulate such a position, one that is substantive enough to support the conclusion that facile dismissal is not an option. This position thus rejected I'll identify as complacent fallibilism, a position involving a deeply problematic intellectual arrogance that is counterproductive for a well-lived intellectual life. Hence, much of our efforts will involve developing the skeptical point of view, beyond that of any simple argument for a skeptical conclusion.

The second stage then turns to the question of what to make of this point of view, and whether what we take to be our best intellectual efforts are nothing more than, as Qoheleth would have it, a chasing after the wind. That's the pessimistic, negative response I'm resisting here, for there may be something to the idea that something less than ideal is still worth having and striving for, while at the same time and in the very process of striving, we cultivate a sense of our limitations. People like that highlight the importance of intellectual humility and of openmindedness, and that kind of integration of attitude and purpose is something to be cherished rather than lamented for not giving us everything we might have initially wanted. The result, then, is an account of the significance of skepticism that does not rely on it being true, nor does it arise in virtue of the quality of argumentation for the view. Instead, it is important both in spite of being false and partially because it is false, for intellectual virtue depends on it.

1.2 A Preview in Outline

The explanation and defense for this thesis is developed across six chapters. We begin from the standpoint of twentieth-century epistemology in the Moorean and commonsense tradition in Chapter 2, noting its threat to the value of skepticism. This history is widely known, culminating in dismissive attitudes toward skepticism that were quite common by the middle part of the twentieth century,

8 INTRODUCTION

especially among ordinary language philosophers. There is a sense in which such dismissiveness toward everything in philosophy was common, supported as it was by the anti-theory quietism of the later Wittgenstein, but my own sense of this history is that the spirit of the age was more contemptuous of skepticism because it requires rejecting so much of ordinary thought and talk. Against the backdrop of this decided lack of sympathy for skepticism, I turn in Chapter 3 to other threats to the value of skepticism that don't rest on anti-theory quietism and appeals to ordinary language, with the goal of explaining how and why we should not rest content with a negative conclusion about the value of skepticism. Reaching this conclusion, though, puts pressure on skepticism, for the backdrop of twentieth-century epistemology places strong demands on skepticism in terms of theory development in order to sustain any account of its significance.

The result of these chapters, then, is to motivate a more careful look at skepticism and, presuming that we can find the kind of theory development required for skepticism, fallibilist contrasts to it. For the latter, I begin by distinguishing between complacent and sensitive versions of the view, and the way in which these different versions of fallibilism involve different responses to the challenge presented to fallibilism from the idea that knowing seems to rule out the possibility of error.

Once this point about apparent infallibility arises, we need a careful account of the idea of infallibility, and that is the task of Chapter 5. It turns out that infallibility is not easy to characterize, but once we make some progress on that issue, we are in a position to begin theory development on behalf of skepticism. I will argue against the idea the infallibility is a logical notion, one to be understood in terms of entailment relations. Instead, I'll defend the idea that infallibility is best understand as a modal notion, one having to do with power and control over the possibility of being mistaken. As we will see, some opacity concerning the notion will still remain, but we will have a clear enough picture of what infallibility involves for use in skeptical theory development.

Such development involves tying this notion of infallibility to the idea of cognitive ideality that skeptics insist on for knowledge, and the proposal I defend maintains that the best way to do so is by appeal to finite extension of ordinary cognitive abilities. In defending this approach, I will compare it to other possibilities, many of which are patently absurd. One such account would be to claim that cognition is ideal when it is God-like, and though that would clearly be ideal cognition, it would be absurd to think that skepticism involves an insistence that knowledge is only present for divine cognizers. Instead, the idea is to focus on (finite) extensions of ordinary capacities to clarify the kind of ideality in question, thereby developing a skeptical account that trades on the gap between our actual capacities and practices and what they would be like if ideal, all the while insisting that we achieve the epistemic *summum bonum* only when our search for the truth couldn't be done any better. Once we have decent characterizations of these extensions, we will have the kind of theoretical development that yields some plausibility to the idea that idealizations involving the elimination of the possibility of error are possible, with one major exception. For among our ordinary cognitive capacities used in the search for truth is ordinary, defeasible reasoning, and idealizing this capacity in terms of the idealization so characterized appears impossible.

It might be tempting to see such apparent impossibility in terms of some confirmation for skepticism, but, I will argue, that would be a confusion. It points, instead, to a debilitating defect for the position if the apparent is real, since the problem arises in the process of trying to say what kind of ideal cognition is being demanded. By way of analogy, consider the regress argument for foundationalism, which attempts to show that there has to be a normatively adequate stopping point for the giving of reasons. The next step is to articulate what might count as a normatively adequate stopping point, and foundationalism has no prospects if we come to the conclusion that such an idea is simply impossible. The apparent impossibility of giving a complete and thorough account of cognitive ideality is exactly of this sort. That is, if the impossibility is real, it shows that theory development of the required sort can't be given. Far from counting in favor of skepticism, it would undermine it. All that would be left is bare argument and conclusion, of precisely the sort that would warrant easy dismissal by appeal to Rawlsian reflective equilibrium or Chisholmian particularism. Thus, instead of counting in favor of a skeptical theory of knowledge, such a result would show that there is no adequate skeptical theory to consider, but instead only a challenge raised by a conflict between pre-theoretical ideas about knowledge that are in conflict. For skepticism to matter, something more is going to be needed.

That is the task of Chapter 6, to show that the appearance in question is deceiving. So, in Chapter 6, I show how to characterize ideality with respect to defeasible reasoning in a way that makes infallibility in this domain reachable through finite extensions of ordinary reasoning capacities and practices. This result is quite surprising, but its success is crucial for the defense undertaken here of the significance of skepticism. Instead of being no more than bare argument and conclusion, theory development will have been done and the resulting position one that competes well with more optimistic epistemologies.

Given such theory development, our focus shifts to the possibility of resisting it. Because of the theory development achieved, there is a fairly compelling argument that no version of fallibilism can be successful if it is a complacent one. So the task is to see if a version of sensitive fallibilism can be found. That is the task of Chapter 7, and in this final substantive chapter, I characterize a view I call "Approximationism" as the right kind of sensitive fallibilism for both resisting skepticism but also incorporating its value.

There are too many people who have been invaluable in this process to mention, but I want to acknowledge the most important ones, even at the risk of unwarranted omission. At the top of my list are my heroes in epistemology, from G.E. Moore in the early twentieth century, to Roderick Chisholm, Keith Lehrer, and John Pollock in the middle part of that century. Equally noteworthy is my intellectual debt and gratitude to Richard Foley and Peter Markie, both mentors *par excellence*, who first introduced to me the central figures noted. In addition, there is a long list of friends and colleagues that have contributed to this project that were in audiences at which this material was presented, beginning with those at Washington University in St Louis for my job talk in 2014, to those who patiently listened to another Presidential Address at the Central States meeting in 2017, as well as those at the Saint Louis graduate conference that same year, followed by a talk at the same university the following year as well as one at the University of Missouri–St Louis, and most recently at the Rutgers Epistemology Conference in 2019. Covid put an end to such high points in my life, but left in place my gratitude for all the help I received from those in attendance at these events. Because I first began the project in my last couple of years at Baylor and worked through the details after moving to Washington University in St Louis, I also thank both institutions and their administrators for their support of my work on this project.

Chapter 2
Skepticism and the Commonsense Tradition

2.1 The Skeptical Task

Sober judgment, founded on conversations with the skeptic in the history of epistemology, affirms that the capacity for error is inescapable. Skepticism arises from this recognition, with the skeptic pressing the point that this capacity for error is our epistemic undoing. Given the assumption that knowledge is the epistemic *summum bonum* or necessary for it, the idea is that knowledge itself is somehow undermined by this feature of our cognitive condition.

At the same time as we all stand convinced of our capacity for error, we also recognize the point of the assumption that knowledge matters. Perhaps we view knowledge as the norm of assertion (don't say what you don't know to be true); perhaps we think that the right premises for practical reasoning are things one knows to be true; and perhaps the acquisition of knowledge is what legitimates closure of inquiry.

Yet, if the skeptic is right, knowledge can't fulfill these roles concerning assertion, inquiry, and practical reasoning. As a result, resistance to skepticism is to be expected, and approaches to skepticism over the past century and a half give examples of ways to resist, culminating in a stance in the middle of the twentieth century that found little of interest in the skeptical project beyond figuring out where it goes wrong. In this chapter, we begin with some stage-setting, as to how one gets to that point, focusing on the burden this history places on skepticism and how the burden might be lifted.

A first way of trying to place the skeptical project in a difficult position is pragmatist in character and begins in the nineteenth century. Such resistance to skepticism points out that we need some epistemic notions and norms to guide belief and action, and if the achievement of knowledge is beyond our reach, then we should find something else that is more useful. Such an approach can be traced to the pragmatist tradition of C.S. Peirce[1] and aspects of it can be found in later pragmatist thinkers, including W.V.O. Quine.[2] Perhaps what matters is justification, or rationality, or warrant, or some other normative notion, instead of knowledge.

---

[1] See, for example, Peirce (1877), Peirce (1878), Peirce (1905), and Peirce (1907).
[2] As developed in Quine (1951), Quine (1960), and Quine (1969).

Skepticism and Fallibilism. Jonathan L. Kvanvig, Oxford University Press. © Jonathan L. Kvanvig (2025).
DOI: 10.1093/9780198924821.003.0002

12 SKEPTICISM AND THE COMMONSENSE TRADITION

This response thus has the somewhat amusing implication that skepticism isn't really that important precisely because it is *true*. The central, guiding idea of this response to skepticism is that, though we might initially have thought that knowledge is what matters and what we seek, once skeptics have their say, we can now see that it isn't what matters and shouldn't be what we seek. So let's turn our misguided attention away from what the skeptic shows we can't get, and focus on what really matters from a purely intellectual point of view: so this response goes.

Such a response is useful only to the extent that the skeptical challenge doesn't eliminate positive normative status as well as knowledge, and skeptics have often argued that the capacity for error not only undermines knowledge but also any purely cognitive preference for a claim over its negation. Against such a generalized form of skepticism, this pragmatist tradition is ineffective. The heart of that tradition involves a ground-shifting maneuver, granting the skeptical conclusion but claiming that we don't really need what the skeptic insists we don't have. Yet, if we never have anything of positive epistemic status, there is no epistemic norm or notion to guide belief and action, and the ground-shifting maneuver has no place left to turn. As a result, it would appear that the pragmatist response can only be effective by resisting skepticism in some way or other, even if granting the skeptic the point about knowledge.

One caveat is in order about this point, though, for in Quine (1969) we find a potential way to avoid having to resist the skeptic entirely, by simply abandoning normativity and replacing it with psychology. Once we realize that any grounding, even through rational reconstruction of some idealized sort, can't be found, Quine notes, "epistemology, or something like it, simply falls into place as a chapter of psychology ..." (82). Here we see some potential for abandoning everything epistemic to the skeptic, and replacing the normativity it involves with the descriptive categories of natural science. By doing so, we won't find norms to guide belief and action, but we'll come to understand exactly how we go about forming beliefs and deciding what to do with reference to the inputs of the senses (or whatever supplements to such a good science tells us are available).

Whereas the first pragmatist response involved ground-shifting within the territory of epistemology, this latter response simply kicks the normative can down the road. For we can't defer to science without also insisting on a distinction between pseudo-science and real science, between marginal science and more respectable science, between science done properly and science gone awry. This point has been made in various ways by critics of the idea of eliminating normative epistemology in favor of the categories used in psychology,[3] and it is worth noting that the view being attributed to Quine in making this kind of criticism is one that

---

[3] See, for example, Goldman (1986), Kim (1988), Kitcher (1992), Kornblith (1994) and Putnam (1985).

he has explicitly disavowed: "they are wrong in protesting that the normative element, so characteristic of epistemology, goes by the board" Quine (1990, 9). More expansively, he remarks,

> Naturalization of epistemology does not jettison the normative and settle for indiscriminate description of the on-going process. For me normative epistemology is a branch of engineering. It is the technology of truth-seeking, or, in more cautiously epistemic terms, prediction. Like any technology, it makes free use of whatever scientific finding may suit its purpose. It draws upon mathematics in computing standard deviation and probable error and in scouting the gambler's fallacy. It draws upon experimental psychology in exploring perceptual illusions and upon cognitive psychology in scouting wishful thinking. It draws upon neurology and physics, in a general way, in discounting testimony from occult and para-psychological sources. There is no question here of ultimate value, as in morals; it is a matter of efficacy for an ulterior end, truth or prediction. The normative here, as elsewhere in engineering, becomes descriptive when the terminal parameter has been expressed. (Quine 1986, 663–665)

So an eliminativist version of naturalized epistemology, jettisoning normativity altogether, is a problematic view, but not Quine's view.[4] For Quine, normativity is found in the engineering relationship between the sensory input (the evidence) and the epistemic goal of predictive accuracy.[5] This normativity about truth seeking is, in Quine's view, epistemology enough, and it doesn't embrace the idea of eliminating normativity from the discipline, and so provides no safe haven from a skeptical critique that claims that no such technology will be better than any other. On this point, we can expect Quine to resist the skeptical claim rather than moving the target and granting the skeptic the point.

In sum, though the pragmatist response to skepticism shows some promise, it is not a promise that can be fulfilled by giving in to skeptical arguments and conclusions across the board. Instead, it can only partially give in to skepticism, when that position is limited in scope to claims about knowledge (or something else identified with or involved in the epistemic *summum bonum*, but not about normativity more generally). So, in the end, the pragmatist response noted must be supplemented by some other form of resistance to skepticism.[6]

---

[4] I omit in the text the more uncharitable idea that Quine disavows something to which the earlier text actually commits him. I won't comment much on this idea, even though it might be true, preferring to focus on Quine's more considered judgment after hearing complaints about what he wrote earlier. I'm inclined to think that charitable interpretation and accuracy align in this case, but if not, the later view is the superior one, and thus more relevant to present purposes.

[5] For an elaboration of this approach to Quine's naturalized epistemology, see Foley (1994).

[6] For arguments that the Quinean view does not provide an adequate response to skepticism about knowledge, see BonJour (1994) and Fumerton (1994), the latter of which labels the circularity that would be involved "pathetic" (338), an apt assessment.

14 SKEPTICISM AND THE COMMONSENSE TRADITION

One way to supplement this pragmatist deflection is by way of an ancient criticism of skepticism involving the problem of paralysis. This problem joins forces with the pragmatist response to skepticism by insisting that we must rely on something to guide thought and action, and skepticism must be rejected at some point in order for such reliance to occur. Examining this supplementation of a pragmatist response will help us to see more of the burden that the skeptical project must carry, and the resources it has for shouldering that burden. It will also hint at the need for a different form of resistance to skepticism in trying to deflect its concerns.

2.2 Pragmatism and The Problem of Paralysis

Recall that the pragmatist resistance to skepticism involves an appeal to whatever is needed to ground proper thinking and decision-making, so that if knowledge can't play that role, something else will be needed. This "something else" may also be within the land of epistemic normativity, and skeptical argumentation can be, and often is, extended to threaten any such appeal as well. So the initial pragmatist demotion of skepticism doesn't succeed all on its own, but it can be supplemented by appeal to the ancient problem of paralysis for Pyrrhonian skepticism. The core of this problem is that when we act, cognition has to play some role in differentiating between possible courses of action, and once cognition is in the picture, any skepticism that eschews all of it will lead to an inability to sort among possible courses of action in any way at all that makes sense.

Pyrrhonians aimed for a skepticism that was significant on grounds concerning the kind of life and community made possible by such a doctrine. Given such a goal, the problem of paralysis has to be avoided, and there is something to learn about the pragmatist attempt to use this problem to undermine skepticism by attending to what Sextus tells us skepticism involves. Sextus tells us that "Scepticism is an ability, or mental attitude, which opposes appearances to judgements in any way whatsoever" (Empiricus, 1933, PH I 8). This ability to find and construct apparent reasons for and against any given claim that one might consider leaves one suspending judgment. If we think of judgment in terms of belief, we can attribute the idea to Sextus that the problem of paralysis can be avoided by letting behavior depend on cognitive elements that are outside the arena of epistemic normativity, noting that belief and judgment are subject to epistemic appraisal but appearance states are not.

Such an approach faces interpretive difficulties, however. Consider what Sextus writes in distinguishing between skepticism and dogmatism:

> When we say that the Sceptic refrains from dogmatizing we do not use the term "dogma" as some do, in the broader sense of "approval of a thing" for the Sceptic

2.2 PRAGMATISM AND THE PROBLEM OF PARALYSIS   15

gives assent to the feelings which are the necessary results of sense-impressions and he would not, for example, say when feeling hot or cold "I believe that I am not hot or cold"); but we say that "he does not dogmatize" using "dogma" in the sense, which some give it, of "assent to one of the non-evidence objects of scientific inquiry"; for the Pyrrhonean philosopher assents to nothing that is non-evident. (Empiricus 1933, PH I 13)

This passage has been the subject of much scholarly dispute. Michael Frede claims that Sextus is here distinguishing between two kinds of bases for beliefs, suggesting that one kind (based on argument and reasons) is barred for the skeptic while the other kind (based directly on how things seem or appear) is not.[7] Jonathan Barnes (1982) and Myles Burnyeat (1980) argue in different ways that the utterances of the skeptic do not commit the skeptic to having beliefs, while Gail Fine (2000) and Casey Perin (2010) argue that the skeptic can have beliefs so long as the propositional content of such is an appearance statement.

My interest here is not so much in the scholarly question of the best interpretation of Sextus, but rather in the question of what options a skeptic has to respond to the deflecting strategy adopted by the pragmatists I've been considering. Pragmatist responses to skepticism seem initially to benefit from the problem of paralysis, relying on the idea that there must be some cognitive element that properly guides ordinary behavior. If skeptical argumentation is extended throughout the entirety of the cognitive domain, paralysis ensues, and that looks like something we should regard as a *reductio* about the significance of skepticism. It is, at the very least, a problem that threatens to reduce the skeptic to silence, for whatever the norms of assertion are, we certainly want to insist on sincerity, and if skeptical argumentation extends so far as to encompass the entirety of cognition, there will be nothing available for distinguishing between sincere and insincere speech acts to which a skeptical account of defensible assertion might appeal.

Such a *reductio* depends on the entirety of cognition being subject to epistemic appraisal, however, and this fact allows the possibility of a response by the skeptic. It is a response that we can see a hint of in the Sextus quote above, for that passage suggests relying on something about appearances rather than something involving judgment, and such a distinction might be put to use in service of guiding behavior. This distinction thus raises the possibility of finding adequate grounding for behavior in cognitive states that are outside the territory of epistemic normativity, and the obvious candidate for such states are appearance states. For notice that a primary difference between appearances and beliefs is that the latter is epistemically assessable whereas the former is not. If it appears to me that the mountains in the distance are the Grand Tetons, this appearance state isn't assessable as rational or not, even though the belief that it typically prompts will be assessable in these

---

[7] See, especially, "The Skeptic's Beliefs," 179–200 in Frede (1987).

terms. So, perhaps the threat of paralysis can be avoided by letting appearances themselves guide behavior, granting that skeptical argumentation is only effective regarding cognitive states that are subject to epistemic appraisal.

An alternative here would be to insist that some cognitive states are rational for grounding rational behavior, but that the kind of rationality in question need not be epistemic. Instead, one might propose a kind of practical or pragmatic rationality that lets beliefs guide action even if those beliefs fail to meet the standards required for epistemic rationality. Defenders of such a position could thereby tout the death of epistemology by noting that the success of skeptical argumentation not only makes skepticism insignificant but also every non-skeptical attempt to explain the nature of epistemic normativity!

Such a path is perplexing at best, however, for practical rationality isn't somehow basic to the normative domain, but arises in virtue of more fundamental axiological characteristics related to the things that lead people to behave in one way rather than another. The typical ideas here are that practical rationality is a function of rational belief and rational desire, though modern decision theory replaces such folk psychological categories with (rational) degrees of belief and (rational) preferences. For such approaches to avoid circularity, the rationality of the cognitive and affective states under consideration must be different from the practical rationality to which they give rise.

To reject this standard way of thinking about where practical rationality comes from, to adopt the proposal above that attributes practical rationality directly to beliefs or other cognitive states, beggars credulity. The proposal is to begin by identifying those actions that are themselves rational from a practical point of view, and then infer the presence of the same kind of rationality for whatever cognitive states led to such actions. The rationality of action, however, would then have to be explained in ways other than by appeal to combinations of cognitive and affective states, and any such attempt makes a complete disaster of our understanding of deliberation. We deliberate when we take into account the things that are relevant for deciding what course of action to undertake, and such an approach requires that the rationality of any such course is explicable in terms of the normative status of the factors that are relevant to decision. Reversing this order of explanation is simply a non-starter.

So the wiser path is one hinted at by Sextus in claiming that sensory states themselves might lead directly to action in a way that provides a cognitive basis for rational action even though the states themselves are not items for epistemic appraisal. Even so, there is a concern about this strategy coming from Wilfrid Sellars's arguments against foundationalism. Sellars famously argued that the regress of reasons is not stopped by resorting to appearance states in contrast to other cognitive states such as belief.[8] For appearance states, even if immune to assessment by

---

[8] The source of this dilemma is Sellars (1956), though clearer explanations of the problem are given by others such as BonJour (1985).

some normative notions, are subject to assessment by other notions that certainly appear to be normative. The appearance of the Grand Tetons in the distance is appropriate in some circumstances but not others. For example, I am currently in my office in central U.S., and such an appearance would not be appropriate to my circumstances. So, even if such an appearance wouldn't be irrational or unjustified, it would be inappropriate to my circumstances, and such language is included among terms of normative appraisal. Moreover, the kind of appraisal in question certainly looks to be of a sort related to the Jamesian goal of getting to the truth and avoiding error. So, perhaps the attempt to find a grounding for behavior in the arena of appearances will fail, because it can only succeed, in our context, by both being a cognitive state and falling outside the domain of epistemic appraisal.

There is a fairly simple response to this attempt to extend epistemic appraisal to appearances themselves, and it is to distinguish between the evidence and its normative force. To say that appearances are subject to epistemic appraisal might be to say that every piece of evidence one might have is subject to epistemic appraisal, or it might be to say that any given piece of evidence can have varying power for implying positive normative status depending on the circumstances in which it arises. It is the latter idea that is at play in distinguishing between the role of context to determine whether a given appearance state is appropriate or inappropriate: in one context it has strong power and in another not much if any.

In the hands of a non-skeptical foundationalist, the power in question will be conceived of in epistemic terms, where the appearance states have the power to confer positive epistemic status on other cognitive states, including doxastic ones. In the hands of the skeptic, of course, no such idea will be employed, but instead, the power in question will be conceived in terms of the power to confer practical rationality on behavior. In such a way, the skeptic hopes to ground rational action partly in terms of cognition, while at the same time insisting that any cognitive state that is normatively assessable falls prey to skeptical argumentation.

Hence, trying to use the problem of paralysis to eliminate the difficulty cited earlier for the pragmatist response to skepticism isn't compelling. That problem was that the pragmatist has to include something further in a pragmatist epistemology beyond changing the focus from things we can't get (e.g., knowledge) to things within our reach that are adequate for guiding action (e.g., justified belief). This initial response to skepticism, suggesting that the position implies its own insignificance, was resisted on grounds that skeptical argumentation often targets not only our possession of knowledge but also our possession of justification. In reply, we imagine the pragmatist saying that generalizing skepticism in this way would undermine the view, because of the problem of paralysis. As we've just seen, though, skeptics have resources in replying to the problem of paralysis by finding a grounding source for behavior that lies outside the domain of normative assessment. Such resistance may be mistaken in the end, but the response has some initial probative value. As a result, pragmatists can't avoid the need for adding something more to their epistemology in the face of skeptical argumentation that not only knowledge but justification itself is under skeptical threat. Thus, pragmatist deflection of skeptical stances isn't going to be adequate on its own for undermining the significance of skepticism.

It is important here to note that we are not trying to assess whether the problem of paralysis itself undermines skepticism. Any skeptical response to the problem will raise questions that will need to be addressed by further discussion. For example, if the solution to the problem is through appeal to appearance states, there is a legitimate concern about whether this basis for behavior includes enough information to distinguish between all the ways that behavior can be either rational or irrational. This concern arises quite naturally for fans of modern decision theory, which explains the rationality of human behavior in terms of mental states such as credences and preferences. This basic framework can be generalized to include confidence intervals in addition to precise credences, but in either case, we can get a subjective Bayesian account of the cognitive dimension of rational behavior that, contrary to making everything depend on appearances, finds no role whatsoever for appearance states in the story of rational behavior. For many, this aspect of Bayesianism is a weakness, but it is one thing to insist on some role for experience in the story of rational behavior, and quite another to embrace the idea that no cognitive aspect is relevant to this story except that of experience. Perhaps the more plausible story is that experiences combine to support credences and confidences, and these in turn combine with (rational) preferences to yield rational action. The burden of trying to tell the story in a way that combines only experience with rational preferences is hard to shoulder.

So nothing noted above is meant to argue for the impotence of the problem of paralysis against skepticism. Instead, the point of the discussion was to see if the pragmatic response to skepticism could solve the need for supplementation, as argued earlier, by insisting that skepticism can't be generalized to the entirety of the domain of epistemic normativity without undermining itself. If successful, this version of pragmatism would then be free to accept skeptical argumentation that isn't self-undermining, and insist that skepticism is insignificant either because self-undermining or because what it shows to be impossible isn't something that matters after all. The conclusion defended here, then, is only that pragmatist deflection alone will not be enough to undermine the significance of skepticism, since fully generalized skepticism isn't that easy to show to be self-undermining. Perhaps efforts to avoid the problem of paralysis in this way will fail in the end, but at this point, the problem isn't conclusive enough to conclude that pragmatist deflection reveals how and why skepticism is only a minor distraction from the worthy project of providing an adequate epistemology.

More can be said on behalf of the skeptic here, however. In the above discussion, skepticism was on defense against the problem of paralysis, and we can gain a better appreciation of the weaknesses of this pragmatist approach to skepticism by noting the ways in which skeptics can go on the offense against the position.

As we've imagined the debate to this point, the skeptical strategy for avoiding the problem of paralysis involves looking for a cognitive basis for behavior that isn't subject to epistemically normative appraisal. In response, we noted that the pragmatist may point to the power and promise of modern decision. If that appeal is part of the best hope for explaining why fully generalized skepticism is self-undermining, skeptics can go on the offensive by questioning why the normativity involved in Bayesianism is the right kind to be talking about when the initial goal was to focus on the epistemic *summum bonum*, its constituents and whatever is necessary for achieving it. The idea here is to note the utter subjectivity of the Bayesian story, and question its relevance to the topic of the debate between skeptics and their opponents.

For purposes of discussion, then, let's assume a Bayesian account that involves only credences, and assesses these credences only in terms of two conditions. The first is probabilistic coherence, requiring that any rational set of credences constitute a probability function (as axiomatized in Kolmogorov (1950 [1933])) and that any change over time to the set obey Conditionalization, the principle that requires that one's new credence level conform to one's old credence level conditional on the total learning that occurs between the two times (where what is learned is a matter of what comes to have maximal credence). Those bothered by the subjectivity of this account of rational degree of belief will shake their heads at the lack of connection in the account to what reality is actually like. More relevant in our context is that a skeptic can make a gift of this sort of rationality to their opponents, granting that skeptical argumentation does not undermine it, but that such rationality is so remote from any epistemic good that is really worth obtaining that finding some aspect of cognition that is epistemically assessable and yet immune to skeptical argumentation would be a hollow victory indeed. In short, pragmatic deflection of skeptical argumentation doesn't work well if the territory we end up in is one where there isn't much of value to be found.

One way to think from this perspective can be put in terms of derived and fundamental value. The idea would then be that the skeptic can grant to the pragmatist that there is value for subjectively rational credences, but that this value is only inherited from the more fundamental value that attaches to rational action. In the context of action, we can distinguish between behavior that contributes to things turning out well and behavior that seemed right at the time but led to disaster. If we think of the latter as rational in spite of the untoward consequences, we will be attracted to a decision theory that adverts to subjectively rational credences, and the sort of value that such rational credences will be due, in part, to the role that such credences play in generating the rationality of actions to which they lead. But that value would then be derived value, whereas skeptical challenge begins at the more intrinsic level. It begins through a joint project with non-skeptics to identify the epistemological *summum bonum*, and then challenges the idea that cognitive success with respect to these things of great value is within our grasp.

The discussion begins by noting the centrality of truth to this domain, and quickly adds a normative dimension to the territory by noting that getting to the truth and avoiding error, while certainly possible, can't be all there is to the idea of cognitive ideality. And thus arises the normative idea of legitimate assurances of being correct, and the value of such legitimization is intrinsic to the account of the epistemological *summum bonum,* as reflected in various preference statements about that domain. We can ask whether we would rather be right or know that we are right; whether to be right by guessing or on the basis of a well-grounded assurance of being right. Such questions reveal that the epistemological *summum bonum,* whether knowledge or something else, has a value that is inherently connected with truth and with something normative as well. The latter we'll call "epistemic normativity," and the important thing to note about it is the way in which its presence involves legitimate assurance with respect to the central value of getting to the truth and avoiding error.

Note the ways in which the Bayesian account might be argued to have at best an orthogonal connection to these concerns. First, having legitimate assurance of having gotten to the truth involves cognitive commitment to the claim in question, and the Bayesian account only has degrees of belief instead of full cognitive commitments. The account can be supplemented by adopting a threshold for full belief to restore relevance to the story just articulated,[9] though some defenses of a Bayesian view (e.g., Jeffrey (1992)) think of the idea of full belief or commitment as an element of an outmoded psychology that is no longer needed. In the latter case, the story will have to be revised so as to introduce some different relation between the notion of truth and the supposed epistemic rationality of combinations of credences.[10] A deeper concern, however, is that the subjectivity of the Bayesian story seems at odds with the ideas that motivate the above account of the highest epistemic goods, for in that story we contrast cognitive accuracy with the same accuracy plus strong, robust assurances of it. How is it that, we might put it, the inappreciable stuff of subjectivity can give us that?

To my mind, the most straightforward way to appreciate this concern is to understand the attraction of the idea that confirmation and prediction are mirror images of each other. A hasty account of the predictions of a theory appeals to the notion of entailment: a theory predicts its consequences by entailing them. The account is hasty because theoretical predictions rest on background assumptions as well, and so theories don't in general entail their empirical consequences. At the very least, however, a theory together with these background assumptions make the consequences in question highly likely to occur, not merely in the sense that we have a heightened expectation of an observation, but that any such heightened

---

[9] For discussion of this Lockean thesis, see, for example, Foley (1991) and Sturgeon (2008).

[10] Here we might think in terms of accuracy-based versions of the view, of the sort we find in, for example, Pettigrew (2016).

expectation is grounded in an objective high likelihood of occurrence. If we combine this objectivity requirement with the idea that confirmation is the mirror image of prediction, we get an account of legitimate assurance of truth only to the extent that the assurance satisfies the same objectivity requirement just noted.

Seen in this way, one can appreciate how a skeptic could view Bayesian epistemology as irrelevantly orthogonal to the concerns that give rise to skeptical argumentation with non-skeptics. To the extent that a Bayesian account identifies something that is worth having, it does so, the skeptic might claim, primarily with respect to practical rather than purely theoretical concerns. So the value it possesses isn't the sort relevant to what is at issue between skeptics and non-skeptics, and hence pragmatist resistance to skepticism, even buttressed by the problem of paralysis, doesn't succeed in undermining skepticism or its significance. For the skeptic need only hold that the normative elements inherent to the epistemological *summum bonum* fall prey to skeptical argumentation, leaving open the idea that there are other possibilities involving normativity that remain untouched by their arguments.

Thus, when the pragmatist proposes to give in to skeptical argumentation and argue for its insignificance by turning to what is important for guiding thought and action, the argument from subjectivity threatens to saddle the pragmatist with rejecting the idea that epistemic normativity itself is important. For we begin, the skeptic may insist, with the great intellectual goods of knowledge, understanding, and theoretical wisdom, and of getting to the truth and avoiding error, and if anything as subjective as the Bayesian apparatus under discussion is invoked as the basis for defending the insignificance of skepticism, the pragmatist will have to sideline standard coherentists, foundationalists, reliabilists, safety and sensitivity theorists, virtue epistemologists, and proper functionalists as well. For all such approaches aim at theories of epistemic normativity connected with these great goods, and if skeptical challenges concerning subjectivity lead the pragmatist to consign such normativity to the same trash pile as was initially proposed for knowledge in light of skeptical argumentation against its possibility, one should long for a less inclusive account of what ends up in the trash pile of epistemology.

To my mind, the lesson is this. The pragmatist is attending primarily to issues about epistemic value, but does so in a way that is insufficiently critical when it comes to the nature of the epistemic states under discussion. As a result, the pragmatist is too accommodating to the skeptic. The idea was to make a gift to the skeptic about what it takes to know, and thereby hope to show that skepticism is insignificant. As with tyrants in general, however, if one cedes territory in hopes of making a good life elsewhere, further demands for more territory are to be expected, and the skeptical threat is tyrannical in precisely this way. By granting to or agreeing with the skeptic about the prospects for knowing, the pragmatist opens the door to having to lose everything of epistemic importance, and that's no way to get to the conclusion that skeptical concerns need not bother us much.

Again, I am not trying to show where the discussion must go, but merely to indicate considerations that prevent any easy pragmatist rejection of the significance of skepticism. For example, I have argued in Kvanvig (1984) that subjectivity of the sort involved in Bayesian epistemology can be endorsed and yet preserve the right kind of connection to great intellectual goods such as knowledge. I'm sure it will come as a great shock to the reader to learn that not everyone was convinced.

The point to note, however, is that there is no quick path to the insignificance of skepticism that arises from the fact that skeptical argumentation threatens to show that some or all of the great intellectual goods are beyond our capacities. The situation is simply too complicated for that. In all, then, pragmatist resistance to skepticism doesn't have the power to explain or justify the ways in which much of twentieth century epistemology was quite uninterested in skepticism and often openly dismissive of it, nor does it clearly yield the resources that I will argue can be found for requiring more of skepticism than is found in simple skeptical argumentation. For that aspect of our story, we turn in a better direction, toward commonsense epistemology derived most directly from the work of G.E. Moore, but also from earlier thinkers, especially Thomas Reid. Such a position is unwilling to cede any territory to tyrants, and claims to be able to show that skepticism is so obviously false that it is hard to see how it can have much significance beyond that of a mere curiosity piece, perhaps best understood as a hyperbolic extension of a properly critical attitude when attempting to find the truth and avoid error.

2.3 Commonsense Epistemology and Its Implications

The commonsense tradition begins by acknowledging our capacity for error, but rejecting the idea that the epistemic consequences of this admission are dire. We find such a combination in earlier periods of history as well, on display in Descartes, for example, who takes seriously our capacity for error and tries to show that the capacity for error doesn't preclude the achievement of metaphysical certainty. Not many in recent times have thought that there is much promise in this project, and much of twentieth century epistemology that resists skepticism traces to G.E. Moore, as well as the earlier commonsense tradition of Thomas Reid. For this tradition, unlike the pragmatist tradition noted above, knowledge is not sidelined but takes center stage, with the commonsense position that we know many things being staunchly defended against skeptical challenges. Moreover, this response to skepticism doesn't aim to show, or needn't aim to show, that Cartesian certainty is the answer to skepticism. Some theorists talk of certainty and proof, as we find in Moore (1939), but that language isn't best understood in terms of Descartes's notion of metaphysical certainty. In addition, even if some commonsense theorist were to endorse Cartesian demands for avoiding skepticism, we can note that nothing about the commonsense tradition requires going in that direction.

2.3 COMMONSENSE EPISTEMOLOGY AND ITS IMPLICATIONS   23

More important in our context is the way in which this commonsense tradition treats, or is inclined to treat, skepticism dismissively. The history of epistemology in the twentieth century, at least until the last couple of decades of it, is dominated by Moorean commonsense epistemology with some seasoning from ordinary language philosophy, two forces that coalesce to make skepticism unimpressive and easy to ignore. Commonsense epistemology presents us with a long list of things that we obviously know to be true, and ordinary language philosophy takes note of the centrality of talk of knowledge in ordinary contexts.[11] In Moore's hands, the list of things that are obviously known to be true is buttressed by attempted refutations of those who deny that we know such things or that the things purported to be known are really true.[12] The most useful Moorean tool, to be sure, isn't in terms of such argumentation, though I won't spend much time defending this claim. Instead, I'll just note that Moore doesn't claim to have wonderful argumentation either: he remarks, in response to skeptical challenge, "I think I have nothing better to say than that it seems to me that I *do* know them..." (Moore 1925, 206). Conceived of as an argument for Moore's positive thesis, such a claim is not adequate, for even if our seemings provide positive evidence for a claim, they certainly do not give conclusive evidence for it all on their own, and especially in controversial areas such as philosophy.

The remark, though, needn't be interpreted in terms of an argument for the conclusion that we know many things with certainty. Instead, it is better treated in terms of the Moorean shift, encoded in my preferred rendition as the motto that one should never give up the more obvious for the less obvious. Perhaps Moore is signaling how obvious is the claim that we know with certainty the claims of commonsense, in contrast with any of the attempted arguments against this claim. So even if his arguments against skeptics are unimpressive on substantive grounds, there is still this lurking methodological dictum that challenges

---

[11] To my mind, on the role of ordinary language philosophy, the most important figure is J.L. Austin. For our purposes, Moore and the commonsense tradition in epistemology will take center stage, but it is worth footnoting the ordinary language influence from Austin, especially from Austin (1946). Two passages are especially relevant. In the first, on 49–50, Austin considers a case of testimonial knowledge that involves having learned that the election is today by reading it in *The Times*. He claims this is genuine knowledge, that the use of the word "know" is correct when reporting such knowledge, even though it is "'liable to be wrong', owing to the unreliability of human testimony ...." This affirmation of fallibilism about knowledge is repeated in the infamous passage that analogizes knowledge claims and promises: The last sentence is a striking assertion, noting our fallibility while denying the propriety of encoding it in the remark that we might be wrong. We will have occasion a bit later to consider other fallibilisms that endorse a similar aversion to such admissions regarding things taken to be known.

"When you know you can't be wrong" is perfectly good sense. You are prohibited from saying "I know it is so, but I may be wrong", just as you are prohibited from saying "I promise I will, but I may fail". If you are aware you may be mistaken, you ought not to say you know, just as, if you are aware you may break your word, you have no business to promise. But of course, being aware that you may be mistaken doesn't mean merely being aware that you are a fallible human being: it means that you have some concrete reason to suppose that you may be mistaken in this case. (Austin, 1946, 98)

[12] For details, see Moore (1925).

any denial of something so obvious. For the methodological dictum implies that skepticism can't be sustained without involving arguments that meet the seemingly impossible standard of employing premises that are at least as obvious as our knowledge that we have hands, that the earth is more than five minutes old, or that we are currently experiencing a world independent of each of our finite human minds.

This anti-skeptical stance was embraced in a bit more subtle form in the work of Roderick Chisholm, especially in his discussion of the problem of the criterion,[13] where his clear preference for Particularism over Methodism and Skepticism relies on the general idea that any approach to the problem will beg the question. As a result, Chisholm says that his approach has presupposed Particularism, and defends this presupposition by claiming, "in favor of our approach there is the fact that we *do* know many things, after all" (Chisholm, 1973, 38).

Two features of this approach are striking. The first is the obvious commonsense aspect to Chisholm's epistemology, and the second is the surprising weakness of this defense of it. The version of foundationalism that results from this presupposition is one of Chisholm's enduring contributions to twentieth-century epistemology, instrumental in changing the landscape from one dominated by coherentism in the middle of the century to one where foundationalism was dominant, at least among internalists, by the end of the century.[14] But in our context, the more important point is the rather casual defense of Particularism through Moorean affirmation of how obvious it is that we know many things. For Chisholm grants that each position begs the question against the other positions, and many will conclude from this admission that no position can be epistemically superior to the others.

It is worth pointing out, though, that there are a couple of responses to this concern available to Chisholm. The first one is a response I am confident he would not find probative, and it is to point out that begging the question is a rhetorical fallacy, not a logical or epistemological one. The paradigm context in which this fallacy occurs is a debate context, and in such a context, it is certainly unwise to appeal to claims whose falsity is trivially implied by the position one's opponent is defending. In contrast, the epistemological issue isn't whether one can convince one's opponent of the error of their ways, or whether one can provide reasons that would be acceptable to those who disagree. Reasons and evidence don't answer to any such standard, and so one might try to disarm the claimed implications of his admission regarding begging the question in a way that leaves open having reasons or evidence for preferring Particularism in spite of the fact that it begs the question against its rivals.

---

[13] See, especially, Chisholm (1973) and Chisholm (1977).
[14] For discussion and defense of this claim, see Lycan (1996).

2.3 COMMONSENSE EPISTEMOLOGY AND ITS IMPLICATIONS 25

The reason I don't think Chisholm would be attracted to this idea is because going this route would be "unseemly":

> What few philosophers have had the courage to recognize is this: we can deal with the problem only by begging the question. It seems to me that, if we do recognize this fact, as we should, then it is unseemly for us to try to pretend that it isn't so. (Chisholm, 1982, 75)

Equally relevant is to note that when the language of begging the question is used, it can often be replaced by language that involves an actual logical or epistemological fallacy, that of circular reasoning. And Chisholm's initial discussion of the problem of the criterion uses that language instead of the language of begging the question, adverting to his preferred paraphrase of Montaigne's formulation of the *diallelus*, the problem of the wheel, or the vicious circle. The heart of the problem is then one of epistemological significance rather than merely a defect in rhetoric.

Rejecting the above view that seeks to undermine the epistemological significance of begging the question, however, leads to perplexity. For if the charge of begging the question levels the epistemic status of each of the views equal to that of the others, it is hard to see how some incrementally favorable reason could raise Particularism to the heights needed for the full endorsement of the position we find in Chisholm.

Here, I think, the best understanding of Chisholm relies heavily on the Moorean shift. The reason Chisholm uses is a claim that is obvious (to him): we do, after all, know many things. And the paraphrase of Moorean methodology that I'm using here says to go with what is obvious, and if there are competing things that are obvious, never give up the more obvious for the less obvious. Understood in this way, the reason Chisholm uses in support of Particularism can swamp the regrettable negativity involved in begging the question against the competition.

Viewed in this way, the problem of the criterion is a hard problem only because it takes considerable explanation to see why the issue can be settled in the way Chisholm proposes. If the issue can be settled by noting that it is obvious that we know many things, one might be forgiven for wondering why the problem deserves extended discussion and what advance Chisholm has made over the one-line Moorean argument cited above. It might be interesting to learn of the fact that everybody is begging the question against everybody else, but at the end of the day, it is the power of Moorean methodology that undergirds Chisholm's preference for Particularism. It also undergirds a rather strong presumption that the arguments for skepticism need not dominate epistemological reflection, and may not be central or very important at all to such reflection.

There is much more that we could say about this issue, but here my goal is only to paint in broad strokes, and by the 1970s and 1980s, things began to change, with strong defenses of skepticism in Unger (1975) and Stroud (1984a). To my mind, the arguments of the former are more probative, but two points were still hard to overcome. The first was the principle underlying the Moorean shift, and no matter how impressive the arguments in support of skepticism, it is hard to see them as passing scrutiny in terms of never giving up the more obvious for the less obvious. Such is the bane of philosophical reflection: what I can see with my own eyes is typically going to be more obvious than philosophical reasoning, even if it is not the most abstruse sort. The second point was a metaphilosophy first introduced by Chisholm in discussing the problem of the criterion, and refined in John Rawls, (1971). For Chisholm, the metaphilosophical options were Methodism and Particularism, with the former relying fundamentally on general principles about how and when we know and the latter starting from particular judgments about what we know. Rawls's method of reflective equilibrium found a middle path between these two options, requiring only some way of eliminating the tension between our general judgments and our particular judgments so as to achieve the equilibrium of a coherent set of attitudes. Given either a Chisholmian or Rawlsian metatheory about how to engage in the project of developing an epistemology, the arguments of the skeptics could easily be treated as nothing more than a step along the path of achieving equilibrium between our general principles and our particular judgments on matters epistemic. So, even though the work of Unger and Stroud resulted in increased attention to skeptical argumentation, it wasn't clear if or exactly why such attention was demanded. Perhaps it was little more than a typical philosophical vice, that of looking for something else to think about when the issues one had been dealing with turn out to have no easy solutions.

So, even if consideration of skepticism became more commonplace, the important question is what route there is on behalf of skepticism to rebut casual dismissal of the sort we find in Moore and Chisholm. For popularity, as we all know, is no sure sign of significance. We look, then, for possible explanations of the significance of skepticism that overcome commonsense-inspired lack of interest.

In the next section, we'll look at the work of Unger and Stroud to see if either provides a basis for such an explanation, and, to presage, we'll not find what we are looking for. But the search will be instructive nonetheless, since it will help to show what is needed in order to find a defense of the significance of skepticism. Doing so will take something different from formulating some new or special argument for the position in order to avoid the casual dismissal that comes from the commonsense tradition, something more in order to be taken as a serious competitor among the great epistemologies vying for our adherence. Note what these great epistemologies would look like if they were nothing more than conclusions, for example, of a regress argument. In that argument, we get skepticism as one possible conclusion, but we also get a foundationalist conclusion, a (kind of) coherentist conclusion, and an infinitist conclusion as well. But these conclusions by themselves don't yield a substantive epistemology. They are beginning points from which a position needs to be developed and articulated. And just so in the history of epistemology. Foundationalists use regress reasoning to identify a starting point for theory construction, giving an account of what kinds of claims or attitudes can be rational without being arrived at by reasoning. More consider adopting or accepting, coherentists turn from regress argumentation to the task of explaining what holistic justification involves so that the idea that all justification depends on linear lines of reasoning is undermined. And even infinitists, few though there be, have more to say than simply endorsing a regress argument that rejects all the alternative possibilities.

So, in the absence of theory construction beyond endorsement of some battery of arguments for the conclusion that nobody knows anything, skeptics shouldn't be surprised when dismissal occurs. To make progress, they need to develop and articulate an epistemological standpoint that fits with and sustains such a conclusion. By doing so, they too will have presented an epistemology with some chance of being a worthy competitor among other epistemological theories, but in the absence of presenting such an account, the arguments they present will be easily accommodated through the method of reflective equilibrium, with no obvious way to insist that one can't proceed rationally by making such adjustments. We turn in the next section, then, to showing why this assessment of the situation is accurate when we attend to the best defenses of skepticism in the last half century.

2.4 Alethic and Epistemic Stories

As noted already, a revival of interest in skepticism appeared in the 1970's, in contrast to the dominant Moorean commonsense tradition together with ordinary language ideas that combined to foster a dismissive attitude toward skepticism. Central to this revival are arguments from Unger and Stroud for the truth of skepticism, and Stroud's work is explicitly an attempt to show that this approach undergirds the significance of skepticism.

Typical accounts of the significance of skepticism rest on its being true or on its epistemic merits, and the goal of this section is to show how recent attempts along these lines fail to yield an adequate response to Moorean methodology, with hints of what needs to be done in a different direction to sustain the central place of skepticism in epistemology. We thus begin with alethic and epistemic accounts, and as we've seen, the pragmatist response to skepticism attacks the first route, maintaining that skepticism about knowledge might be true, but if it is, it just means that knowledge isn't really what matters from a purely intellectual point of view. This pragmatist tradition can join forces with recent attempts to argue that knowledge isn't really what we are after anyway, as we find articulated in Kaplan (1985) and Jeffrey (1992). The action-guiding central role of cognition is much better satisfied by some epistemic notion linked to decision theory, leading to the idea that something in the neighborhood of a coherent credence function is what matters. Other options, though, replace the centrality of knowledge with something else. Perhaps what we want or ought to want is objectual understanding of things, as I have argued elsewhere.[15]

The central role that such responses to skepticism share is that of putting pressure on the idea that skepticism is significant if true. That is, they challenge alethic stories concerning the significance of skepticism. As we have seen, these attempts to show that skepticism isn't important are hard to sustain unless on can find some epistemic territory free from skeptical threats. A more direct challenge to alethic stories about the significance of skepticism comes from noting how strange is the idea of that we can reveal the significance of a claim or position by showing that it would be important if true. Think of pure, unbridled speculations about catastrophes that could happen, but for which no evidence has been or will be found. Such speculations are not significant just because they'd be important if true. So even if the pragmatist rejoinder fails to impress enough, we shouldn't be attracted to the idea of linking the significance of skepticism merely to its being true. Instead, if there is a link to truth and falsity to be found in a decent account of the significance of skepticism, we should expect to find it in the arena of argumentation and evidence rather than mere truth.

Note as well that this is what we see when we look at the renewal of interest in skepticism in the 1970s. The significance of skepticism depends, not just on the question of its truth, but on its epistemic credentials as well. This turn in the discussion doesn't abandon the idea that the significance of skepticism is related to truth, of course, for the discussion assumes that the epistemic goal is, or involves, getting to the truth and avoiding error. So, if we are to find significance for skepticism that is related in some way to truth, it will have to be in in virtue of the epistemic arguments for the view, arguments that serve the goal of getting to the truth and avoiding error.

This point is precisely what is challenged, however, by the Moorean shift and its methodology. How can any skeptical argumentation survive this attack? To resist this methodology, the arguments used have to rely on premises that are at least as obvious as the idea that we know many things. One might think that this approach is a lost cost, but it is worth noting that the revival of skepticism in the 1970s involves argumentation that advertises itself along these lines. So, to give this defense of the significance of skepticism due consideration, let's consider how such attempts proceed, starting with the appeal to commonsense in Stroud's defense of skepticism in Stroud (1984b).

---

[15] See Kvanvig (2003), Kvanvig (2006b), Kvanvig (2009b), and Kvanvig (2013). It should be noted that the importance of knowledge might still be defensible, compatible with this point of view, if understanding is a species of knowledge. Such a claim faces serious obstacles, though, as argued in Kvanvig (2003), Kvanvig (2009a), Pritchard (2009), and Pritchard (2010).

In that work, Stroud presses the dreaming hypothesis, arguing that the truth of that hypothesis is incompatible with knowledge, and that if such incompatibility is present, one needs to rule out that hypothesis in order to know anything else. Moreover, this ruling out idea is one that Stroud insists is part of our commonsense understanding of knowledge, of what is needed in order to know. But, Stroud claims, one can't rule out the dreaming hypothesis is false, so we at least appear to have here an argument for skepticism that aims to shoulder the burden imposed by the Moorean shift.

To be fair to Stroud, it should be mentioned that the argument isn't presented so as to convince us to become skeptics. Stroud denies that anyone should seriously consider endorsing skepticism: "... philosophical scepticism is not something we should seriously consider adopting or accepting" Stroud (1984b, 1). Instead of taking his work to be an argument that we don't know anything at all, he claims instead that it is an argument that threatens our ability to have a complete understanding of all of our knowledge, taken as a whole:

> We want an account of our knowledge of the world that would make all of it intelligible to us all at once. We want to see how knowledge of the world could come to be out of something that is not knowledge of the world. Without that, we will not have the kind of doubly general explanation we seek. I think skepticism in epistemology now represents, and perhaps always did represent, the possibility that such an explanation is impossible; that we cannot consider all our knowledge of the world all at once and still see it as knowledge. Given that project, the threat is that skepticism will be the only answer. (Stroud, 1984b, 8)

The idea, then, is that somehow skepticism threatens to make it impossible to explain or make intelligible to us how the totality of our knowledge arises, presumably, from sense experience—from that which is not knowledge.

This may be a subtlety that we can ignore. To see why, suppose we are never inclined to "consider all our knowledge of the world all at once." This phrase seems to be identified with the project of explaining how knowledge arises from non-knowledge. So, suppose we never consider the general epistemological project of constructing such an explanation. One reading of the quote here would have us conclude that knowledge would then abound, it would be present pretty much to the extent that Mooreans claim. And then, consider what happens when we undertake the epistemological project. If Stroud is correct, we will not succeed. What follows from this failure? Well, if skepticism doesn't follow from it, it is hard to see what significance to attach to the view. Perhaps what follows is the relatively quotidian point that we hardly ever know that our positive philosophical viewpoints are correct, and even if this failure rises to the level of an impossibility, that's not a significant skepticism to swallow, unless this impossibility threatens to undermine all of our other knowledge as well. So, even if Stroud doesn't wish to counsel endorsing skepticism, it will be hard to find any significance to the arguments he is giving if they don't in fact threaten to show that we don't know anything.

Here's an alternative way of making this point, noting that Stroud's subtlety may leave a Moorean commonsense viewpoint unperturbed. After all, it isn't part of the Moorean stance to insist that our philosophical projects can be successfully discharged. Instead, the heart of the Moorean stance is that we know many things, and needn't be troubled by skeptical arguments to the contrary. This commonsense standpoint is fully compatible with the existence of knowledge deserts–topics and issues regarding which we are simply incapable of discerning the truth and hence incapable of knowledge (even if we are inclined in such deserts to vociferous defenses of a position!).[16]

In addition, the arguments that Stroud gives present every appearance of being arguments for a skeptical conclusion. So it is hard to see how to take those arguments to be arguments against a capacity for achieving a philosophical understanding without also taking them as showing what it would take to know any given claim or theory. And if we take the arguments that way, they are arguments for the truth of skepticism, even if it would somehow be a mistake seriously to consider adopting or accepting it.

So, I propose to take Stroud's arguments at face value, and if we do that, we construe them as arguments for a skeptical conclusion. The initial argument, to repeat, is an argument involving the dreaming hypothesis, and it is an argument that depends crucially on a closure principle about knowledge,[17] and Stroud begins the task of uncovering such a principle by considering some examples from ordinary life. In our context, this approach can be viewed as an attempt to articulate a commonsensical viewpoint that can survive the Moorean shift of never giving up the more obvious for the less obvious, so what we are looking for here is an explanation of what the closure principle is and how obvious it really is.

Here are some of Stroud's examples. He claims that one must know that a bird is not a canary in order to know that it is a goldfinch; that one must know that the witnesses aren't lying in order to know that the suspect was in Cleveland; and that the Duke must know that he is not dreaming in order to know that he is speaking in the House of Lords. One generalization from these examples is a simple closure principle: if Q is incompatible with P, then you must know that Q is false in order to know P.

The obviousness of all this is hardly defensible, however, and it is easy to imagine Moorean eye-rolling at these examples. Consider the bird example first. If you have to know that the bird isn't a canary in order to know that it is a goldfinch, presumably you also have to know, for every other kind of bird, that it's not that kind

---

[16] I borrow this language about knowledge deserts from Keith DeRose. See, for example, DeRose (2018a) and DeRose (2018b).

[17] For discussion and clarification of what a closure principle is and why considerable license has to be taken in labeling the principles in the main text as closure principles, see Kvanvig (2006a).

of bird either, and that requirement is not part of ordinary life or thinking. After all, harder comparisons don't undermine easier ones: one can tell that a whippet isn't a beagle, but have a hard time distinguishing between a whippet and an Italian greyhound. That's a prosaic possibility in ordinary, commonsense thinking. From this perspective, it may not even be true that if you know that something is a goldfinch, you are in a position to come to know, for every other kind of bird, that it's not that kind of bird. Regardless of this last point, however, the point to note is that it is a fiction to think that you can't tell that something is a goldfinch unless you also know that it isn't a canary or that it isn't any other kind of bird.

So the first example fails to survive Moorean scrutiny. What about the second case? It involves learning through testimony, from eyewitnesses who claim that the suspect was in Cleveland. Once again, though, one can learn something through testimony without first considering and ruling out the possibility of deception. To think otherwise makes a disaster of basic learning in early childhood. It is on the basis of such learning that humans come to realize that sometimes appearance isn't reality and sometimes people lie, deceive, or are simply mistaken. So, perhaps, it may be true that if you know via testimony that the suspect was in Cleveland, you are in a position to conclude that the witnesses aren't lying (on the assumption that they are saying that the suspect was in Cleveland). But you don't have to know this first, or concomitantly with, knowing that the suspect was in Cleveland.[18]

Beyond the particular examples invoked is the need for a generalization on them, and here the Moorean standard is going to be even harder to overcome. For even if the examples were more convincing, it isn't the examples themselves that are part of the skeptical argumentation. Instead, it is a generalization on them that plays this role. And even if the examples were as obvious as the claim that we know many things, it will be hard to hold the same view of any generalization on them. There are infinitely many ways to generalize on any given set of examples, and even if there are some cases where we know exactly which is the right generalization, that is not always the case. When it isn't the case, Moorean advice to never give up the more obvious for the less obvious will generate suspicion about the generalization proffered.

Here such suspicion is especially germane, since first thoughts about how to generalize lead to indefensible proposals. The proposal noted above, that if two claims are incompatible, you can't know the first without also knowing that the second is false, is one of them. It is much too demanding, for it implies that you have to know all the logical consequences of anything you know. Since the denial of any such logical consequence is incompatible with the purported knowledge

---

[18] A caveat: one can imagine special epistemic requirements imposed in legal cases that are not part of ordinary life, so that the standards jurors must satisfy to conclude that a person is guilty might include reaching a decision about whether the accused was in Cleveland and whether those who affirm this claim in testimony are being truthful. Obviously, however, nothing follows from this possibility about ordinary contexts.

claim, the principle implies that one must know that such a denial is false. Moore's ghost laughs at such epistemological pretense.

In the face of such difficulties, Stroud considers a weaker principle: if you know that Q is incompatible with P, then you have to know that Q is false in order to know P. But this weakened principle is in a worse position, since it doesn't even fit the examples with which Stroud begins. The suspect-in-Cleveland case doesn't fit this principle, since one might never have considered the issue of whether the witnesses are lying, and as a result not have a belief at all about whether that claim is compatible with the claim that the suspect was in Cleveland. In such a case, the revised principle wouldn't require the ruling out of the lying hypothesis that Stroud wants. A similar point plagues the first example, for one might be looking for goldfinches before ever knowing anything about canaries, leaving the principle unable to explain the ruling out requirement Stroud insists on for this example. It is also worth noting that Stroud holds that the Duke could both be dreaming he was speaking in the House of Lords while actually doing so, so it is hard to see how the Duke's knowing that the Duke is dreaming would be incompatible with speaking in the House of Lords. So the weaker principle isn't really a generalization from the examples being used.

It would be understandable at this point to experience the kind of bemusement or even exasperation toward which Mooreans are inclined, thinking that no amount of fiddling with details is going to get us to something that is anywhere close to as obvious as that we know many things. But let's assume we have a free afternoon with nothing else to do, so we decide to humor the skeptic a bit more.

So we suggest that the skeptic try again to formulate a closure principle with the imagined skeptical implications, and it isn't hard to see that there will be a multitude of such principles. If we stick to the direction that Stroud takes, we will focus, not on claims that are incompatible alternatives to the target claim, but rather on claims that are alternatives to one's knowing the target claim instead. So he proposes that if Q is incompatible with one's knowing P, then one must know that Q is false in order to know P.

But here the argument overreaches, since if anything is incompatible with your knowing P, it is the denial of that very claim! That is, you're not knowing P is incompatible with your knowing P. So, by the above principle, you must know that it is false that you don't know P in order to know P. If we assume that knowing that it is false it isn't the case that you know P implies knowing that you know P,[19] we end up with an unsavory KK principle, according to which knowing requires knowing that you know. In addition, even if resistance is warranted about the equivalence of knowing that you know with it being false that you don't know that you know, the concerns about the KK principle in question will extend quite

---

[19] That is, in symbols: $K{\sim}({\sim}(Kp)) \rightarrow KKp$, an application of double negation inside the scope of a knowledge operator.

easily to this double negation variant of it. I won't say that every version of a KK principle is unsavory, though suspicion is generally warranted, but this one certainly is problematic.[20] Among other difficulties that have been raised against it, it succumbs to a problem that plagues many epistemic principles, the problem of small children and animals. Such individuals know many things, but they do so unreflectively and thus fail to have reflective beliefs about what they know or don't know. In addition, the principle triggers information explosion: you can't know anything without knowing infinitely many things, and that is surely an unsavory dish.[21]

A Moorean might be forgiven for pointing to a pessimistic induction about the prospects of finding a defensible generalization on the examples, but wiser Mooreans would see that such an induction would depend on an unfortunately small data set. Even so, it is worth noting that this game of trying to find a generalization not subject to obvious defect doesn't address the more fundamental problem that any generalization must not only be free from defect, but must also be at least as obvious as the commonsense observation that we know may things. That standard yields a daunting challenge to efforts to find an adequate generalization, but there remains a natural alternative to consider that we haven't considered yet, one arising by analogy from the first refinement of the initial closure principle we considered. There, the problem was that the first proposal required logical omniscience, and a natural way to avoid this problem involved introducing a knowledge operator into the antecedent of the initial principle. We can do the same here, to offer another possible closure principle for Stroudian argumentation. Doing so yields the claim that if you know that Q is incompatible with your knowing P, then you can't know P without knowing Q is false.

Before demolishing this latest stronghold, our imaginary patient Moorean notes a virtue of this principle, for it avoids the problem of small children and animals. Unreflective knowledge doesn't trigger any application of this principle, thereby allowing it to be compatible with knowledge by small children and animals. Even so, patience has its limits, for this latest proposal still suffers from the problem of information explosion. Among normal adults, it is hard to find people who don't know that their not knowing P is incompatible with their knowing P. Even so, one can know that not knowing P is incompatible with knowing P, and yet not know that one knows. The latter might take some epistemological investigation of

---

[20] KK principles were introduced into the literature in the groundbreaking work on epistemic logic, Hintikka (1962).

[21] It is noteworthy that Hintikka's KK principle is said to hold only for conclusive knowledge of the sort that can never be undermined by further learning, as explained in (Hintikka, 1970, 145–146), so counterexamples about ordinary knowledge don't threaten his version of the principle. I point this out but will note as well that that there are no instances of this kind of knowledge, at least for ordinary, fallible human beings, and it is pretty clear that Hintikka's defense of his KK principle relies on the assumption that there are instances of this kind of knowledge to be found. Further useful discussion about KK principles can be found in Hemp (2006) and in Greco (2015a) and Greco (2015b).

at least a mildly substantive sort; the former requires only some rather banal logical information. So the antecedent of the latest principles, even though not universally satisfied by all knowers, is satisfied quite generally, and in a way that makes this principle succumb to the same kinds of objections that undermine typical KK-principles.

At some point along the way, the Moorean will weary of the game, and want to do something else. If there were some idea on offer that looked like an obvious truth and also threatened skeptical conclusions, we might hold such a Moorean accountable for an intellectual failure or vice. But nothing in the discussion has looked even remotely promising in terms of this conjunctive demand, and so turning away from the effort to focus on other philosophical tasks is expected and perhaps also fully warranted.

It is this attitude that I have been wanting us to notice. It is at least a mildly dismissive attitude toward skepticism and arguments for it, and it is hard to see what good reason could be given against such an attitude that didn't involve further theoretical development of a skeptical epistemology. What we get, when the focus turns to the general principles involved in any given argument for skepticism, short-circuits the needed connections. Rather than making further attempts to provide a closure principle that generalizes on commonsense attitudes about knowledge, while at the same time clearing the Moorean hurdle of being at least as obvious as that we know many things, a better strategy would be to develop the skeptical position itself. Such an approach would no longer rely merely on argumentative attempts to undermine commonsense, but would aim at presenting a fully developed theoretical alternative to commonsense epistemology. Defenders of commonsense would see immediately how such an approach conflicts with the platitude that we know many things, but it is one thing to face only a generalization on some simple examples and quite another to find a theoretical framework that identifies at least what ideal knowledge might look like and how it might be acquired. Such an attempt would at least shift the ground of discussion from the difficult tasking of finding the significance of skepticism in some simple argumentation that generalizes on examples in a way that competes in terms of obviousness with the idea that we know many things. While Mooreans have no proof that this task is impossible (except one that starts with the claim that we know many things!), they have two things they can appeal to that are hard to overlook. The first is the failure of the closure principles above, and this pattern of failure can at some point justify the induction that we are wasting our time. The second is the relevance of the obviousness standard, for the search for a closure generalization proceeds with a blind eye to this requirement. Moorean commonsense epistemology places items we know to be true in one hand and abstract philosophical principles in the other, asking how the latter could ever compete with the former in terms of obviousness. In the face of this methodological principle, epistemologically sophisticated Mooreans will reasonably view mere skeptical reasoning as an interesting philosophical pastime for a free afternoon, but largely irrelevant to their day jobs of developing and defending theories about the great epistemic goods and the normative standards we face that are epistemic in nature.

The same pattern emerges in the other outstanding work reviving an interest in skepticism, that of Unger (1975). We find first an argument for skepticism that ties knowledge to absolute certainty. Unger spends some time arguing that knowledge requires absolute certainty, but all his argument needs is that if you know, it's OK for you to be (absolutely) certain. Perhaps Moore would agree, since (as we have seen already) he ties together knowledge and certainty. But questions arise because of the qualifier: what is the relationship between certainty and absolute certainty? According to Unger, there is no difference, since certainty falls into the category of an absolute term. For absolute terms, gradeability isn't possible, so if certainty falls into this category, one can't be certain of two different things while also being more certain of one than the other.

It is at this point that Unger's argument starts to look very much like mere fodder for reflective equilibrium, for the notion of certainty being employed leads straightforwardly to the Dogmatism paradox. According to this paradox, if you are certain of something then no new information could dislodge this certainty, and thus you could be and should be dogmatic about it. Unger exploits this connection to argue that it is never OK to be certain, but the rest of us will be more inclined to see this connection as a *reductio*. For it is no part of ordinary, commonsense attitudes to reject the possibility of being wrong regarding what we know to be true, and given such attitudes, any premises that lead to the idea that knowledge implies dogmatism will be resisted. As such, it will function in the same way as other epistemic paradoxes, leading to more careful understandings of key epistemological terms and their implications, but never rationally forcing one to abandon the idea that we know many things. If one never abandons the more obvious for the less obvious, the most natural targets for refinement will be the general epistemological principles that give rise to the paradox, and so Moorean methodology will reinforce the same attitude toward this argument and the associated paradox as we found with Stroud's argument.

So Unger's argumentation won't, by itself, do much to dislodge Moorean dismissiveness, but there is a further feature of Unger's discussion that can't be dismissed in this way, and which will play an important role in our discussion of different kinds of fallibilism. For central to Unger's work is this notion of knowledge being an absolute term. Knowledge is an absolute term because it is linked to certainty, which is itself an absolute term, Unger maintains.

If we try to fit these ideas into an argument that can elude Moorean dismissiveness, these considerations won't have much probative value. But, as we will see, there is a different role that they can play, one that will occupy our attention in future chapters. They will become important if we find some other way of establishing the significance of skepticism, and the approach I'll argue for is that development of the skeptical position itself is necessary for such significance, in contrast to approaches that rely only on alethic and epistemic considerations themselves. In the process of such theory development, this notion of absoluteness will be important, so some preliminary discussion here will help set the stage for future chapters.

Unger relies on an appeal to absolute notions, with the paradigm example being that of flatness. Flatness, Unger claims, is absolute, not a gradeable notion at all. Either a thing is absolutely flat, or it isn't flat at all. If knowledge is absolute in this way, and Unger insists it is, then one's knowledge is either absolute or it isn't knowledge at all.

As I will argue later, there is a kernel of truth to be found here, but we'll need something more than what Unger provides to find it. For Unger's approach appeals to an ordinary language tradition and linguistic tests for determining whether a term is absolute. Note, however, that linguistic tests relying on the adverbs 'relatively' and 'absolutely' won't definitively reveal which terms are absolute and which aren't. The last table I built is flat, but not absolutely flat. And when I say that it is flat but not absolutely so, I'm don't mean that it is close to being flat. I try to say what I mean, and in this case I did. You can't make a case about absoluteness by telling people they really didn't mean what they said.

The point to note here is that there are several hurdles facing this appeal to absoluteness. There is, first, the phenomenon of hyperbole, so if the first use of a term is hyperbolic and the second is literal, we should expect to find a difference between the two where the second is described as absolute. Your love for someone or something might be unconditional, but not absolutely so, for example, and one explanation of how what you report can be true is for the first part to be hyperbolic and the second not.

There is also a point that generalizes on the distinction between restricted and unrestricted quantification in ordinary language. When you say that there is nothing in the fridge, we might try to interpret your language as an instance of hyperbole (if we charitably aim to find a truth here), but perhaps a better story is that the quantifier is a restricted one with an unstated restriction provided by the context. On the latter story, the claim is (literally) true, while on the former story it is (literally) false.[22] For those attracted to the latter story, as I am, we find here an example of polysemy that reminds us that even universal quantification

---

[22] Here I rely in a distinction between what is literal and what isn't, even though this distinction itself may be problematic. See Lakoff (1993) for discussion. And lest we think that it is a recent phenomenon to corrupt the distinction by using "literally" in a metaphorical way (as when the announcer of an NFL game reported that the when the running back carried the ball up the middle, the linebacker "literally took his head off"), there is this passage from Frances Brooke's 1769 novel *The History of Emily Montague*: "He is a fortunate man to be introduced to such a party of fine women at his arrival; it is literally *to feed among the lilies*."

itself isn't absolute. Thus, if one says that there is nothing in the fridge, but also that one doesn't mean that there is absolutely nothing in the fridge, the remark might be understood as involving two different but related meanings for the quantifier.

In addition, there is a difference between extreme terms and absolute ones, and it is a difficult question how to tell the difference. One would expect that the adverb 'absolutely' would help in discerning the difference, as when we distinguish between being exhausted and being absolutely exhausted. But such adverbs can sometimes be best understood in terms of emphasis rather than qualification: to say I'm absolutely exhausted might just be a way of emphasizing my condition rather than qualifying it in some way.

These points combine to help us see the folly of letting our philosophy be driven by claims about how we talk or should talk.[23] During the heyday of ordinary language philosophy, it was common to think that one could settle lots of important philosophical debates by appeal to linguistic data. What a crazy idea! We can be thankful that we have moved away from this idea, for even though linguistic data isn't irrelevant to philosophy, it is a strange view that aligns word and world so tightly that one could figure out, for example, what constitutes normativity just by attending to language.[24] So when a skeptic proposes that there is a distinction between absolute properties and other properties that are not absolute by relying on the idea that we can tell the difference by noting which adverbs can be attached appropriately to a term for that property, we should be skeptical!

The points above coalesce around the vexed distinction between semantics and pragmatics, and the central point to note is the theoretical nature of any project designed to tell us the difference. What is needed, that is, is full-blown theoretical inquiry, and no appeal to syntax or ordinary language is going to be able to substitute for it. In our context, what is needed is an explanation that doesn't rely on claims about how we talk, but rather about the phenomenon itself, beginning with an account of absoluteness. Here the basic idea seems to be in terms of a limit, so that once the limit is reached, gradeability disappears entirely. Once we understand absoluteness in terms of a limit of some sort, we then look for properties that obtain only at a specified limit, and here things get a bit trickier. Unger claims

---

[23] A favorite Kripke quote on the matter:

> The philosopher advocates a view apparently in patent contradiction to common sense. Rather than repudiating common sense, he asserts that the conflict comes from a philosophical misinterpretation of common language .... I think such philosophical claims are almost invariably suspect. What the claimant calls a "misleading philosophical misconstrual" of the ordinary statement is probably the natural and correct understanding. The real misconstrual comes when the claimant continues, "All the ordinary man really means is...". (Kripke, 1982, 65)

[24] For a less strident explanation of this rejection of ordinary language philosophy, see Kvanvig (2014), the section "Theory and Value-Driven Metatheory" in the Introduction.

that nothing can be flat and yet capable of being flatter, that nothing can be certain and yet capable of being more certain. To support these assessments, we need an explanation of the limit that applies in each case, so as to rule out instantiation short of it.

Identifying the limit isn't an easy task, and the point I'm working toward is that doing so will involve constructing a theoretical model or theory that supplies the needed identification. For example, if we want an absolute notion related to temperature, we find the notion of absolute zero, relative to a theory of temperature that understands it in terms of mean kinetic energy. So, absolute zero is really absolute, not relatively absolute.[25]

For other properties, things can get complicated. Think of a container being empty, as when one finds oneself on a hike, needing a drink, and finding only an empty canteen. A natural idea here might be that the canteen is empty if and only if it constitutes a perfect vacuum, but that is unpromising. It would imply that canteens are never empty, and we shouldn't endorse that idea, since it is obviously false. Yet, if there are absolute terms of the sort Unger is looking for, this term would seem to be one of them. So what is the limit idea relative to which we identify emptiness as absolute?

At least in the imagined context, the emptiness in question involves a lack of water, so we might think of replacing the idea of a perfect vacuum with that of the absence of any H_2O molecules. That too yields an inappropriate idea for the limit relative to which we would want to identify emptiness as absolute, for any positive humidity level implies the presence of water molecules.

We might move then to the idea that water vapor is different from liquid water, and the limit idea for emptiness in this context concerns liquid water, not water vapor. That point is correct as far as it goes, but the line between vapor and liquid isn't precise. So, using this distinction would require some account of what to say when it is neither determinately true nor determinately not true that there is liquid in the canteen. In such a case, is the canteen empty of water? Our imaginary hiker will certainly come to this conclusion, and I'm inclined to agree.

I'm inclined here to favor precisifying in the manner of supervaluationism, so that once we precisify the line between vapor and liquid, the limit concept yields empty when the precisification comes down against there being any liquid and it yields not empty in the other case. In such a case, though, the property of emptiness is fundamentally understood in terms of the model we are using, rather than

---

[25] A perplexing thing to note, though, is a story at ScienceDaily from January 4, 2013 (https://www.sciencedaily.com/releases/2013/01/130104143516.htm), which reports the creation of a gas that has negative Kelvin values. Perhaps this means that absolute zero isn't absolute, though I note that the report quotes one of the physicists as claiming that the gas isn't colder than zero kelvin, but hotter. I will leave it to others to try to make sense of all this, but one suspicion that comes to mind is that the language of cold and hot can have a meaning independent of the theory that identifies temperature in terms of mean kinetic energy.

simply in terms of the canteen and what is in it. We are relying on an account of emptiness where that property is understood in terms of emptiness-relative-to-a-precisification-in-a-model. The latter is our absolute notion, leaving open the question of whether the former is as well. What we will end up saying about the property of emptiness is that it is properly modeled by an absolute notion, and so answers to the idea of absoluteness in some way.

We'll be developing this idea further in the course of our investigation—the idea that we model the notion of a limit and then think of the property in question in terms of some relation to the model—and it is worth noting that similar points arise for the property of flatness. Note first that a flat surface can lose that appearance under magnification. But the loss of the appearance isn't always a matter of a solid surface no longer appearing flat, but can also be one in which solidity itself is lost. So, when we want to get precise about flatness, we need to do some idealizing. We turn to Euclidean geometry and develop a model for flatness in terms of parallel lines and parallel planes. Every two-dimensional plane is automatically flat, and a three-dimensional surface is flat when its surface has all of its lines parallel with lines of some two-dimensional plane. The resulting notion of flatness is a mathematical idealization and involves the notion of a limit that is central to the idea of absoluteness: if the surface of an object is flat on this model, it couldn't be flatter. But the role of idealization in this story should lead us to ask whether we should distinguish between flatness itself and flatness in the model, and the answer is obvious. For the approach taken only models objects that have precise boundaries and are composed of points that exhibit mathematical density, so that no empty space can be found between any two points. So flatness-in-the-model may be a useful approach to understanding flatness, but it would be a mistake to identify the two. We can thus grant that we can make sense of an absolute notion of flatness without already having determined the relationship between this absolute notion and the property of flatness itself. To come to a conclusion about this relationship involves something more, something having to do with approximations to ideal flatness—flatness-in-the-model—and whether any such approximations can be close enough to be correct.

This point will take careful development in later chapters, especially when it comes to the idea that knowledge itself is absolute. Just as with flatness, our understanding will be furthered only once we have an understanding of what the ideal is under which the notion is supposed to be absolute. To get to that point, we again need more than skeptical argument and conclusion. We need theory development on behalf of the skeptic, and such theory development aims, in particular, at clarifying what this ideal for knowledge really is. To put the point in the language used above, we'll need a model where we can specify a limit for identifying knowledge-in-the-model as absolute. If no such account can be found, so much the worse for skepticism, since the alternative explanations of the significance of skepticism in terms of alethic and epistemic stories stumble under the load of Moorean methodology. But if such an account can be found, we'll be in a position to ask and address the questions about approximations to the ideal and whether any such approximations are close enough to be correct.

So, even though Unger's argument for skepticism can legitimately be met with the same attitude we noted when considering Stroud's argument, the discussion of absoluteness, and the associated concept of ideality advances the discussion beyond these arguments and conclusions. For it signals the need for theory development, as I've been arguing, and as we will see as well, what kind of fallibilism is needed to respond to a skeptical theory so developed.

At this point in our discussion, then, we see pointers in two directions. The first is that alethic and epistemic explanations of the significance of skepticism disappoint. For them to succeed, the arguments given would have to survive the scrutiny imposed by Moorean methodology, and it is easy to see a pattern developing, where the "NOT OBVIOUS ENOUGH" placard gets raised by the judges at some point in the argument.

It is worth noting, however, that something seems amiss in this approach to the significance of skepticism, and this recognition points in the general direction alluded to above concerning proper theory development. After all, consider all the various philosophical theories and systems with which we are acquainted, and which we recognize as significant approaches to the topics they address. Our attributions of significance are not alethically or epistemically driven. If our focus is on truth, we would end up with the view that only one view in a given area is significant, and if we focus on arguments themselves, it would be difficult to explain how one and the same person could find to be significant views that compete with the one thought to be best. For if the epistemic factors favor a given view, they disfavor all competitors. It is not hard to see that that's not how significance works. Even if arguments in favor of a thesis need to play some role in the story of significance, something different is going to be needed to complete the explanation.

In response, it would be reasonable to conclude that the alethic and epistemic stories pursued in this section are simply on the wrong track. Instead of looking for some significance in skepticism by examining specific arguments for skeptical conclusions, we should look for some significance for skepticism that is independent of the question of whether it is true. As I understand the matter, this point is a lasting contribution from Moore and the commonsense tradition he represents: skepticism, to the extent it is significant, is significant in ways that are independent of its truth value and independent of compelling or persuasive argumentation for the view. Once we learn this lesson and look for a different and better explanation of the significance of skepticism, we won't completely ignore the question of truth, of course, for if skepticism is mere idle speculation of the sort people engage in at bars over a few drinks, we shouldn't expect to find the view to be of philosophical significance. Yet, because we most often recognize philosophical theories to be important while at the same time either rejecting them or remaining agnostic about them, we should expect the same for skepticism if there is any such significance to be found. We look, that is, for a story of the significance of skepticism that would give us a reason to be dissatisfied with Moorean dismissiveness toward the view and some understanding of why such dismissiveness is to be avoided.

Such significance requires effort by or on behalf of skeptics, for something more will be needed beyond bare thesis and arguments for it. Instead, we should expect to find significance for positions once they are developed, not merely because of some argumentation for a bare thesis. It is the path recommended by attention to Ungerian skepticism, where the notion of an absoluteness for some properties is crucial, but where the discussion of this feature relies too heavily on ordinary language claims. The only proposal we've seen that might suggest a less demanding path to follow is in Stroud's suggestion that his arguments aren't supposed to turn us into skeptics, but have a different function. As we saw, it is hard to see how his approach could succeed in defending the significance of skepticism in a way that is independent of the truth of the skeptical position, even if the account doesn't aim at inducing belief.

The best conclusion to derive from these points, then, is that an account of the significance for skepticism will need to await what we find once the burden of theory development on behalf of skepticism is shouldered. We will show how such theory development should proceed in Chapters 4 and 5, for the challenges to success are considerable. But if we assume that these challenges can be met, we can give a brief preview of where our discussion will lead us in the search for the significance of skepticism. This more general significance links aspects of skepticism both to a proper understanding of the best form of fallibilism but also to a central aspect of a well-lived life, that of humility, including intellectual humility, and appropriate expressions of it.

The approach we will develop, after completing the task of theory development, takes a path through the virtues of limitation, such as humility, to explaining and defending the value of skepticism that rebuts the ordinary language, commonsense response to it that treats it merely as fodder for reflective equilibrium. This approach will thus lead us both to an account of the significance of skepticism, but will also show why a proper form of fallibilism needs to reject Moorean dismissiveness toward skepticism.

2.5 Conclusion

So the significance of skepticism is not found by considering the skeptical thesis itself or arguments for that thesis. Finding such significance can only be accomplished by seeing how to develop the idea that knowledge itself is somehow tied to an ideal standard that is chronicled in the development of a skeptical theory or position. Moreover, even though there is an enduring contribution made in commonsense epistemology that dovetails with this demand for theory development, this epistemology has been associated history with a dismissive attitude toward skepticism and the argumentation for it.

Once the prospect of finding significance for skepticism elsewhere than in truth and quality of argumentation, the question arises as to whether fallibilist resistance to skepticism can only appear in a form accompanied by Moorean dismissiveness toward the view. As we have seen, the dismissive attitude is perhaps warranted in the face of attempts at defending the significance of skepticism in the ways considered in this chapter, but once we look for a different kind of account, we will also need to consider whether there is a version of fallibilism that can be less complacent than one involving Moorean dismissiveness. Perhaps Moorean dismissiveness would still be warranted after we complete theory development, but the guiding principle goes against this possibility, for if dismissiveness remains appropriate, it is hard to see how we'll have found any significance for this object of disdain. So, in the process of theory development for skepticism, we'll also be developing an understanding of fallibilism that aims at avoiding Moorean dismissiveness, for it is in the dance of these two positions that the significance of skepticism is revealed. Hence, in the next chapter we'll focus on fallibilism and it varieties, including but not limited to complacent versions of it that embrace Moorean dismissiveness.

Chapter 3
Versions of Fallibilism

3.1 Introduction

The point of the last chapter was to reveal the pressure on skepticism to embrace a need for theory development, and the goal of this chapter is to document how versions of fallibilism that resist skepticism face similar issues. We saw, in the last chapter, how a methodological defense of commonsense epistemology, focused on the Moorean principle that one should never abandon the more obvious for the less obvious, makes it difficult for skeptical argumentation to provide us with no more than another impetus for achieving reflective equilibrium among our considered judgments. Moreover, such equilibrium will still honor the Moorean dictum, and hence the result will not be a form of skepticism. The consequence of all this is an expectable attitude of dismissiveness toward skepticism and the arguments in favor of it, leaving epistemologists free to contemplate skeptical argumentation when they have nothing else to do, but with little motivation for taking skepticism seriously when the important tasks in epistemology need to be addressed.

Suppose, however, that skepticism can be developed in a way that yields a possibility of finding significance in skepticism in a way that is independent of the truth or falsity of skepticism and one which does to depend immediately on the quality of some argument for skepticism. Such an account would forestall any immediate dismissiveness, for it wouldn't come in the form of an argument to which the Moorean principle could be applied. As a result, it would put pressure on the attitude of dismissiveness, while at the same time allowing those attracted to such a position to ask about the details of commonsense opposition to it.

In addition, while our focus to this point has been on asking more of skepticism than thesis and bare argument, it is equally true that there are pressures on the commonsense alternative to skepticism that are often given short shrift by defenders of the view. The point of this chapter is to show what these pressures are, and so before taking up the task of theory development for skepticism, it is useful to appreciate the difficulties faced by fallibilists as well as those we have seen faced by skeptics.

In order to get to the issues faced by fallibilists, the question arises whether we might wish to develop a version of commonsense epistemology in terms of Cartesian infallibilism. The foolhardy direction counsels adopting the stronger position and trying to defend the view that our epistemic assurances simply couldn't be better than they in fact are for the many things we know to be true. In recent times,

Skepticism and Fallibilism. Jonathan L. Kvanvig, Oxford University Press. © Jonathan L. Kvanvig (2025).
DOI: 10.1093/9780198924821.003.0003

positions that either use the label of infallibilism or have been so-characterized have been championed,[1] but they make no pretense of claiming that our epistemic assurances are maximal, of the sort that achieve the Cartesian ideal. So, as I'll explain in more detail later, they aren't really taking the foolhardy path. Once the less heroic route is taken, one which abandons the idea that our epistemic assurances would satisfy Cartesian reflection in front of his stove, we enter the territory of fallibility. For fallibilists, the epistemic worry central to skepticism is legitimate: things could be better, epistemically speaking, and our preference for maximal assurance about where and when we'll encounter knowledge deserts goes unsatisfied.

Once in the territory of fallibilism, a weaker form of infallibilism may be defensible, but it would be, as Jason Leddington (2018) claims, an embracing of fallibility for infallibilists. That is, regardless of whether one claims that our epistemic grounds guarantee the truth of what we know, we still will have to be willing to claim that we might be wrong even about what we know. It is this component of fallibilism that is the concern of this chapter, since it gives rise to the possibility that fallibilism itself is an intellectually unstable position. Notice, for example, that Moore doesn't really spend any time trying to articulate how his commonsense epistemology compares with full-blown infallibilism of the sort we find in Descartes. Instead, he is content with insisting on knowing for certain that he has hands, among many other items of commonsense that he endorses. Moreover, when we attend to the great ordinary language philosopher J.L. Austin, we find an admission of a liability for error in cases of testimonial knowledge because of the unreliability of human testimony, even though the claim that the election is today is something one knows on the basis of having read it is the newspaper. This conjunction is obviously an affirmation of fallibilism, but Austin also is a bit uncomfortable with it, as he also writes, "'When you know you can't be wrong' is perfectly good sense. You are prohibited from saying 'I know it is so, but I may be wrong'.... If you are aware you may be mistaken, you ought not to say you know ..." (Austin, 1946, 98). One wonders what to make of this astonishing combination of views. In the newspaper case, he admits to being aware of the possibility of error, but in the latter passage, he says that in such cases you ought not say that you know. But that is precisely what he did.

The point, however, isn't about whether Austinian consistency can somehow be defended here, but rather about a potential instability in fallibilist attitudes and positions. Moreover, one doesn't need to be a skeptic to see the danger that is lurking, for the claims that Austin makes, viewed separately, aren't in conflict with what commonsense ideas could or would support. Nothing about commonsense prohibits trusting sources of information that are less than maximally reliable, and

---

[1] The two best-known are McDowell (1994) and Williamson (2000). For critical discussion, see Brown (2018) and Pritchard (2012). Williamson replies to Brown in Williamson (forthcoming).

such trust is often understood rightly, in this perspective, as how learning occurs, where to learn something new is to come to know. In addition, and in contrast, this everyday understanding doesn't lead us to expect others to note the possibility of error as a matter of course. It is, instead, perplexing, at the very least, to hear someone endorse a claim and point out at the same time that they might be wrong. This strange combination of claims carries with it no guarantee of consistency, so one wonders whether and how fallibilists can be committed to both views without significant theoretical work to show how the combination is consistent.

In response to this puzzling combination of views, fallibilisms can be developed that are more complacent about the tension in this combination of views, or more sensitive to those who question their coherence, as do skeptics but also many non-skeptics. Moore doesn't address the tension, making it easy to predict that someone attracted to Moorean commonsense philosophy would be expected to be rather complacent about the apparent tension, never really taking seriously the idea that anything short of Cartesian infallibilism is going to be incoherent. Austin's remarks, however, show that he's aware that expressing fallibilist theses is perplexing, and thus that those who endorse fallibilism have some explaining to do.

So the goal of this chapter is to engage in fair play regarding both sides of the dispute between skeptics and fallibilists. In the process, we'll delineate between various forms of fallibilism in response to this tension in the view, to see what the view requires and what options are available for endorsing it. The ultimate goal here is to look for a version of the view that is compatible with the defense of the significance of skepticism to be developed later, but we can't get to that stage of this project without completing the groundwork of this chapter involving identifying possible versions of fallibilism that are not required to be both dismissive of skepticism and complacent in the face of the tensions in the view. So let's begin with the notion of fallibility itself, to see what these possibilities might be.

3.2 Generic Fallibilism

In one way, it is a bit surprising to find the language of fallibility used in contrast to the Cartesian idea of looking for metaphysical certainties, since the generic idea of fallibility refers to a liability to err. Such a property is a property of persons, and Descartes certainly never intended to undermine the demon or dreaming hypotheses by defending the idea that human beings are not liable to err. Instead, he meant to oppose a kind of fallibility that can be applied to any number of epistemological items: justification, rationality, knowledge, understanding, wisdom, warrant, positive epistemic status, etc. The fallibility of people has the status of a banality, and any skeptic who thought that skepticism is the immediate consequence of this fact would be easy to resist.

46 VERSIONS OF FALLIBILISM

So let's begin from the idea that fallibility involves a capacity for error, but not merely as a property of cognizers but rather as a feature of cognitive attitudes or of actions that are the correct means to our goals (or the goals we ought to have). We then note that such a capacity is surely not adequate on its own for sustaining skeptical conclusions. If it were, skepticism would reduce to the view that nobody who isn't God-like can know anything, requiring for knowledge the absence of any capacity for forming false beliefs on any topic. That is a position deserving of not only a dismissive attitude but derision as well. To avoid this unfortunate consequence, skeptics need to focus instead on fallibility as applied to epistemological items.

Among these epistemological items, the skeptic initially targets one in particular: knowledge. Among the antinomies and paradoxes of philosophy, skeptics insist, would be any talk of fallible knowledge. Perhaps there are such things as fallible justification, fallible rationality, fallible warrant, and fallible positive epistemic status, but there simply cannot be any such thing as fallible knowledge.

But why, a commonsense epistemologist might ask, should we think any such thing? The start of an answer might point to Moore himself, who in Moore (1939) clearly acknowledges a demand for certainty in order to know. He requires of his proof of an external world that the premise he uses is a claim known to be true, and in defending that he does know that his premise is true, he says, "How absurd it would be to suggest that I did not know it, but only believed it, and that perhaps it was not the case! You might as well suggest that I do not know that I am now standing up and talking—that perhaps after all I'm not, and that it's not quite certain that I am!" (Moore, 1939, 145). Skeptics will perhaps smirk at the bluster here, but the point to note is that Moore connects what is certain with what is known. To know something is for it to be certain, and not just for one to be psychologically certain of it. For note that psychological certainty would be most naturally expressed in terms of personal attribution. But Moore's language is more objective: he implies that *it* is certain, not (just) that *he* is certain. In addition, Moore also equates a denial of knowledge and certainty with the possibility that perhaps he isn't standing up and talking (at the time that he was doing so), leading one to wonder if knowing for certain can be understood fallibilistically. For the last remark ("perhaps ... I'm not [standing up here and talking]") would most naturally be thought of as pointing out a possibility of being in error, and that possibility would seem to be precisely what is involved in the idea of fallible knowledge. So, Moore's claims provide some precedent for thinking that commonsense epistemology might not, after all, be comfortable with talk about fallible knowledge.

Reinforcement on this point can be found in David Lewis as well. He writes:

[I]t seems as if knowledge must be by definition infallible. If you claim that S knows that P, and yet you grant that S cannot eliminate a certain possibility in which not-P, it certainly seems as if you have granted that S does not after all know that *P*. To speak of fallible knowledge, of knowledge despite uneliminated possibilities of error, just *sounds* contradictory. (Lewis, 1996, 549)

Note that Lewis here is not voicing a strange or exotic thesis, as happens when he avers that every possible world is as real as our world. Instead, he's voicing something that we are supposed to recognize as an attractive claim, the same claim we see in J.L. Austin, to the effect that when you know you can't be wrong. For Lewis, the language is a bit more cumbersome, adverting to talk about eliminating possibilities of error, but the generic idea is the same. Austin gives full endorsement to the claim "'When you know you can't be wrong' is perfectly good sense", while Lewis is slightly less committal, claiming only that it *sounds* contradictory to say you know but might be wrong.

Lewis's remarks here echo the history of epistemology. Defenders of fallibilism regarding knowledge, prior to the rise of probabilism in the nineteenth century, are hard to find.[2] But Lewis's remark must be resisted by fallibilists, and Lewis himself ultimately does so as well.[3] The question is how to resist, and I want to distinguish between complacent resistance, leaving us with complacent fallibilism about knowledge, with appropriate resistance, leaving us with a form of fallibilism that can be sensitive to the difference between fallibilism about knowledge and fallibilism about justification. The road to a sensitive fallibilism begins by acknowledging the tinge of infallibilism in knowledge that Lewis notes, refusing the kind of complacency we find in those who ignore or facilely dismiss the tinge. Any such fallibilism, I'll argue, is too simple, since it will fail to explain the important difference between fallibilism about knowledge and fallibilism about justification. But

---

[2] To my knowledge, the first clear defender of fallible knowledge in the history of western philosophy is Philo of Larissa (159/8–84/3 BC). See Brittain (2001) for the evidence and discussion of it.

[3] Well, maybe. Lewis explicitly claims he is defending a version of infallibilism, but I think the details don't lead to this conclusion. First, he appeals to restricted quantification to undergird the claim that correct attributions of knowledge involve all possibilities of error being eliminated, leaving ones that we are "legitimately ignoring" untouched. To my ear, that sounds like a version of infallibilism in name only. A further interpretive issue here is that Lewis isn't really talking about knowledge, but about sentences that use the language of "knows". For Lewis and other contextualists, the truth-value of such sentences varies by context. One upshot of such a view is that the Disquotation Schema must fail:

(DS) "S knows that p" is true iff S knows that p.

It will fail for the same reasons that it fails for contextual terms more generally. Think, for example, about indexical language. The sentence "I am Obama"is true in some contexts of utterance and not in others. So take one such context, one in which Obama utters the sentence "I am Obama", and then apply (DS) to it. You are then in a position to deduce that I am Obama. But I'm not. I'm Jon Kvanvig.

Once we see that (DS) isn't preserved for contextual terms, remarks that contextualists make about "knows" and its cognates do not imply anything about the range or nature of knowledge. For that, one needs a substantive epistemology. (For sustained discussion of this point, see the interchange between Ernest Sosa and Keith DeRose in Tomberlin (1988)).) So, remarks about the language of "knows", when understood contextually, don't connect in any direct way to the disagreement between fallibilists and infallibilists.

My discussion in the text thus abstracts from the contextualism Lewis develops, and focuses instead on the initial claim about knowledge itself. It isn't merely that claiming knowledge while granting the possibility of error sounds bad, it is more relevantly a matter of whether an inability to eliminate possibilities of error immediately implying that one doesn't know.

48 VERSIONS OF FALLIBILISM

complacency can still arise, I'll maintain as well, when the tinge isn't dismissed. In such a case, the tinge will need to be accommodated in some fashion, but I will urge that fallibilists should prefer a theory that not only accommodates the data about concessions but also predicts it.

3.3 Fallibilism's Central Issue

The central issue for fallibilism, then, arises primarily when we try to conjoin a claim of knowledge with an awareness or admission of fallibility, one concerning the chance or possibility of error. We can call such an attitude a concessive attitude, and a verbal expression of this attitude a concessive assertion.

There is a third category, a concessive attribution, where one person attributes knowledge to another while noting the possibility that the other person is mistaken. Our initial tack on each of these will be to treat them similarly, though the possibility remains that reasons might be found during investigation for differentiating between them. I note the different categories of concessions because contextualist views in recent epistemology typically do not view concessive attitudes and assertions in the same way they view concessive attributions.[4] Our starting point, however, will focus on concessive attitudes.

Concessive assertions are not always epistemic. For example, consider the claim that "Democrats will control the Senate by 2030, but I could be wrong," or the claim that "Putin can't win the war in Ukraine, but I might be wrong (because I've been wrong on these sorts of things so many times in the past)." Both claims (at least if they are sincere) involve concessive attitudes, and both raise eyebrows when asserted. They are, in some sense, infelicitous, but there is no use of the concept of knowledge or any normative epistemic term in them. Because of the infelicity of the remarks, one is tempted to wonder whether the speaker meant to report *thinking* that Democrats will control the Senate, rather than it actually being so. In the second case, one might wonder whether the intention was to report feeling certain that Putin can't win.

The same inclinations arise when the remarks become overtly epistemic. If one says, "I know Democrats will be out of power by 2030, but I could be wrong," or "I know Putin will lose, but I might be mistaken," the same inclination to rephrase is felt, with one exception. For there is a standard use of "knows" where it is best understood to involve only subjective certainty.[5] Once this possibility is

---

[4] The versions of contextualism I have in mind here are defended by Stewart Cohen, Keith DeRose, and David Lewis. See, for example, Cohen (1987), DeRose (2008), and Lewis (1996).

[5] This use raises the issue of whether "knows" is a factive verb. For discussion, see Hazlett (2010). For the most part, this issue is orthogonal to the dispute between skeptics and fallibilists, since for both positions the focus is on knowledge that is factive, so our discussion will tend to ignore the issue of the best way to understand non-factive uses of "knows".

acknowledged, the epistemic examples can be seen to be less troubling than the original non-epistemic cases. But if we imagine ourselves in a context where this possibility is to be discounted, the same perplexities arise for both epistemic and non-epistemic concessions. The point to note, then, is that there is some interpretive discomfort at the actual language, leading hearers to want to re-phrase what is being said, or charitably take it in some special, perhaps non-factive, sense.[6] So, concessive attitudes and assertions need not involve the epistemic concept of knowledge, and can be equally troubling whether in this epistemic form or in a non-epistemic, merely factive, form.

Compare these first two concessive attitudes with other epistemic concessive attitudes. One might say, "I have good reasons for thinking there are no white ravens, but I could be wrong." Such a remark is a straightforward expression of fallibilism about reasons, and it involves no infelicity of expression at all. There is no felt pressure to re-phrase what is being said or to look for some unusual sense of the terms employed. The same would be true if one had talked about being justified in thinking there are no white ravens, or warranted in believing the same. That is, no infelicity of expression results from conjoining these claims with a concessive admission of one's own fallibility on the issue.

These points show that the infelicity of epistemic concessions is found when the epistemic notion in question is factive, as it would be for factive knowledge. In addition, we see the same infelicity when mere factivity is involved: that is, when the knowledge operator isn't present and all we have is the same propositional content. So factivity would seem to be the crucial feature here, and we get confirmation of this point by noting that the awkwardness of concessive attitudes and assertions generalizes to other attitudes as well. Consider factive attitudes such as regret, happiness, disappointment, or anger. One can't regret the flooding in India unless there was flooding in India; one can't be happy one's work has appeared in print unless it has; one can't be disappointed with a rejection by a journal without there being such a rejection; and one can't be angry with the divisive state of politics unless it is in such divisive state. Of course, when factivity fails, there might be something else about which these emotions are present, but it wouldn't be the circumstances as described. Moreover, when factivity is present, concessive admissions sound bad. "I'm angry you shot my dog, but you might not have;" "I regret not having read your book already, but I might have read it and forgotten that I did;" "I'm happy to report that you won the Lakatos prize, but maybe you didn't;" "I'm disappointed that the Tarheels lost in the championship game, but perhaps they won." Talk about inducing perplexity in hearers!

---

[6] There is a growing cottage industry on this issue of concessions, including Littlejohn (2011), Dodd (2010), Dougherty and Rysiew (2011), Hetherington (2013), Dougherty and Rysiew (2009), Stanley (2005b), Stanley (2005a), Benbaji (2009), Dodd (2006), Rysiew (2009), Fantl and McGrath (2009), and more recently, Simpson (2022) and Stoutenburg (forthcoming).

50 VERSIONS OF FALLIBILISM

Not as commonly noted, however, is the way in which concessive attitudes function with other great epistemic goods besides knowledge. As background to this point, let's separate the theory of epistemic value from the theory of epistemic normativity. The latter contains normative notions such as justification, rationality, warrant, and epistemic probability. The former contains the great epistemic goods of knowledge, understanding, and (theoretical) wisdom, all of which are factive or semi-factive. What I want to point out is the way in which concessive attitudes function for the latter two, having already noted the infelicity of concessive attitudes and attributions when it comes to knowledge.

Understanding comes in both objectual and propositional forms. One can understand, say, the modern synthesis that combines elements of Darwinism with processes of random genetic mutation, and one can also understand that the modern synthesis isn't Darwinism itself but rather Darwinism plus something having to do with random genetic mutation. Suppose, then, that a person claims the latter, but conjoins it with a concession of fallibility: "There are things that I understand, and my understanding includes something about the modern synthesis in biology, that it isn't Darwinism alone, though I could be mistaken about this point." Such a remark is perplexing, as infelicitous as a similar remark about knowledge.

A bit less troubling, however, are concessive attitudes about objectual understanding. If you say, "I understand the global economy, but I might be wrong about it," there is an air of infelicity again. But it could be removed by pointing out that one only means that one could be wrong about some of the minor details of the global economy. This point fits with the characterization I gave in Kvanvig (2003), claiming that objectual understanding is semi-factive. To have such understanding, one has to be in large part correct, but not about all the details. So even though the air of infelicity can be removed in this way, it remains the case that objectual understanding, like propositional understanding and propositional knowledge, is not easily conjoined with concessions of fallibility.

What of theoretical wisdom? The same points apply here. A quick gloss on the nature of theoretical wisdom will aid in appreciating this point. Theoretical wisdom involves a recognition of what matters and what doesn't, what is worth spending one's time pursuing and what isn't.[7] As such, it is a factive notion as well, and fallibilistic concessions sound faulty. Examples are a bit hard to see and appreciate, because of the rather general impropriety of claiming to have some wisdom, but one way to get such examples is to put the language in the mouth of a recognized saint. So, for example, if Mother Teresa espouses the view that Jesus was right about the insignificance of the cares of this world, she might say, "I have gotten to the point of seeing the wisdom of Jesus's view that the cares of this

---

[7] This idea is a medieval one, Eleonore Stump tells me, where understanding is knowledge of causes and theoretical wisdom is knowledge of what is important.

world are insignificant, though of course I could be wrong about that," we would be perplexed.

So the infelicity of concessive attitudes, assertions, and attributions pervades all of these great epistemic goods, including not only knowledge but understanding and wisdom as well. Since we have also noted the infelicity of concessive attitudes about simple truth claims as well, the attractive explanation appeals to factivity itself: each of the great goods displays a factive character to it, and we should expect that the noted infelicity is triggered when factivity is involved. It is not simply a feature of knowledge, but also of other epistemic goods, in addition to being present in non-epistemological contexts such as those involving simple truth claims as well as claims about emotional states that themselves have a factive character. In each case, concessions are infelicitous and the common denominator is factivity, leading to the idea that the simplest explanation is that the source of the infelicity is factivity itself.

Those familiar with Timothy Williamson's defense of the knowledge norm of assertion, as found in Williamson (2000) and building on the earlier Williamson (1996), will note how the factivity explanation competes with one relying on the knowledge norm of assertion. On the knowledge account, one shouldn't say what one doesn't know to be true, and so even for mere alethic concessions, the claim shouldn't be made unless the first conjunct is known to be true. (The implication of this view is that an epistemic concession shouldn't be made either unless one knows that one knows that the first conjunct is true.) Furthermore, for factive emotions, the story gets a bit more complicated, but Williamson argues that such states involve the factive state of knowledge as well, and so the expressions will also count as expressions of a related knowledge state, and hence be subject to a knowledge norm. Without intending to settle a dispute between the knowledge norm explanation and the factivity story, we can note the simplicity of the latter view over the former. In addition, on the factivity story, concessions about knowledge, understanding, and wisdom trigger infelicity directly, without a Rube-Goldberg circuit that runs through knowing that one knows, or that one understands, or has some choice bit of wisdom to impart.

Regardless of what is used to explain the infelicity in question, however, what is important is that such infelicity puts pressure on fallibilism while at the same time fitting quite well with infallibilism. For if knowledge is infallible, we should predict the infelicity of concessive attitudes, assertions, and attributions; but if knowledge is fallible, there are no obvious routes to such a prediction. It is in response to this prediction that we find distinctions between sensitive versions of fallibilism and complacent versions of it. Though we will see that there are gradations of sensitivity to be found, the first step for distinguishing the two is in terms of the approach taken to the data predicted by infallibilism. A strong instance of complacency denies the data, whereas more sensitive versions of fallibilism admit that the data is genuine and try to craft a version of the view that isn't undermined by the data. In the next section, then, we examine this distinction among types of fallibilism more closely, as a first step toward defending the need for a sensitive version of fallibilism and the precise degree of sensitivity that is best.

Before doing so, however, a bit of clarification is in order about the notion of prediction itself. The relevant notion of prediction here is epistemic, rather than psychological. When a theory yields a prediction, it generates epistemic grounds for the prediction itself. The psychological notion of prediction, from the mouth of Nostradamus or Jeane Dixon, generates no such grounds and can occur without the speaker having any such grounds either.

Beyond being epistemic in character, predictions are also defeasible. That is, a theory can make a prediction, the prediction turn out to be incorrect, and yet the theory fail to be refuted or undermined by that fact. For predictions can fail not only because of a fault in the theory but also for other reasons. Epistemologists came to see this point after Quine's articulation of this holistic doctrine in Quine (1951), one which he attributes to Duhem (1914), though the transmission lines are not direct.[8] Quine's holism goes much further than either Duhem's holism or the defeasibility point here, for Quine maintains that any statement can be preserved in the face of contrary experience if one makes enough adjustments elsewhere in one's system of beliefs. Duhem maintains only that recalcitrant experience is ambiguous enough that it never points with singular clarity at any particular claim that is thereby refuted. So predictions are calculated, experience consulted, and then some judgment or epistemic calculation must be made to conclude where the fault lies. It is often the prediction itself that is fingered, but the prediction might not be at the problem. Historically famous cases of such can be found in the discoveries of planets beyond Saturn, where observational data did not fit with the predictions of Newtonian mechanics.

Regardless of whether defeasibility leads to the radical holism of Quine, the point to note in our context is that the prediction of infelicity that comes from infallibilism is an important one, but one that leaves some room for response by fallibilists, given the defeasible character of the prediction. We turn, then, to these fallibilist responses, which range from complacency to more sensitive ones.

3.4 Sensitive and Complacent Fallibilisms

As I use the terms, a central difference between complacent and sensitive fallibilism is found in their different treatments of the infelicity of concessive attitudes.

[8] See note 2 in Howard (1990), where Quine is quoted as claiming that he hadn't heard of Duhem when he first wrote "Two Dogmas of Empiricism," but instead was motivated by his own "common sense, plus perhaps some influence from Neurath's congenial figure of the boat." It is noteworthy that numerous references to Duhem can be found in Neurath (1983), the published collection of his important papers, so the best story to tell is one that has the influence on Quine by Duhem to be indirect, coming through direct influence from Duhem to Neurath and from Neurath to Quine.

3.4 SENSITIVE AND COMPLACENT FALLIBILISMS   53

At one extreme is a complacent fallibilism that treats concessive knowledge attributions—and also concessive attributions concerning understanding and wisdom—as unproblematic, no more a cause of concern than concessive attributions concerning epistemically normative properties and states. Such complacency toward this tinge of infallibility fits well with Moorean dismissiveness of skepticism, so we'll be understanding both the more general dismissiveness toward skepticism and the more specific dismissiveness toward the infelicity of concessive attitudes under this type of complacent fallibilism.

The idea that such infelicity needs no response whatsoever, though certainly possible, isn't the most promising version of fallibilism, nor is it the only version of the view that counts as complacent. To reject the data concerning infelicity without explanation would not be epistemically responsible, given the, at least apparently, troubling character of the attitudes. That leaves the question of how to embrace fallibilism and yet offer an explanation that still is to be categorized as complacent.

A further form of complacency arises by first reminding us that it is factivity itself that triggers the impropriety of concessions, as noted above. This idea then leads to the possibility of treating the infallibilist tinge noted by Lewis in terms of a simple scope distinction. The idea Lewis notes is that when you know, you can't be wrong. Such a claim hints at infallibility, but it is also of a form that is known for generating modal fallacies. In particular, it is subject to a scope ambiguity, where the modal operator can take either wide or narrow scope. On the wide scope reading, the claim simply reports the factivity of knowledge: it is necessary that (if you know, you are correct).[9]

This factive reading provides no support at all for infallibilism. It amounts to nothing beyond the claim that factive knowledge entails truth, and no fallibilist thesis is threatened by such a claim. For such complacent fallibilists, scope confusion underlies any infallibilist tinge in knowledge, and so even though it might sound problematic to say you know but can't eliminate all possibilities of error, that is simply because we are prone to modal confusion. If we generalize this idea

---

[9] Well, almost correct. As noted already, ordinary language employing talk of knowledge has a use of the term that is clearly non-factive, expressing psychological certainty instead of something factive.

On the notion of operators taking wide scope, the language is fairly widely used and understood, so I'll explain it only in a footnote. Sometimes a logical particle governs an entire expression, and sometimes only part of the expression. In the former case, the particle takes wide scope, and in the latter case it is narrow scope. Though the modal confusion was recognized in medieval discussions as involving a confusion between the necessity of the consequence and the necessity of the consequent, contemporary discussion of this distinction traces to Bertrand Russell's discussion of negation in Russell (1905), where the sentence "The present king of France isn't bald" can be interpreted in terms of this distinction (Russell's language is about primary and secondary occurrences of the negation, but the language of wide and narrow is much more intuitive). If the negation is given narrow scope, the sentence says that there is a king and he's got plenty of hair. If it is given wide scope, what is denied is that there is a king who has hair, which of course is the preferred reading.

For the example in the text, narrow scope says something beyond factivity. It claims that if you know, then it's not possible that you are mistaken. This claim is remarkably robust, requiring knowers to be God-like in cognitive abilities. As we will see, such a claim implies infallibilism but is a much stronger claim as well, and stronger in a clearly objectionable way.

54 VERSIONS OF FALLIBILISM

to the infelicity of concessions more generally, we explain away the infelicity in terms of a scope confusion. Once so accommodated, the infelicity puts no pressure on fallibilism, so complacency toward concessive attitudes, assertions, and attributions is unobjectionable.

Such an accommodation is a bit too easy, though. If the appeal of infallibilism were a matter of modal confusion, we should expect one of the two scope readings to be what the infallibilist is after, even if it is a claim that should be rejected after close inspection. The problem is that the wide scope reading is too weak to express the infallibilist idea, but the narrow scope reading is too strong. It is the claim that if you know, you couldn't exist while being mistaken on the matter in question, and that claim is too strong because it implies that knowledge obtains only where the knower is cognitively God-like, being unable to make a mistake (on the matter in question). Such a claim says, then, that knowledge requires personal infallibility. As we saw earlier, though, the fallibility of persons is a banality, not by itself suitable for sustaining skepticism. After all, even if infallibility were present for some of our beliefs, it is no implication of that idea that we'd lack the power to form a false belief about the matter. Even if there are ways to guarantee that we are correct, that doesn't mean we are incapable of following a different path and ending up in error. So whatever we make of the adage that when you know you can't be wrong, the simple scope distinction doesn't address the tinge of infallibilism in the adage nor in the infelicitous attitudes, assertions, and attributions discussed above.

One further point is worth noting about trying to defend fallibilism by appealing to this scope distinction. The idea was that if the infelicity of concessions arises because of factive elements, we might find attractive the idea of explaining away the infallibilist tinge in knowledge solely in terms of factivity. Doing so puts all the weight of this explanation on the wide scope reading of the adage in question, but it is worth noting the contrast between the banality of this wide scope reading and a dissimilarity when it comes to alethic concessions, as when someone says, "it is raining but it might not be." There is no banality related to such a concession, for if there were, it would be something like "when something is true and you endorse it, you can't have gotten it wrong." That claim isn't even remotely plausible, and the only nearby claim that is plausible is the claim that if a truth is believed, that true belief can't also be a false belief. But that claim is plausible solely in virtue of non-contradiction and bivalence, needing no appeal to scope distinctions in order to uncover the banality. So even if factivity is the central aspect involved in understanding the infelicities of concessions, that conclusion provides no basis for the idea that fallibilism can avoid the issue of troubling concessions merely by pointing out a scope confusion.

Such a scope-distinction fallibilism attempts to explain away the infallibilist tinge in knowledge in terms of a false presupposition. Once the presupposition is identified as false, we explain away the discomfort associated with concessive attitudes and attributions. To this point, we've seen one unattractive way of pursuing the false presupposition idea, in terms of a modal confusion, but we'll find other ways of trying to identify a false presupposition underlying infallibilism, so there are other attempts at complacency to consider. In contrast, more sensitive fallibilisms embrace the difference between concessive attitudes about epistemically normative properties and the more troubling concessive attitudes about factive states such as knowledge, aiming to understand this infelicity properly in a way that does not require abandoning fallibilism.

To move toward more sensitive versions of the view, I'll first consider complacency in a fallibilist stance arising from various ways of trying to explain away the data concerning concessions. Understanding these kinds of complacency and the problems they face begins with the theoretical framework that generates the problem, one involving the proper way to understand the notion of possibility involved in the concessions.

This framework begins by identifying this kind of possibility in terms of epistemic possibility, though we should be careful at this point not to assume much content to the idea of the epistemic here. A better way to think of the matter is to treat the term as a placeholder for a kind of necessity that is obviously different from notions of metaphysical or logical or nomological or accidental necessity. None of these give plausible understandings of the kind of possibility envisioned. Instead, the kind is identified as epistemic, since it seems to be about success and failure when it comes to our attempts to find the truth and avoid error, in a way that comes and goes as new information is acquired. For example, one can correctly remark that James Bond might be in Zurich, given one's current state of information regarding his whereabouts, but also correctly remark an hour later that Bond can't be in Zurich, given that one has just seen him in the hallway. This variability isn't found for any of metaphysical, logical, or nomological necessity, and it is a quite different kind of variability from that involved in accidental necessity, the kind of necessity that claims about the past possess. So we label the modal notion "epistemic", to flag its variability with respect to information possessed. We are then in a position to consider the initial plausible story about this kind of possibility, a story that fully supports Lewis's sense that concessions sound contradictory. So let's take a look at this standard story and the additional pressure it puts on fallibilism.

The standard story about epistemic possibility, playing a central role in seminal work on epistemic logic, Hintikka (1962), defines it in terms of knowledge. In particular, it identifies it with an absence of knowledge of the negation:

Epistemic Possibility (EP): $\diamond_e p =_{df.} \sim K \sim p$

In English, EP claims that p is epistemically possible means that $\sim p$ is unknown. Using our example above, at 10 a.m. there was a possibility of Bond being in Zurich because you didn't know that he wasn't in Zurich. By 11 a.m., however, it was no

56 VERSIONS OF FALLIBILISM

longer possible that he was in Zurich at 10 a.m. because you just saw him in the hall at 11 a.m. (and, I'm assuming, we are in a location that we know to be several hours away from Zurich).

Given this understanding, a concessive knowledge attribution is semantically contradictory, since knowing $\sim p$ entails not knowing p. So the standard story about epistemic possibility makes the infelicity of concessive attitudes as logically strong as it could be. This semantic account of the infelicity renders such attitudes contradictory, and such a semantic account leaves no room whatsoever for escaping the infallibilist implication of infelicity of concessive attitudes, assertions, and attributions.

In quoting Lewis concerning the data of infelicity, we see that Lewis is a bit guarded about the data and the idea of contradiction that results from this semantic account of epistemic possibility. In that passage, Lewis only claims that any concessive attribution "sounds contradictory," rather than claiming that they are contradictory, and we can use Lewis's discussion to reveal one idea for how a fallibilist might resist the standard story about epistemic possibility. He does so through two devices, appealing to contextualism and restricted quantification. As noted above, I don't think the appeal to contextualism will help here, if our interest is in the issue of what we know and whether that knowledge is fallible or infallible, just as I don't think that an understanding of how indexicals work will help with the philosophical problem of personal identity.[10] But the idea of restricted quantification might. When we note the apparent contradiction of concessive attitudes and attributions, perhaps we are thinking in terms of epistemic chances or possibilities of error, and perhaps the proper semantical treatment of this notion requires ruling out all such chances or possibilities. If so, as Lewis thinks is the case, we have the quantifier 'all' to interpret, and the idea of restricted quantification can be used to defend that (to put the point tendentiously) perhaps, and surprisingly, "all" doesn't always mean *all*! Lewis writes:

> Our definition of knowledge requires a *sotto voce* proviso. *S knows* that *P* iff *S*'s evidence eliminates every possibility in which not-*P*—Psst!—except for those possibilities that we are properly ignoring. (Lewis, 1996, 554)

This appeal to restricted quantification is independent of any appeal to contextualism. On Lewis's contextualism, the class of possibilities that are properly ignored varies by context, so much so that when we focus on claims about what we know, the possibilities that are properly ignored diminish to the point at which no attribution of knowledge can any longer be correctly made—hence the propriety of terming our knowledge "elusive". It is elusive because it is ubiquitous until we

---

[10] To remind, contextualism is a theory about our use of the word "know" and its cognates, a theory of "knowledge", rather than a theory of knowledge. A theorist can offer both kinds of theories, but contextualism about "knows" and its cognates needs supplementing by something else to give us the latter kind of theory.

start reflecting on it, where it tends to disappear entirely. Well, again, not quite, since the implications of such a contextualist point is not one about knowledge but rather about the truth value of claims about knowledge, so it isn't really knowledge that is elusive, but the truth of the claims we make about it. In short, it is about "knowledge" rather than about knowledge. But the point about restricted quantification remains, and it does not require contextualism. For if contextualism were false and the truth-value of claims about knowledge were invariant, the quantifier concerning possibilities eliminated by one's evidence could still be a restricted quantifier.

Once we characterize the concessions claimed to sound contradictory in terms involving a quantifier, we should wonder why we should side with Lewis in treating the quantifier as a restricted one. Lewis maintains that it is restricted, but doesn't actually defend the view that it is. Instead, he uses the idea that it is a restricted quantifier to avoid interpreting concessive knowledge attributions as actually contradictory. When interpreted in the stronger way, of course, skepticism looms immediately, for as noted already, trying to avoid skepticism without endorsing fallibilism is arguably hopeless. So, if we try to find a defense of this appeal to restricted quantification, a quite natural idea would be a Moorean/Chisholmian one that we know many things, after all, with the only issue being how to understand such concessions so that they are compatible with the obvious point that we know many things in spite of sounding contradictory.

Appealing to restricted quantification is a convenient way to secure this result, but perhaps too convenient. While it is true that many, even if not all,[11] quantifiers are restricted ones, they tend to be rather obviously so: it is sometimes correct to complain that there is nothing in the fridge, and though it is sometimes fun to pretend that the quantifier is unrestricted when the complaint is voiced, it's obvious that it isn't. But the tinge of infallibilism in knowledge, already acknowledged by Lewis, shows that it simply isn't obvious that the quantifier in the characterization of knowledge is restricted as well.

To illustrate this point, when Johnny Cash sings,

> I've been everywhere, man
> I've been everywhere, man
> Crossed the deserts bare, man
> I've breathed the mountain air, man
> Of travel I've had my share, man
> I've been everywhere.

we don't pause in confusion or perplexity about whether he's visited parts of the universe outside our light cone, but immediately see this quantificational claim as the combination of hyperbole and restricted quantification it is.

---

[11] For a compelling argument that some quantifiers have to be unrestricted, see Williamson (2003).

58 VERSIONS OF FALLIBILISM

To return to the example about what's in the refrigerator, the concessive analog would be:

There's nothing in the fridge, but there are shelves and a light bulb in there.

A somewhat strange conjunction, but it is not infelicitous. In reply, one's hearer might say, "Ah, you prevented a weak joke!" The point to note is that mastery of language involves competence in recognizing restricted quantification, and the fridge example is just such a case. But if restricted quantification is at work in epistemic cases, it would be an outlier example, not falling under the usual competence feature of natural language mastery. As such, the view looks suspiciously like special pleading, of just the sort that philosophers and lawyers are good at, but which does little more for a position than save it from outright and decisive refutation. To put the point another way, the fact that the restricted quantification in question is an outlier with respect to normal competency requirements on the mastery of language remains a mark against the view even if it doesn't count as decisively refuting the view.

So Lewis is on the side of the fallibilist, and tries to explain away the infelicity of concessions, but does so without adequate buttressing for the *explanans*. In addition, it is worth noting the pressure such an escape route epistemically necessary, it isputs on the account of epistemic possibility. In intensional logics, the dual rules are typically thought of as basic principles for the logic in question,[12] but given Lewis's proposal of employing restricted quantification in an account of knowledge, we'll need to formulate an intermediate principle before we can endorse an account of epistemic possibility in terms of there being no uneliminated possibilities of error that aren't properly ignored. For if an account of knowledge allows there to be possibilities that are properly ignored, these very possibilities should still count as epistemic possibilities, leading to a required abandonment of EP, the standard Hintikkian account of epistemic possibility.

Lewisian ideas thus mesh nicely with those of a growing number of philosophers who aren't happy with this standard account of epistemic possibility.[13] So

---

[12] Since the nature of duality is widely understood, I leave this brief explanation to a footnote. It arises initially in standard first-order logic, where the universal and existential operators are duals of each other. What that means is that we can define either in terms of the other, thereby simplifying the underlying structure of the logic. For these quantifiers, the dual rule is:

$\forall x \Psi \dashv\vdash \neg \exists x \neg \Psi$

More generally, where X and Y are logical particles related by a dual rule, we get:

$X \dashv\vdash \neg Y \neg$

The logician's interest is piqued here because dual rules appear quite generally across a wide variety of logical systems, as noted in the text.

[13] For additional discussion of and resistance to the standard account, see, for example, Hintikka (1962), Teller (1972), Fetzer (1974), Teller (1974), DeRose (1991), Huemer (2007), Yalcin (2007), Sorensen (2009), Yalcin (2009), Egan and Weatherson (2009), Reed (2013), and Knobe and Yalcin (2014).

3.4 SENSITIVE AND COMPLACENT FALLIBILISMS   59

what a Lewisian account of concessions needs is an alternative to EP, and one that fits much of what Lewis writes is the following:

EP$_{ev}$: $\diamond_e p$ $=_{df.}$ where E is one's total body of evidence, there is a possibility in which $\sim p$ is true that is not ruled out by E (that is, the denial of this possibility is not entailed by E).

Fallibilists typically want to maintain that there are always, or typically, possibilities of error that are uneliminated in the sense involved in EP$_{ev}$, so the sound of contradiction point that Lewis makes is sustained. Moreover, this account fits nicely with Lewis's remarks, since he uses the language of evidence explicitly: "S's epistemic possibilities are just those possibilities that are uneliminated by S's evidence ..." (552). In addition, it is a charitable gloss on the "ruling out" language to understand it in the manner of the parenthetical clause above. Without some such clarification, one might interpret the notion of ruling out in terms of knowledge itself, so that one can rule out anything entailed by what one knows. In such a case, knowing p would automatically rule out any possibility in which p is false, and all discussion of the importance of restricted quantification would disappear. Instead, his infallibilist concern is about a body of information that doesn't include the target proposition itself but instead contains whatever information is being used or relied on to confirm the truth of the target proposition. So, we need to understand the notion of ruling out in terms other than something involving knowledge, and the language of total evidence and what it entails fits well with Lewisian themes.

So we have an alternative to the standard account of epistemic possibility, and it is one that a Lewisian might use to both embrace the infallibilist tinge in knowledge and also resist infallibilism. The tinge remains because knowledge still requires ruling out epistemic possibilities of error, but restricted quantification lets some of these be properly ignored even though, according to EP$_{ev}$, they really are epistemic possibilities.

Even so, as is obvious, it takes much more to supplant the standard account than simply providing an alternative to it. For the standard account is standard because it has many features that are needed in a fully adequate account of epistemic possibility. One such virtue we have noted already: it makes epistemic possibility relative to bodies of information possessed by knowers. EP$_{ev}$ does so as well, but there are other features of an adequate account of epistemic possibility that it lacks. It has important formal shortcomings and also falls short on metatheoretical grounds, and these failures make it difficult to see how EP$_{ev}$ could be used to characterize fallibilism and make sense of concessive attitudes, assertions, and attributions. We will thus be led down the path of trying to find an account that lacks these shortcomings, a task that we will find daunting.

3.4.1 Alternatives to the Standard Account and Their Weaknesses

First, let's consider the formal issues that EP_{ev} raises. For intensional logics, we expect to find two operators, a strong and a weak, related by a dual rule. Thus, for example, for modal logic, necessity is a strong operator and possibility a weak operator, with the dual relationship given by the identity or interderivability between the necessity of a claim and the lack of the possibility of that claim not being true. Or, again, for deontic logics, we have a strong operator involving forbiddenness and a weak permissibility operator, related by the dual rule identifying the permissibility of an action or state of affairs with the failure for its absence to be forbidden.

So when we turn to epistemic logic, we expect to find the same formal features. The usual assumption here is that the weaker operator is the epistemic possibility operator, with some stronger operator an epistemic necessity operator. We can then speak of what might be and what must be, what may occur and what has to occur, understanding all such locations to be epistemic in character rather than metaphysical, nomological, or logical. Given a starting point in terms of epistemic possibility, we can then ask what the stronger operator is, one that is related to epistemic possibility by a dual rule, one that tells us that if p is epistemically possibility, then it mustn't be that $\sim p$. The common assumption in the literature of epistemic logic is that this stronger "must" operator is that of knowledge itself, in large part, I expect, because that is part of the point of calling the logic an *epistemic* logic. This relationship is precisely what is encoded in EP, so the standard story about epistemic possibility has the virtue of sustaining this formal feature.

This explanation that identifies a strong epistemic operator with knowledge is not completely compelling, but the assumption is nonetheless natural. An alternative to it, though, would be to consider severing the link between epistemic necessity and knowledge, thinking of the former in other terms. The first question to ask about such severing, though, is whether the proposed notion of necessity could coherently be logically weaker than knowledge, and here the idea should be rejected immediately. For if this idea were endorsed, we'd have a view on which something might have to be true and yet not known to be true. Such an implication should be rejected out-of-hand, so a first thing to note is that if one wishes to distinguish between epistemic necessity and knowledge, one will have to do so in a way that nonetheless endorses the claim that knowledge is a logical consequence of epistemic necessity. In other words, one must endorse the idea that, as a matter of logical necessity, if a claim is epistemically necessary, it is known to be true.

This result leaves in place the possibility of distinguishing the notion of epistemic necessity from knowledge by maintaining that it is stronger than knowledge, perhaps explicable in terms of some notion of ideal knowledge. Such an identification could be secured trivially by defining the notion of ideality in terms of epistemic necessity, for example. Whether or not such an identification is endorsed, however, what we would end up with is that what one knows to be true need not be what epistemically must be true, and though what epistemically must be true is incompatible with the epistemic possibility of not being true, this incompatibility would give us no reason for claiming that knowledge itself is incompatible with such an epistemic possibility.

On behalf of the idea that epistemic necessity is different from knowledge, I note that there is a similar concern in deontic logic. In addition to operators concerning what is permissible and what is forbidden, we would like to identify an operator concerning what is obligatory. An initially promising idea is that what is obligatory is to be understood in terms of a denial of there being any way of opting out. That is, where it is obligatory to do A, it is forbidden to fail to do A.

Even so, we find the following kind of language concerning what is forbidden. You ask, "Do I have to do that?", and a reply that is sometimes voiced is this: "No, you don't have to but you ought to." There are potential ways to explain away such utterances without positing a difference between a deontic "must" and obligation itself, but positing such a difference is one theoretical option.[14] So there is some precedent for considering the idea of taking the strong operator in an intensional logic to be something other than the most natural ordinary language concept one finds, whether it be the deontic concept of obligation or the epistemic concept of knowledge.

Are there better reasons for identifying the strong epistemic operator with knowledge? Consider again the situation where you affirm at 10 a.m. that Bond might be in Zurich, but upon seeing him in St. Louis, you take back the affirmation, saying, "I was wrong, he must not have been in Zurich at 10 a.m." It follows from this "must" claim that Bond was not in Zurich at the time in question. It is pretty clear that the necessity claim implies a knowledge claim, as argued above, so the issue to address concerns the other direction. We ask, then, whether in this example if you claim to know that Bond wasn't in Zurich at the time in question, are you also committed to the claim that he mustn't have been there then. Attributing such a commitment is as natural an idea as the link Lewis notes between knowledge claims and being able to rule out possibilities of error, making the identification between epistemic necessity and knowledge quite attractive.

So, it would seem, Lewis might endorse something like EP_{ev} while still insisting on an identification of knowledge with epistemic necessity. In fact, however, proceeding in this way runs into problems about the factivity of the strong epistemic operator. For if the epistemic "must" is the dual of epistemic possibility, we should expect it to be factive. Not all intensional logics have this feature: witness deontic logic, where we should never expect the strong deontic operator to imply truth. But for modal logics, as well as epistemic ones, we should have such an expectation. So, if we look at EP_{ev} through the lens of a dual rule while also endorsing

---

[14] For discussion, see McNamara (2010).

Lewis's idea of restricted quantification concerning the ruling out of possibilities of error, we get that the epistemic "must" applies whenever any possibilities of error that exist are properly ignored. The difficulty is that it is compatible with this claim that there is a possibility of error that is also an actuality, in which case, the claim in question must be true while at same time also being false. One could avoid this awkward possibility by insisting that nothing actually true can be properly ignored, but doing so should raise eyebrows. First, note that a "possibility of error" might involve only alternative hypotheses to what one actually believes, and if that is all we mean by a possibility of error, then of course every actually true alternative hypothesis would count as a possibility of error that can't be ignored. But that is because such an actually true hypothesis would reveal that one's belief is mistaken, and so trivially something that isn't known to be true. The more substantive notion of a possibility of error is that all such knowledge-undermining possibilities would need to be ruled out to characterize the tinge of infallibilism that Lewis notes. On this wider understanding, however, there is no reason to hold that what is actual can't be properly ignored. That is the lesson of external but misleading defeaters. Such a defeater is something that is actually true but beyond one's purview, but since it is misleading, it doesn't undermine knowledge.[15] It is thus properly ignored, for if it were not ignored, it would become internal and its defeating power would be displayed so that knowledge is undermined. As a result, insisting that nothing actual can be properly ignored is not a suitable way to avoid the problem of factivity that is raised by replacing EP with EP_{ev}.

This problem of non-factivity for the strong epistemic operator is a result of the combination of claims that Lewis wants to endorse, so may not be a problem for EP_{ev} itself, but rather for a theory of knowledge that uses this idea of properly ignored but uneliminated possibilities of error.

So the first complication to be faced when substituting EP_{ev} for EP or using it as a basis for sustaining the latter, is that it looks like factivity for the strong epistemic operator is going to be lost. This problem results from Lewis's proviso that some possibilities of error can be properly ignored, so one might consider retaining EP_{ev} and dropping the idea of restricted quantification. Doing so brings us to a deeper concern about this proposed replacement for EP, arising because of the theoretical baggage that EP_{ev} brings on board.

If we assume that knowledge is the strong epistemic operator, we can put the second complication in the form of a question. When we infer knowledge from the lack of an epistemic possibility for the negation, the question is, "What hath evidence to do with knowledge?" The thought behind the question is whether we're all supposed to be evidentialists now, and the implied criticism is that no decent account of epistemic possibility should require accepting one particular theory of knowledge over some other theory of knowledge. For those unwilling to make

---

[15] For extensive discussion on misleading defeaters, see Klein (1981).

the assumptions that epistemic necessity and knowledge should be identified, a similar criticism could be launched, according to which no account of epistemic possibility should require one approach to epistemic necessity over others. In both contexts, then, we get a metatheoretical constraint on an account of epistemic possibility, to the effect that our account of epistemic possibility should be independent of the question of which first-order theory of knowledge (or epistemic necessity) is correct.

This constraint extends to accounts of fallibilism as well, given the close relationship between fallibilism and epistemic possibility, for fallibilism is a metatheoretical category that is supposed to include those first-order epistemologies that reject skeptical standards for knowledge. The most common characterizations of fallibilism, in terms of a lack of entailments provided by one's evidence or justification or grounds for belief, fall prey to this metatheoretical constraint, since such accounts are not theoretically neutral on the nature of knowledge. One such account is EP_{ev}, once we drop Lewis's idea about interpreting it in terms of restricted quantification. So it, as well as other entailment accounts, fails the theoretical neutrality test.

All such accounts also fall prey to another objection, widely known in the literature, that any appeal to entailment or guarantees of truth will not be able to explain how fallible support occurs for necessary truths.[16] The problem is that a necessary truth is entailed by everything as well as nothing, leading to the conclusion that any basis for belief in a necessary truth will be an infallible one.

A possible response to this worry could be developed by arguing for an alternative logic on which necessary truths are not so easily entailed, but this is a difficult road to travel. For it isn't enough to note that there are non-standard logics that avoid this problem. Instead, what is needed is a full-blown defense of such a non-standard logic in order to relieve the proposed entailment account of fallibilism and epistemic possibility on offer from this objection. Even if one succeeded in this effort, the lack of theoretical neutrality would still plague any such proposal, turning such a gargantuan success into a mere hollow victory.

There are more general problems for an entailment account of fallibilism as well. In generic form, the problem with such an approach to infallibility is that it many theories of knowledge that are intuitively fallibilist in character can end up being counted as versions of infallibilism. If we want to use this language to describe such views, we could describe them as versions of Cheap Infallibilism, not worthy of properly characterizing the lofty epistemic status the skeptic claims we can't have. I've characterized some views of this sort elsewhere,[17] and it is worth noting what a wide range of positions end up counting as versions of Infallibilism

---

[16] Reed (2012, note 13) cites a number of epistemologists aware of this criticism, the earliest of which is Lehrer (1974).

[17] See Kvanvig (2011b) and Kvanvig (2014, 89–103).

64 VERSIONS OF FALLIBILISM

when it is quite clear that they are really fallibilist accounts at bottom. They do not, that is, identify knowledge with the lofty ideal of the skeptic, and no skeptics worth their salt would slouch away in defeat after seeing such proposals.

For example, if the system of information is your evidence and one endorses the Williamsonian idea (see Williamson (2000)) that your evidence is identical with your knowledge, then all of your knowledge is trivially infallible on the truth-entailing conception of infallibility. For, of course, what you know is entailed by any body of information that includes what you know.

In spite of this entailment, however, the story of fallibilism is writ into the process of coming to know, the process of climbing the mountain to such an achievement. Even if reaching the summit gives one the resources to rule out all possible alternatives, there is nothing in the process of coming to know that undermines fallibilism or yields the kind of infallibility the skeptic insists is needed in order to reach that summit. So the truth-entailing feature of this account of evidence isn't the kind needed to yield genuine infallibilism of the sort skeptics have always claimed is required for knowledge.

There are weaker notions of evidence that generate similar results. For example, suppose you think that evidence doesn't need to be true in order to count as evidence. You might also find an analogue of the deduction theorem for first-order logic plausible for epistemic logic. That is, relative to a given background system of information or context, one might expect the following to be true:

$$DT_\epsilon: \Phi \vdash_\epsilon \Psi \text{ iff } \vdash_\epsilon (\Phi \to \Psi)$$

Roughly, the argument from one claim to another is a good epistemic argument (in a given context) if and only if the conditional between the two is itself epistemically supported (in that context). This analogue of the deduction theorem for first-order logic thus puts both the antecedent of the conditional and the conditional itself within the system of evidence in question, allowing a Cheap Infallibilism that involves the entailment of the consequent when the system contains adequate evidence for it.

This form of Cheap Infallibilism is untouched by the fact that the antecedent of the conditional might be false (given the assumption that evidence doesn't need to be true to count as evidence). For the issue isn't whether evidence can mislead, but simply whether it entails the truth of what one knows to be true. On this picture, there is no possibility of anything that one knows to fail to be supported by evidence that entails this knowledge.

Yes, this is a mystifying position, but the point to note isn't the strangeness of the position but rather that it isn't really a form of infallibilism. It isn't a form of infallibilism even though it makes entailment from one's evidence a feature of its account of knowledge. The conclusion to draw, as before, is that the entailment understanding of infallibilism classifies such a theory incorrectly.

3.4 SENSITIVE AND COMPLACENT FALLIBILISMS   65

Note that it won't help here to modify the proposal so that one insists that nothing can be evidence unless true (whether or not one disagrees with Williamson about requiring that it be known). This emendation would help avoid the feature of the above view that allows the presence of entailing evidence for false beliefs, but it would remain a Cheap Infallibilism nonetheless. For, so long as one still insists that nothing is evidence that doesn't conform to DT, adding the truth requirement in order for something to be evidence will still make the body of evidence one that entails the truth of whatever is supported by that body of evidence. Such a view wouldn't collapse the distinction between justification (by your evidence) and truth, but it would make the former a subset of the latter.

So, even if false evidence is disallowed, a theory can be developed that is a Cheap Infallibilism only, on the entailment rendition of the line between fallibilism and infallibilism. It would not be a full-blooded infallibilism that the skeptic says we need for knowledge but can't have and which infallibilists such as Descartes granted we need for knowledge and maintained we can have. It is this skeptic-satisfying conception that fallibilists intend to dispute, and thus defenders of the views above might enjoy claiming to have defended a kind of infallibilism, but without something further, skeptics are right to view them as fallibilists in sheep's clothing.

I note in passing how an evidentialist can avoid such a Cheap Infallibilism. The conception of evidence that avoids this problem with the entailment criterion for infallibilism is one that denies DT_ε. Perhaps the most plausible way to do so is to start with the idea that evidence is factive but can be adequate evidence for something that is false. Then DT_ε must be rejected, since the conditional itself would be false.

It strikes me as a mark against this view of evidence that it must deny DT_ε, for DT itself has rather illustrious standing for first-order logic and we have good reason to expect that analogues of it will be equally auspicious for intensional amendments of that logic. More circumspectly, though, the idea that evidence must be factive even when non-entailing is not by itself a strong enough reason to reject DT_ε, even though it may be the best way to develop that point of view. A more decisive disconfirmation of DT_ε would require much more than mere incompatibility with a controversial idea about evidence.

A deeper concern about this proposal in our context, however is this. Even though the theory under consideration would clearly be an instance of fallibilism, this fact would provide no benefit at all to the entailment criterion for a construal of infallibilism. For the distinction between fallibilism and infallibilism is a metatheoretical category distinction, and thus needs to classify theories correctly regardless of which particular theory of evidence or knowledge is being proposed. The fact that there is at least one evidentialist theory of knowledge that it correctly identifies as fallibilist in character is of little value to the criterion since it classifies so many other possible theories incorrectly.

66 VERSIONS OF FALLIBILISM

We can generalize on the issue involved here. On any theory of knowledge, even one that skeptics agree has high enough standards for knowledge, there will be partial stories that can be told about the epistemic standing of any of our beliefs that leave open whether those beliefs are true and whether if true they count as knowledge. That fact doesn't allow us to determine whether a given theory of knowledge is fallibilist or infallibilist. Moreover, moving from partial elements involved in the theory to total accounts for any given belief can overreach in a way that masks whether the theory is fallibilist or infallibilist. Williamson's approach is a good example of why, but it is only one such example. The most telling point above is that it doesn't matter if knowledge is evidence or whether or not evidence has to be true or accurate. All this needed is a very simple analogue of the Deduction Theorem for first-order logic, one couched in terms of the epistemic consequence relation that holds between what is known and the grounds for such knowledge. What is needed is an account of the distinction between fallibilism and infallibilism that doesn't force us to deny this analogue of DT in order to defend the account in question.

There is thus an enormous reservoir of reasons to distance ourselves from entailment accounts of infallibilism and to look elsewhere. Entailing evidence or epistemic support isn't sufficient for infallibilism, and if one wants to insist that it is nonetheless necessary for infallibilism, it is too easy to find such support even in obviously fallibilist epistemologies. As a result, it is not a requirement that can do the work needed in sorting various theories of knowledge correctly into the categories in question.

If we look for something better, the best replacement for the entailment conception of fallibilism is, to my mind, the formulation by Baron Reed in Reed (2012). That formulation claims that one can know p on the basis of some justification j and yet such a belief on that very basis could have failed to be knowledge. This proposal handles the problem of fallibility regarding necessary truths, and it offers an alternative to EP_{ev}:

EP_j: $\diamond_e p =_{df.}$ where j is the basis for one's belief p, it is possible to believe p on the basis of j and yet not know p on the basis of j.

This approach has the advantage of characterizing epistemic possibility in the fashion of a dual rule by defining it in terms of knowledge, which we are assuming to be the operator of epistemic necessity.

Nevertheless, it appears at first glance, to found on the metatheoretical constraint already discussed, for it uses the language of justification in its formulation. It thus appears to be biased in favor of justificational theories of knowledge, in much the same way that EP_{ev} is biased in favor of evidential theories of knowledge.

Reed shows a sensitivity to this issue, though his response to it occurs in a different publication than the source cited above. In Reed (2007, note 2) he writes,

3.4 SENSITIVE AND COMPLACENT FALLIBILISMS 67

> I should also note that I am using the term "justification" in a broad sense, so that it may cover a wide range of epistemological theories, thus including both externalist theories like reliabilism (in which probability is explicitly one of the central elements) and internalist theories like moderate foundationalism and coherentism (which allow for a belief to be justified even though it is not certain) ... The only restriction is that justification, as understood here, is a necessary condition for knowledge rather than, say, merely rational acceptability.

Reed thus thinks of his language about justification as a kind of generic placeholder for a necessary condition on knowledge, rather than some specific idea that would be rejected by non-justificationist approaches to knowledge, such as we might find with safety and sensitivity theories of knowledge.[18]

Yet, this functional approach to a justification condition, identified solely in terms of being a necessary condition for knowledge, has problems of its own. To see why, note that the standard approach to knowledge characterizes it in terms of belief, truth, some normative epistemic notion, and a clause to pacify Gettier. We can then find a necessary condition for knowledge by combining the latter two. If we adopt Reed's functional approach to justification, this new condition fulfills that role, and also makes any true belief that satisfies this condition one that is known to be true. The purely functional approach to justification would then imply that it knowledge can be identified with justified true belief.

This result, even if a reason to prefer formulating Reed's proposal in language other than that of justification, doesn't undermine the proposal directly, but does raise the following issue for the view. For on this functional approach, the account can only be adequate if justification, understood to be the combination of the normative condition plus the Gettier clause, were compatible with the belief being false, so that one could base one's belief on this combination and yet not know. To appreciate this point, let's use "X" and "Y" as placeholders for the two conditions in question, and consider approaches to the nature of X that are obviously fallibilist in character. In order to classify these approaches correctly, a purely functional account of justification on which the combination of X and Y satisfies this functional role would have subject all such theories to the requirement that the combination of X and Y is compatible with false belief, given the beginning assumption that the combination of X and Y together with true belief is knowledge.

Yet, this requirement that the combination of X and Y be compatible with false belief conflicts with many first-order theories of knowledge on this issue, for many such theories are designed precisely to undermine this possibility.[19] Others argue

---

[18] For a sensitivity approach, see Nozick (1981), and for approaches involving safety, see Sosa (1999) and Pritchard (2005).

[19] One such theory is developed in Lehrer (2000), together with a further argument that denying the possibility of false belief while satisfying the proposed justification and Gettier conditions is exactly what we want from adequate accounts of X and Y.

that the significance of the Gettier problem is precisely the denial of this possibility.[20] So it would be an inadequate metatheoretical constraint to insist that no approach to the Gettier problem can involve the claims that the combination of third and fourth conditions guarantees truth for belief. As a result, giving a purely functional role to the notion of justification in EP$_j$ doesn't succeed in removing the concern that the language of justification is not metatheoretically neutral concerning first-order theories of knowledge.

One might wonder if there is some hope to be found against this objection by appeal to the notion of basing involved in the account. Perhaps one might hope that one simply couldn't base a belief on whatever elements are involved in this combination of normative and anti-Gettier conditions. Such hope disappoints, I'm afraid. When reflection kicks in regarding putative cases of knowledge, the reflective basis for belief can come to include elements that wouldn't be present in unreflective cases, and when those reflecting are also epistemologists, the reflection in question can alter the basis of belief to include not only the elements of the normative clause itself but also the failure of those elements cited in the Gettier clause that would undermine knowledge. Moreover, some first-order approaches to the Gettier problem insist that in arriving at a believed conclusion, one must also infer, and base one's belief in part on, the claim that there is no ultimately undermining information one does not possess.[21] So the metatheoretical independence of first-order commitments shows that the objection can't be answered by relying on special features of the basing requirement.

So the attempt to let the language of justification be a functional placeholder will not work as a way to avoid the metatheoretic requirement of neutrality regarding theories of knowledge when specifying which of them count as versions of fallibilism and which do not. Hence, even though EP$_j$ has an advantage over EP$_{ev}$ by linking epistemic possibility and epistemic necessity in the fashion of a dual rule, both of these approaches have difficulty with the metatheoretical constraint concerning neutrality between competing theories of knowledge.

Moreover, it is not clear how to solve this latter problem. To do so, we'd have to have a metatheory that told us exactly what parts are needed for an adequate theory of knowledge, but I know of no such metatheory nor can I see any reason to think that there must be such a metatheory. With regret, I would expect that we find and will continue to find contentions here as we do everywhere else in philosophy.

Perhaps fallibilists could pass the buck to skeptics on this issue, claiming that the onus is on skeptics to say what infallibility amounts to and why it is required for knowledge. The idea, then, would be to wait for theory development on behalf

---

[20] As in Sturgeon (1993) and Zagzebski (1994).

[21] A good example of something along these lines is Harman (1973), with Harman (1970) a precursor of the view. See also Harman (1980).

of a skeptical point of view, and then adopt a simple definition of fallibilism in terms of a denial of skepticism.

Well, that won't quite work, since one doesn't have to be an infallibilist to be a skeptic. But, if we imagine the theoretical apparatus the skeptic contructs, we might still be able to follow this idea by defining fallibilism in terms of key denials of some part or parts of the theoretical apparatus in question. In light of this possibility, for the present, we can agree to table any demand for stopping our inquiry until we have an adequate account of fallibilism and the related notion of epistemic possibility.

A minor concern with this buck-passing idea is that it forces a change in direction on the central issue of this chapter, one that concerns what a fallibilist can say about the infelicity of concessions. The buck-passing strategy gives up on the idea that we can make progress on the infelicity issue by figuring out the right fallibilist alternative to EP. By passing the buck on this effort, we can no longer hope for progress along this path.

Given the difficulties encountered along that path, however, suspicions abound that it is a dead end, anyway, so let's live with the disappointment engendered and try to make progress on the infelicity issue by considering that issue directly and independently of the definitional possibilities. To do so, we'll look at the variety of responses to the problem to give us a better idea of when a version of fallibilism should be counted as complacent rather than sensitive. So let's take a look at what might be said directly in response to the problem of concessions, continuing to hold before our minds the Lewisian remark about the tinge of infallibilism to be found in epistemic language.

3.4.2 Infelicity and Varieties of Complacency

Our goal is to reveal the deficiencies in complacent versions of fallibilism in the face of the data concerning the infelicity of concessive attitudes, assertions, and attributions. More sensitive approaches to this data try to explain how and why these things are infelicitous, without succumbing to the skeptical point of view and the implication of the standard account of epistemic possibility that such attitudes and attributions are semantically inconsistent. Failure to shoulder this burden results in complacency, perhaps a settled enough complacency to deny that there is anything troubling at all about concessive attitudes and attributions.

This distinction between complacent and sensitive fallibilism is not as precise as we might wish, but an analogy might help make it clearer. In discussions concerning the problem of evil, philosophers of religion distinguish between a theodicy and a defense.[22] For the latter, the goal is to show that the problem of

---

[22] The distinction is due to Plantinga, as it appears in Plantinga (1967) and Plantinga (1974), as well as in subsequent writings.

evil does not show that the conjunction of the existence of God together with a recognition of evil is a contradiction. That is, a defense purports to show that the existence of evil doesn't refute the claim that God exists. A theodicy, however, has higher ambitions. It attempts to make the ways of God plain. That is, it attempts to show why suffering and misery are part of the created order. Its goal isn't merely to disarm arguments attempting to show logical inconsistency, but a deeper understanding of the way in which suffering and misery are part of a divine plan.

Just so, a sensitive fallibilism isn't content merely avoiding logical inconsistency with the data concerning concessions. Instead, a sensitive fallibilism wants to be able to explain what is infelicitous about the concessions in question, in a way that fits nicely with fallibilism itself. On this approach, the language of concessions isn't to be understood semantically in terms of a denial of knowledge of the negation, but instead conveys (non-semantically) the idea that one doesn't know whether the claim in question is true.[23] Developing this idea typically relies on a standard conception of fallibilism, according to which one's epistemic grounds for belief provide no guarantee of truth. So, for example, one might think of epistemic possibility in terms of a denial that one's evidence entails a given claim, or that the claim in question has some non-zero probability on the evidence in question.[24] A related position, somewhat inspired by Lewis's idea that sometimes we neglect negligible counterpossibilities, maintains that in conceding the possibility of error, one is communicating the idea that the chances of it aren't negligible after all, that the chances are significant.[25] In either case, epistemic possibility is not defined directly in terms of an absence of knowledge of the negation, but is understood in some other way that leaves open the option of an appeal to Gricean maxims about the theory of communication to explain how and why the concessions imply (non-semantically) a claim that contradicts the knowledge claim.[26]

One such Gricean maxim is the maxim of relevance, and one way of being irrelevant is to bring up truths unrelated to the conversational context. If the chances of error are insignificant or negligible, that should tell us, so the story goes, that they are irrelevant to the conversational context. So if one brings up some possibility of error, a Gricean story would be that we are communicating that the chances aren't insignificant and hence can't be ignored. In such a case, we have an account with at least initial plausibility for why concessive attitudes and attributions are infelicitous. That story maintains that the concessions in question

---

[23] See, e.g., Dougherty and Rysiew (2009). Further discussion of CKA's can be found in Stanley (2005b), Dodd (2006), Rysiew (2009), Dodd (2010), Dougherty and Rysiew (2011), and Littlejohn (2011).

[24] As defended by Dougherty and Rysiew (2009). See Reed (2012) for documentation of those who endorse the lack of entailment conception of fallibilism, and for reasons to reject such understandings of the view.

[25] As defended in Fantl and McGrath (2009) and also in Brown (2018).

[26] Grice, (1968).

aren't semantically problematic, but are problematic on non-semantic, pragmatic grounds.

A crucial question for such approaches is their replacement notion of epistemic possibility, and in describing these pragmatic approaches, I've been skirting the issues raised in the last section about the difficulty of finding an adequate account of epistemic possibility to replace the standard account. On the standard account, the weaker possibility notion is defined as the dual of the stronger necessity notion, typically understood as knowledge. So a pragmatic account of concessions need an account of epistemic possibility, and we have already seen two problems that need to be addressed. The first concerns the factive nature of epistemic necessity, the dual of epistemic possibility, and the second concerns the metatheoretical requirement that our account shouldn't commit us to some particular theory of knowledge over other theories. As a reminder, if we want to define epistemic possibility in terms of non-entailing evidence, it isn't clear how knowledge is going to be the dual or epistemic possibility, nor is it clear that the dual will factive, nor is it obvious that our account is suitably theory neutral.

When we try to glean some understanding of epistemic possibility from these pragmatic explanations of the infelicity of concessions, we don't seem to get the results we need. For example, when the assumed approach to epistemic possibility is in terms of a denial of entailing evidence or in terms of there being some non-zero chance of error, the dual of such an idea would be that if p must be true, one's evidence entails p or that $\sim p$ has no chance of being true, but neither of these claims are factive.

Let's take each claim in turn. For the entailing evidence account, it is easy to see that an entailment relation between two items doesn't also entail the truth of the entailed claim. If we want the latter, we'd have to add the idea that no false claim could be evidence. In such a case, we can defend the truth of the entailed claims, for if one starts with truths and those truths entail a given claim, the entailed claim must be true as well. Yet, the contention that nothing false could be evidence is something that would have to be added to the bare semantics to get the factivity result, and it is certainly not an obvious claim.[27] The relevance of this point is that, whichever side we wish to take on the factivity of evidence, such factivity is not a semantic fact, but rather a substantive theoretical one. As such, it is not part of the content of the idea of possessing entailing evidence, and since it is not, an account of epistemic possibility in terms of entailing evidence does not yield the factivity result we seek.

On the other approach above, the one that understands epistemic possibility in terms of a non-zero chance or probability of the negation of the claim, we could get factivity if and only if zero probability entails falsity and a probability of one entails truth. But neither claim is adequately supported, since any measure that conforms

---

[27] For recent literature on the issue, see Mitova (2018).

to the probability calculus leaves open the possibility of things happening that have no chance or probability of happening. The examples aimed at showing this fact typically involve a space of possibilities with an infinity of options, one of which will occur. Perhaps, for example, we have a target divided into segments corresponding to the real numbers between zero and one inclusive, and then throw a dart with an infinitely fine point on it, so that it can hit, at most, one of the segments. When the thrown dart hits a segment, something will have happened that, on any standard mathematical conception of probability, had zero chance of happening. That is so because, if we treat each point in the space as equally probable to be hit, then we are forced to assign a probability of zero to each of the options, on pain of the sum of all of them exceeding one. So a probability of zero doesn't entail falsity, and by implication a probability of one won't entail truth. For if p has a probability of zero but is true, $\sim p$ will have a probability of one and will be false.

So on either option, the semantical treatment alone fails to undergird the factivity of epistemic necessity.[28] Some might try to evade the problem by questioning whether we need epistemic necessity to be factive. A first point to note is that, when it comes to intensional logics more generally, we get a pleasing endorsement of dual rules quite generally, even though some of the strong operators aren't factive. Logical necessity is the dual of logical possibility; nomological necessity is the dual of nomological possibility; moral obligatoriness is the dual of moral permission; the past tense operator is the dual of the future tense operator, etc. Since some strong operators on this list aren't factive, it makes sense to wonder about which strong operators are factive and which aren't. For the first two on our list, factivity holds; for the latter two it does not.

Hence, demanding the implication of truth for the strong operator in an epistemic logic doesn't follow from any general demand on strong operators in intensional logics. It obtains, of course, when the logic is understood to be about some kind of factive knowledge, but if epistemic possibility is a weak operator designed to represent some ordinary language role about what might be the case, once we have this operator defined, someone trying to evade the problem of factivity might insist that we simply define a strong dual operator, and then aim to discover whether or not that strong operator is factive. Discovering that it isn't factive, it might then be claimed, isn't a death-blow to the logic, but rather a discovery about the nature of epistemic necessity. It would simply show that the strong operator wasn't to be understood in terms of knowledge or any other factive epistemic notion.

Thus, the first point to note is that more work needs to be done to defend the claim that there is a problem here if the strong epistemic operator, one expressed using the language of what *must* be, is not truth-implying. The earliest epistemic

---

[28] As argued first in Littlejohn (2011).

logics, tracing to Hintikka (1962), satisfy this demand, but historical priority by itself establishes nothing. The kind of logic aimed at is an epistemic one, and there are lots of epistemic notions other than the notion of knowledge.

Many will view the idea of a non-factive epistemic operator as a non-starter, perhaps saying what we are inclined to say about the factivity of logical, metaphysical, nomological, and accidental necessity. "Why think these notions are factive? Well, Anything that has to true will be true, and the claims that are governed by these operators are thus true because *they have to be true*." It is worth noting, however, someone expressing reservations:

> Some philosophers insist that, by definition, a law of nature, whatever else it may be, must be a true proposition. I can't think why. (Inwagen, 1988, 48)

The reservation expressed here is, let us say, underdeveloped. Is the worry about whether laws of nature are nomologically necessary? On this score, I would have thought that the answer is trivial, given that the meaning of "nomological" concerns the kind of necessity possessed by laws of nature (if there be such). Skeptics about modality have sometimes rejected the idea that the laws of nature are necessary, but that position is hard to defend, once we notice that laws can entail empirical generalizations without being entailed by those generalizations. So, I'd be surprised if the concern expressed in this quote were one about whether laws go beyond mere empirical generalizations. Or, more relevant to our context, is it resistance to the idea that nomological necessity is factive? We get no further clarification or discussion of this point, but the latter idea is one possibility. If it is, I trust the reader will see the idea with the same incredulity I experience, tempted to repeat: "Well, of course they are true, because *they have to be true*."

A more charitable take on van Inwagen's skepticism stresses the "by definition" qualifier, noting that if a claim is true by definition, we need a semantics to undergird this attribution of analyticity to the claim. If that is the concern being expressed, it is one that we can readily endorse, for the precise nature of the distinction between the analytic and the non-analytic is a troubling one. In our context, what matters though is not whether the factivity of the strong operator obtains in virtue of some analytic connection between that operator and the concept of truth, but rather the factive element itself, and whether the link between the dual of an proposed notion of epistemic possibility must, in the sense of metaphysical necessity, be true. And on this point, the answer is obvious: of course they are true because they have to be.

One might be tempted to resist here by resorting to a hackneyed joke about how to predict who will do their duty and who won't. "Will that person do their duty?" you are asked. And you reply, "Of course they will, because they *must*!" Perhaps we mustn't use such lame jokes!

74 VERSIONS OF FALLIBILISM

Note, though, that the reason it's such a lame joke is precisely that all of us can tell the difference between the "must" of obligation and the "must" of laws of logic, nature, and metaphysics. If one can't see the difference, I don't know what to say, but if you see the lame humor in this joke, I think you do see the difference.

In our context, though, there is a further reason to prefer a dual of the notion of epistemic possibility that is factive. For we are interested in disputes between skeptics and non-skeptics in epistemology, and are using the language of epistemic possibility in that context. So, we are clearly in a domain where any logic we might use will be one that is epistemic in virtue of having something to do with getting to the truth and avoiding error, as knowledge is. In that context, it is pretty clear that we will want an interpretation of the strong epistemic operator that is truth-implying, since the goal is obviously factive and the kind of success that is in dispute between skeptics and non-skeptics is one that is factive as well.

Moreover, as we noted earlier, factivity itself is at the heart of the impropriety of concessions, whether or not those concessions are epistemic. So even if there is some basis that has not yet been given for taking seriously the idea that epistemic necessity isn't factive, our discussion can still proceed under this assumption since factivity is central to the need for fallibilism to address adequately the data concerning concessions. In this context, concessions about the possibility of error are problematic because they threaten the truth of any claim involving the strong epistemic operator, and this threat arises precisely because the proper assumption governing this context is one in which this operator is factive.

So the issue of factivity puts pressure on an account of epistemic possibility in terms of non-entailing evidence or the chance or probability of error, because factivity isn't preserved for the dual of such a possibility. Perhaps though we can supplement the accounts of epistemic possibility under consideration to avoid the problem. Why not, for example, do nothing more than add a reference to factivity into one of the two accounts above? This idea, then, is to define epistemic necessity in terms of factive epistemic state *FES*, where *FES* involves an evidential condition in which one's evidence does not entail truth. As should be obvious, *FES* might be knowledge itself, but we needn't assume that it is—we only need it to play the role of a state to which the strong epistemic operator applies. Given such an account, we can then identify epistemic possibility in terms of the dual of epistemic necessity: epistemic possibility obtains for p just when it is not epistemically necessary that $\sim p$. If we wish to use a possible worlds semantics to characterize this notion of possibility, we'll say that there is a world that is epistemically ideal with respect to p (so that p is true in this world and the evidential basis responsible in part for the ideality of this world with respect to p is also present) and in which *FES* does not obtain.

Two virtues of such an account come to mind immediately. First, it is an account of epistemic possibility at least in the spirit of the two mentioned above, on which epistemic possibility is understood in terms of non-entailing evidence or a chance of error. Second, we might even end up identifying *FES* with knowledge, though not on semantic grounds, for that would require a semantic connection between evidence and knowledge. If we think of *FES* in terms of knowledge, the resulting account of epistemic possibility says something in the neighborhood of a standard idea since Gettier: that there are epistemically ideal worlds in which one's justified true belief regarding p is gettiered. Moreover, the account of epistemic necessity and possibility both preserves the duality relationship between the two in addition to generating a semantic explanation of the idea that epistemic necessity implies truth.

Note that such an account would be very close to that proposed by Reed discussed at some length in the last section. The main difference is that Reed's account doesn't advert to the concepts of evidence or probability or chance. Whether and to what degree this feature is an advantage, we need not pursue here, since the point of note in our context is that the demand for a factive notion of epistemic necessity can be satisfied by all these proposals.

Even so, both proposals appear to yield the required factivity at the cost of theory neutrality. We saw this point in the last section, where it was argued that there is no purely functional account of justification available for use in the account we look for, and here it looks like theory neutrality is sacrificed in relying on the conceptual apparatus of evidence or probability is equally problematic. That is, if we think of epistemic necessity in terms of knowledge, we should not burden our treatment of this operator with some semantic link between it and the concepts of knowledge or probability. This point was made about the concept of evidence previously, and the same point holds when it comes to the concept of probability, with one exception. Instead of relying on, say, a mathematical notion of probability, one could propose to use the idea of epistemic probability as a placeholder for something that will be needed to add to true belief in the process of characterizing knowledge. As we saw in discussing Reed's functional characterization of justification, the distinction between a Gettier condition for knowledge and some other third condition, which is not only a possible account of knowledge but one of the leading contenders, will undermine such a purely functional approach.

At the end of the last section, we offered a buck-passing way forward in attempting to characterize fallibilism, changing direction to focus more directly on the problem of concessions and the variety of possibilities fallibilists might propose in the face of the data about concessions. At the most complacent end, we find fallibilists who see no problem to be addressed at all, a position that has so little to recommend it that it deserves to be ignored. One way to move away from such exaggerated complacency in terms of the Gricean distinction between semantic and pragmatic implication, and the problem we are discussing here is that by doing so, fallibilists end up saying things about the notion of epistemic possibility itself, and in a way that causes problems for a related understanding of epistemic necessity. Note also that doing so conflicts with the buck-passing strategy proposed at the end of the last section, for if we found an account of epistemic possibility and epistemic necessity in the process of defending a Gricean story about the impropriety of concessions, we could use that account to clarify the nature of fallibilism directly. But the lesson of previous discussion was intended to convince us that such a direction wasn't going to work, and here we see the same point all over again.

Moreover, if we focus on what could be done in this Gricean direction while at the same time trying not to commit ourselves on any particular characterization of epistemic possibility, our results will underwhelm. Such an account will merely insist that the standard account of epistemic possibility is mistaken, and mistaken in a way that can be generalized so that no adequate replacement could be found that renders the concessions semantically inconsistent. After insisting on these points, one could then go on to talk about Gricean implications that are not semantic, but the problem is that we would have nothing more than an undefended insistence that the implications in question are not semantic.

As I see it then, there is good news and bad news about the Gricean story. The good news is that it opens up a possible direction for fallibilists to explain the infelicity of concessive attitudes, attributions, and assertions, one that would be impossible on the standard semantics for epistemic logic. The bad news, however, is that it does so in a way that travels the same dead-end road of the last section, in committing to a replacement for the standard account of epistemic possibility. In addition, when this repetition is noted, any attempt to get by without proposing a replacement results in speculation depending on an undefended insistence that the infelicity found is pragmatic only.

So, whereas the Gricean account of infelicity is to be commended for being less complacent than a version of fallibilism that simply denies that there is anything that needs explaining when it comes to the purported data about the infelicity of concessions, the path toward a duly sensitive version of fallibilism isn't going to be found in this direction. We should thus ask whether the data about concessions can be challenged in a way that shoulders an explanatory burden, but without implying any particular replacement notion of epistemic possibility for the standard account of it.

Here, I think, the answer is "yes", and it is an answer that fits concerns I've expressed elsewhere about the history of epistemology and the regrettable consequences of focusing this history on conversations with the skeptic.[29] The idea behind challenging the data more directly is to blame the skeptic for the appearance of impropriety in concessive attitudes, assertions, and attributions. The history of epistemology has been one long conversation with the skeptic, and the idea here is that having such conversations has led to a common, but false,

---

[29] I use this idea to argue for a more central place for the concept of understanding in epistemology, in Kvanvig (2003).

presupposition about knowledge. That presupposition is that in order to know, you must be able to produce a defense of your view adequate to convince a reasonable skeptic of the truth of your view. Since skeptical resistance won't be assuaged at any point short of infallible grounds, we can call this "the infallibility presupposition". The idea, then, is that expressions of fallibility flout this presupposition, and so sound inapt. Moreover, the presence of the presupposition is the result of these conversations with the skeptic, not anything about the nature of knowledge itself. The concessive expressions themselves are true and would be completely untroubling were it not for this false presupposition.

Note that if this is our complete story about the concessions in question, the proper conclusion to draw is that our ways of speaking need to be educated in the new fallibilism and that we need to change the way we speak so that the truth of fallibilism can be expressed straightforwardly in our concessions without what they convey being infected with a false presupposition. Once we succeed in getting speakers of the language to drop the false presupposition, concessions about what we know will be no more infelicitous than concessions about what is supported by good reasons.

This approach, like the pragmatic versions of sensitive fallibilism above, can advert to the kinds of conversational constraints discussed by Paul Grice (1968). One such constraint induces a kind of agreement bias in favor of granting one's interlocutor whatever points are being made so as to further the goals of the conversation. When one's interlocutor is a skeptic, that inclines us to agree with demands for absolute certainty and the like, at least provisionally for the sake of conversation. Through centuries of such conversations, the bias hardens to the point of a presupposition, making us uncomfortable with claiming to know while also acknowledging that we might be wrong. That is the problem, the false presupposition theorist insists. It's a philosophical explosive device packaged in the nice wrapping of conversational propriety.

The complacency of this view isn't as bad as if one simply waved aside the skeptics, telling them that they are wasting our time. But it is troublingly complacent nonetheless, at least as troubling as an appeal to restricted quantification, where the restricted nature of the quantifier isn't revealed by competence in the language. For on the false presupposition explanation, we find an urge for absolute certainty which is held to be unrelated to any of the great epistemic goods, the goods of knowledge, understanding, and theoretical wisdom. It is hard to see how the desire for such certainty could be a mere artifact of the influence of bad epistemic company, and thus hard to see how skepticism could be so far off the mark as to make this be the sole explanation of such an exaggerated preference. To the extent that this artifactual story of the attraction toward absolute certainty is found wanting, to that extent we should find the false presupposition explanation unsatisfying, and any version of fallibilism defined in terms of this approach to concessive attitudes and attributions complacent.

The false presupposition fallibilist might be right, and it may be a position we are forced to adopt later on, but our initial impression of it ought to be that it is a rather radical take on what seems to be a legitimate issue. The issue is that skeptics don't seem to be making things up when they point to our desire for maximal assurances of being correct, but instead are identifying accurately some important aspect of the human cognitive condition, even if they have trouble saying exactly what that aspect is. In the end, fallibilists might have to say that any such sentiment is present only because of the long history of talking to the wrong people, but we won't be in a position to adopt a debunking explanation of this sort without failing to find a more sensitive way to develop fallibilism.

So let's conclude this brief consideration of this approach by provisionally acknowledging the intellectual pressure against the false presupposition explanation of the infelicity of epistemic concessive attitudes, assertions, and attributions, even though this version of complacency avoids the problems that have plagued the earlier versions relying on Lewisian ideas and Gricean elements. To the extent that we find the false presupposition approach to be an option, we should note that, while it remains true that skeptics need to take steps in theory development to avoid being nothing more than fodder for reflective equilibrium, it is equally true that fallibilism is in a slightly uncomfortable position, in need of formulating a sensitive version of it but lacking, at this point, a way to do so. We thus wonder whether and how a skeptical theory can be developed, but we are equally puzzled as to whether and how a sensitive version of fallibilism can be developed.

Thus, our current position is one of being unimpressed with false presuppositions explanations as well as with other complacent versions of fallibilism, but also dissatisfied with using this lack of success as much of a benefit to skepticism. The fallibilist still has work to do to explain the difference between the expressions of fallibility about what we know and expressions of fallibility about the adequacy of good reasons for belief. The skeptic, on the other hand, needs to do serious theoretical work to show how and why knowledge really is, in some important sense, tinged with infallibilism. All of this points, at least from our current perspective, to the conclusion that we cannot rest content with either a complacent fallibilism or an undeveloped skepticism.

3.5 A Way Forward

Suppose then that we agree about the tinge of infallibilism in knowledge and also experience the concern about a fallibilism that is too complacent. What is needed is some way of leaving open the possibility of fallibilism without complacency, but how can we do that? Moreover, is there a way to do it that doesn't simply ignore the burden of theory development by skeptics?

An answer to this question can be developed by attending to two central claims in a powerful argument for global skepticism. The first claim is the idea that knowledge is an absolute term. Part of this idea is that knowledge doesn't come in degrees, that it is ungradeable in the same way as other concepts such as truth and being. As is to be expected, there are dissenters on this point, but I propose to grant it here.[30] The other part of the absoluteness idea is what Ungerian skepticism relies on, and it involves the notion of absoluteness in terms of an extreme that cannot be surpassed.

We have also seen perplexities that arise when we try to characterize such absolute notions, resulting in a need for some kind of theoretical modeling of the feature in question. For flatness, for example, we have seen that we can model in geometric terms, abstracting away from the difficulties posed by uncomfortable metaphysical realities concerning, e.g., material constitution, vagueness, and indeterminacy. So, even if absoluteness is granted for a particular term or concept, characterizing such absoluteness involves the typical modeling of a phenomenon involved in theoretical work.

Once the ideal is so characterized in the epistemological realm, a second feature is needed in order to sustain skeptical outlooks. This feature generalizes on the usual issue encountered when a given phenomenon is modeled theoretically, where the question always arises as to the degree of fit between the model and reality. For example, given a geometric model of ideal or perfect flatness, the question arises as to whether any actual physical surfaces are close enough approximations to the ideal for it to be correct to attribute flatness to them. Just so in epistemology as well. Once we have properly characterized the absoluteness involved in knowledge, the argument for skepticism will also need to maintain that no approximations to the ideal is ever a close enough approximation to sustain the correctness of claiming that some item of information is known to be true. In short, knowledge is absolute and a "close approximations" defense of fallible knowledge fails.

With this kind of skeptical stance as background, we can see what needs to be done to embrace fallibilism without doing so complacently. A complacent fallibilism rejects the claim that knowledge is absolute, claiming that there is no infallibilist tinge to be found, and that perhaps the best explanation that can be found regarding this mistake is due to an infection of false presupposition. A sensitive fallibilism agrees with the skeptic about the infallibilist tinge involved in knowledge, welcoming and participating in the elucidation and theoretical development of this idea. It is a cooperative venture, since both positions will be in trouble without it. We have seen as much regarding skepticism itself, and the same

---

[30] The literature is too vast to catalog here, but some noteworthy contributions to the literature include Sainsbury (1988), Hetherington (2001), Smith (2008), McDaniel (2013), and McDaniel (2017), with each of these pointing to additional literature challenging absolutist assumptions.

80 VERSIONS OF FALLIBILISM

is true for the sensitive fallibilism we seek, for without a substantive skeptical position to take seriously, a complacent fallibilism appealing to a false presupposition will be more attractive. The project of the next two chapters is thus a cooperative one between skeptics and sensitive fallibilists. It is a dance between the two that neither will want to avoid. Of course, after the dance ends, the two will part company on the "close approximations" point. The skeptic says that no cognitive successes are close enough to the cognitive ideal for knowledge, while appropriately sensitive fallibilists will disagree.

In this way of approaching the issue between skeptics and fallibilists, three possibilities remain open initially. It might turn out that there is no way to characterize the notion of ideal knowledge the skeptic hopes to use to show that it is something beyond our reach. As we will see, such a threat to skepticism arises most clearly and directly regarding knowledge of the future, but it is a threat that arises as well in older philosophy of science concerns about finding adequate support for theoretical, as opposed to observational, claims. These, and other, regions of concern all fall under what is commonly referred to as the problem of induction, but I'll avoid that terminology here and will focus specifically on the issue of knowledge of the future. I'll avoid the terminology about induction, since the issue is not really about a specific kind of argumentation that we might label as such, but rather about a more generic notion of epistemic support that is defeasible in character. Moreover, I'll focus on the idea of knowledge of the future, since it is as clear a case as there could be where any epistemic support we find will be defeasible in character and the problem can be discussed without the need for any characterization of a theory/observation distinction. In short, this kind of knowledge provides a good test case for the challenge faced by the skeptic, one concerning how to engage in theory development of the sort needed to put pressure on fallibilist rejections of skepticism.

We will explore this point in depth in later chapters, but for now a brief taste of the problem is worth providing. The idea that we focus on is that perfect knowledge, of every sort, is tinged with an absolutist character. Yet, knowledge of the future is obviously inferential: there is no such thing as a crystal ball that allows one to see into the future, since the future is not-yet. As Peter Geach (1977) noted, the future is not like a red carpet to be rolled out, allowing the possibility of peering into the fabric while it is still rolled up. No, the future doesn't unfold, it comes to be. So any knowledge we have of the future won't be perceptual but will instead have to be inferential. There are no crystal balls to peer into, no powers of foresight that are perceptual or quasi-perceptual in nature for detecting what will happen, since the future is the realm of what is yet to be, not what already is.

Or so my presentist predilections tell me. For those more inclined toward the spatializing of time involved in the view that all of the spacetime manifold in its totality is what there is,[31] any fully perceptual account of knowledge of the future is still going to be hard to defend. For one thing, perception is, by its nature, a point of causal contact between a perceiver and a perceived, and it would be surprising indeed to find out that we need to make sense of backward causation in order to understand the possibility of knowledge of the future. So, whatever the ultimate metaphysical story, knowledge of the future is best understood, not in terms of a perceptual model, but rather in terms of inference.

Among inferential relations, we find both deductive and non-deductive varieties, with related formal investigation of both monotonic and non-monotonic consequence relations. Standard first-order logic, as well as typical intensional logics, are monotonic logics, typified by a consequence relation that cannot be undermined by additional premises. Non-monotonic logics study a consequence relation that can be undermined by additional premises, making them a more natural way of developing a formal system by analogy to the phenomenon of defeasible learning. Given the existence of both kinds of inferential relations and the possibility of formal investigations related to each, it would be a regrettable epistemic imperialism to ignore one of these possibilities when it comes to inferential knowledge, including knowledge of the future.[32] So the skeptic, to shoulder the burden of characterizing the connection between knowledge and infallibility, must do so while at the same time not exhibiting such imperialist tendencies. And that is the rub! How could non-monotonic, defeasible reasoning ever be characterized in such a way that some perfect form of it implied infallibility? As we will see, things are not as hopeless as they might seem initially, but that is a story for later chapters to tell.

This caution against epistemic imperialism is needed most clearly when attending to Humean arguments against knowledge of the future. Hume wanted to know how we know the sun will rise tomorrow, and acknowledged that the grounds for such a belief are, broadly speaking, inductive. But when evaluating the quality of these grounds, Hume first transposes induction into deduction, wanting to add an additional premise about the future resembling the past. That is precisely an imperialism to avoid. Introverts aren't extroverts needing to grow up, and neither is an non-monotonic set of reasons really a monotonic one when fully developed. So if inductive arguments about the future are problematic, the Humean skeptic needs to do more than point out that such arguments don't function well when evaluated by deductive standards. In particular, such a skeptic needs to identify the ideal standard for knowledge with respect to reasoning patterns that are formalized in terms of consequence relations that are non-monotonic. We will see

---

[31] Since one's stance on time won't matter much for our topic, I'm being a bit casual here, and more careful discussion can be found in Mellor (1998), Sider (2001), Rea (2003), Zimmerman (2011), Miller (2013), and, most recently, Dyke (2021). The language of spatializing time is taken from Taylor (1955).

[32] I borrow the language of epistemic imperialism from Alston (1993).

that doing so is the most difficult part of developing a skeptical theory of knowledge, and in virtue of which the skeptical position deserves attention and respect in ways that bare skeptical arguments and conclusions do not.

Sensitive fallibilists will welcome the theory development needed to sustain the first skeptical premise, since it will provide useful grounds for why an explanation is needed of the infelicity of concessive attitudes and attributions concerning knowledge, while complacent fallibilists may take comfort at the seeming dilemma faced by any such attempt by skeptics to avoid the charge of epistemic imperialism. So part of our task in articulating and defending a version of sensitive fallibilism is that of formulating skepticism so that it doesn't succumb to this charge. For if skeptical theory development founders on the issue of epistemic imperialism, we will have strong grounds for siding with complacent fallibilists in endorsing the false presupposition view, perhaps in conjunction with aspects of the Gricean approach as well, concerning concessive attitudes and attributions. If, that is, skepticism depends on refusing to acknowledge the importance of the distinction between monotonic and non-monotonic consequence relations, we have every right to treat the apparent impropriety of these concessions as an intellectual overreach prompted by a philosophical mistake. Yet, if skeptics can somehow manage to carry out theory development without ignoring or dismissing or downplaying the significant difference between monotonic and non-monotonic consequence relations, we should side with more sensitive fallibilists in thinking that the impropriety of concessive attitudes and attributions concerning knowledge is not illusory nor a product of lending an ear to the wrong people.

We are not, at least at this point, ready to adjudicate on this issue between fallibilisms that embrace complacency and those requiring more sensitivity, even though it is hard at this point to see any way for skeptics to live up to the demands being placed on them and thus avoiding this basic imperialism argument for complacent over sensitive fallibilism. The path we will follow, then, is one where both the sensitive fallibilist and the skeptic walk together. If this part of the path can be successfully traversed, we must be either sensitive fallibilists or infallibilists about knowledge; if navigation is impossible, complacent fallibilism triumphs, and Moorean dismissiveness vindicated.

There is one more option to note other than those just mentioned. If no adequate account of the infallibilist tinge in knowledge can be developed, we might conclude, not that complacent fallibilism is to be embraced, but rather that the notion of knowledge is not really coherent after all. So instead of claiming that we do have knowledge and that there is nothing inapt about claiming to know while admitting that we might be wrong, we might embrace a fallibilist epistemology that focuses on cognitive successes other than knowledge because of the incoherence of the idea of knowledge. One can view this approach as falling broadly within the pragmatist tradition that responds to the challenge of skepticism by questioning the significance of it. If the infallibilist tinge in knowledge renders it unattainable because incoherent, it is no great loss to stop thinking about knowledge when it comes to characterizing the connections between mind and world that count as great successes from a purely cognitive point of view.

If, however, the infallibilist tinge can be coherently characterized, then we can still include knowledge as one such success, and it will then be an open question whether such an important success is within our grasp. That is, we will need to assess the plausibility of sensitive fallibilism in comparison with the skeptical implications of infallibilism. In the process, we will also consider some of the recent positions that claim to be, or have been characterized as, infallibilist in character. As we will see, these positions do not do justice to the infallibilist tinge Lewis notes, relying on an indefensible view about the relationship between infallibility and a notion of entailment. That view, as discussed above, is that lack of entailment from evidence to conclusion is the defining feature of fallibilism and the presence of such an entailment the defining feature of infallibilism. Neither claim is correct, and the positions we'll discuss are thus best thought of as versions of fallibilism as well, even if using language of a stronger position.

We thus approach the issue of the absence of infallibility in two stages when thinking about fallibilism concerning knowledge. The obvious stage is that of characterizing the kind of fastidious standards the skeptic insists are needed for knowledge. As we will see, this task is one of providing an adequate model for infallibility, and once the model is in place, the next question concerns the relationship between the model and reality itself. To the extent that the model idealizes, we can anticipate that the reality modeled will never or not typically match the ideal. That leaves two options in place, where the first one is that, in reality, knowledge is elusive, not only when we reflect on it (a Lewisian theme) but always and everywhere. The other option begins with the possibility that because models are not the reality modeled, the question arises as to whether our claims about what is known are close enough approximations to the model to count as being correct. Pursuing this idea will lead us to a version of sensitive falliblism, which is our ultimate goal here.

The exact requirements for a less complacent defense of fallible knowledge are not as clear as we might like, but that fact can be shelved for now, since the issues involved in knowledge of the future remain unaffected by the details. If we can complete this project, we find a way of making an advance over Lewis's own *sotto voce* approach, as well as moving beyond the idea that the infallibilist tinge is simply a false presupposition arising from having spent too much time in bad epistemic company. To avoid both kinds of complacency, we seek something better. We seek an account on which it is part of the nature of ordinary, fallible knowledge to reveal itself as a poor shadow of something better and higher. It is not merely that the ordinary possessors of knowledge long for the security and comfort of opinions that can withstand any amount of scrutiny whatsoever, even though we certainly do. It is that the knowledge we possess is also but a shadow of something more real, even if it is to be regarded as something real in itself. Skepticism

84 VERSIONS OF FALLIBILISM

is sustained by this feature, both in terms of power and value. As we will see, the best versions of fallibilism require accommodating the pull of infallibilism in such terms.

I speak here in metaphors only, though, and our present concern requires nothing more perspicuous. Before getting to the second stage at which these ideas are made less metaphorical, we need to complete the first stage of characterizing the skeptical ideal itself. One word of caution is in order here, though, to prevent the idea that what is being defended here is a version of contextualism. It can be combined with that view, but it need not be. Contextualism is a very specific way of accommodating the idea of variability or relativity concerning when to attribute knowledge and when not to, but it is far from the only view that addresses such issues. Subject-sensitive invariantists do so as well, as can purely intellectualist views that refuse to mix practical and intellectual concerns when it comes to the nature of knowledge or other forms of epistemic propriety.[33] So the version of sensitive fallibilism to be developed won't be committed to contextualism or any of these alternatives to it.

Of course, since the proposed procedure is at most a sufficient condition and not a necessary one for avoiding complacent fallibilism, there may be other ways to embrace fallibilism about knowledge without being complacent about it. We need not claim that there is no other path for defending sensitive fallibilism other than the one followed here, but if there is, it falls into the "something we know not what" remainder of the logical space of sensitive fallibilism, as far as I can tell. I'd welcome learning the details of what such an approach might be, and here simply acknowledge that the approach to defending fallibilism taken here is in no position to claim to be the only possible approach. Instead, the only claim is that it is a plausible route to take, and any other route, though possible, is shrouded in mystery. I know of no other way to embrace fallibilism about knowledge without doing so in a complacent way.

3.6 Conclusion

We have seen in the chapter the basis for our investigation of the next two chapters, including our focus on knowledge of the future. That basis involves the proposed path that begins by characterizing the infallibilist tinge in the notion of knowledge and then investigates whether a sensitive version of fallibilism can be developed that honors this tinge and yet is capable of defending the idea that we know many things by being in a state that is a close enough approximation to what infallibilists

---

[33] Defenses of contextualism can be found in Cohen (1987) and DeRose (2008), and the best-known versions of subject-sensitive invariantism are Hawthorne (2004), Stanley (2005b), and Fantl and McGrath (2009). I discuss these views in favor of a version of intellectualism in Kvanvig (2011a).

claim to be correctly characterized as knowledge. The first step challenges the kind of complacency about skepticism displayed by Moorean dismissiveness toward the view, and the second step shows respect for the theory development accomplished on behalf of skepticism in the process of characterizing the infallibilist tinge. Sensitive fallibilism acknowledges the skeptical point that none of our intellectual accomplishments are perfect, and shoulders the intellectual burden of explaining how our accomplishments are close enough to being ideal, while at the same time using all of this machinery to explain how and why concessive attitudes and attributions about knowledge are both correct and infelicitous.

In this setup, there are four possible positions to take regarding the problem to be addressed, on the assumption that an optimistic version of infallibilism is chimerical. Given this assumption, the first option is skepticism itself, and the effort needed on behalf of this view begins with the project of theory development, refusing to settle for basic arguments for a skeptical conclusion that are easy to treat dismissively in terms of merely presenting the need for reflective equilibrium so that our considered judgments about the nature and scope of knowledge fit well with the bedrock obviousness of the fact that we know many things. This same theory development could be used for optimistic versions of infallibilism that claim both that knowledge is infallible and that we know many things, but as already noted, we'll side with the history of epistemology in abandoning this idea. The other broad category is fallibilism, of which we note three varieties. The first two arise in response to the problem of fallibilist concessions about knowledge, and they are complacent fallibilism and sensitive fallibilism. The second agrees with the skeptic that there is something more troubling when such concessions are made about knowledge than when they are made about epistemically normative properties such as rationality, justification, warrant, and the like. The most promising version of complacent fallibilism disagrees, seeing the difference between the two domains as disappearing once we rid ourselves of the false presupposition about knowledge induced by discussions with the skeptic. Both of these kinds of fallibilism agree that there is such a thing as knowledge, but they disagree about its nature. The third kind of fallibilist agrees with the skeptic that nothing could be knowledge without having the tinge of infallibility, but also holds that what this shows is that the idea of knowledge is incoherent. As a result, epistemology done properly in this fallibilist vein should focus on cognitive successes from a purely intellectual point of view that are other than knowledge, for they are the only ones with any hope of being important.

By developing the skeptical position over the next couple of chapters, we'll find grounds for rejecting any fallibilism that finds the notion of knowledge to be incoherent, and thus justify our focus on complacent versus sensitive versions of fallibilism. We turn then to the project of augmenting bare skeptical argumentation so as to develop a model of how ideal knowledge of the future can be characterized.

Chapter 4
Infallibilism and Idealizations about Knowledge

4.1 Introduction

The background now in place involves commitment to two significant tasks, one regarding skepticism and the other regarding fallibilism. Fallibilists will be off the hook if skepticism can't be developed into a position that articulates the gold standard for our attempts to ferret out the truth, for without such theory development, fallibilists can be complacent, relying perhaps on the false presupposition idea that it is conversations with the skeptic throughout the history of epistemology that is the problem, not anything having to do with obvious idea that we know many things. Even so, sensitive fallibilists lose out if things go this way, for without theory development on behalf of skepticism, there is nothing to which sensitivity needs to be shown. If skepticism can be developed, however, fallibilists will need to find a way around the problems noted in the last chapter that threaten to undermine the effort to develop a sensitive version of fallibilism, one that takes seriously the need to explain and predict how and why concessive attitudes and attributions about knowledge are both correct and infelicitous.

One central problem for sensitive fallibilism concerns the notion of fallibility itself, and we found in the last chapter that it is difficult to find a theory-neutral account of this notion. As a result, we decided to kick the can down the road and wait on the skeptic to elucidate the high standard claimed for knowledge, hoping to be able to characterize the relevant sort of fallibility simply in terms of the negation of this high standard. This idea makes good sense, since the language of infallibility is quite common in skeptical characterizations of what knowledge demands. We begin, then, with the attempt to characterize these high standards.

4.2 Skepticism and High Standards for Knowledge

We begin, then, with the stage of inquiry that involves a characterization of perfect, absolute, infallible knowledge. Such knowledge is, at the very least, ideal knowledge, and though one might question whether any such thing is possible, our first task is to characterize it so that we can investigate whether it is possible and whether it is an accurate characterization of all knowledge or only a perhaps

Skepticism and Fallibilism. Jonathan L. Kvanvig, Oxford University Press. © Jonathan L. Kvanvig (2025).
DOI: 10.1093/9780198924821.003.0004

4.2 SKEPTICISM AND HIGH STANDARDS FOR KNOWLEDGE   87

unachievable ideal. We have many slogan-like ways of pointing toward such a characterization: besides the language of infallibility, we often hear talk of being incapable of being wrong, being able to rule out all possibilities of error, being epistemically certain (or having an epistemic probability of one), being metaphysically certain, and, more rarely, talk of incorrigibility. But all of these slogans are inadequate when put to the task of a careful articulation of infallibilism about knowledge.

Some brief explanations why are in order. First, we won't get very far using the concept of infallibility to characterize infallibilism, though of course such an account would be correct. In addition to accuracy, though, we need something informative, so let's look at the other items on the above list. Suppose we focus on being incapable of being wrong. Such an account would be too strong. Our knowledge of our own existence might be infallible even if we grant the possibility of getting oneself into the unusual situation of believing that one doesn't exist, and certainly one shouldn't think that doxastic recalcitrants and their simple refusals to believe show that nothing can ever be known infallibly. Moreover, consider the Cartesian project of trying to rescue our typical cognitive edifices from skeptical clutches. Descartes's idea is not to argue that we are incapable of being wrong, but rather that we have control over whether we are wrong: we can avoid the possibility of being wrong by making sure that our will doesn't outrun the understanding when it comes to figuring out what is true and what is not. So the stronger view about being incapable of being wrong is too strong, since the Cartesian project clearly involves a commitment to finding an acceptable version of infallibilism.

Other exaggerations can be found as well, including the idea that infallibility involves the impossibility of having a reason to doubt. The problem with such a proposal is that it must rely on some restrictive notion of what it is to have a reason, one that eludes us. For, testimony can give you a reason to doubt anything. Just find someone that you take to be an epistemic superior who tells you that your opinion is a mistake. That's a reason to doubt. When Descartes's evil demon tells you that you aren't a thinking thing and that you don't exist, it's a mistake to maintain that this testimony doesn't give you a reason to doubt these claims. Such a reason to doubt may be relatively easy to undermine by Cartesian reasoning, but that point won't reinstate the idea that infallibility involves the impossibility of having a reason to doubt, since an undermined reason is still a reason.

Some will chase the rabbit of refinement here, hoping to replace the language of reasons for doubt with that of non-undermined reasons for doubt. It should be obvious this is a waste of time, but I'll take the time to say why it won't work. Take any fully justified belief that you have. It will be a belief for which you have no non-undermined reasons to doubt. But it won't be infallible for all that.

So let's focus elsewhere to see why other common characterizations don't work, one of which we have seen already, concerning the ability to rule out any possibility of error. First, as we saw in the last chapter, any true mathematical belief is one for which all possibilities of error are automatically ruled out, but not all true mathematical beliefs are known to be true, much less known infallibly. A defender of this idea might object that such beliefs aren't a counterexample to this proposal, since it focuses on the idea of ruling out of possibilities, and ruling out can't obtain by default, but instead must count as an accomplishment of some sort. I'm not sure this claim makes any progress on the example, since if there are no possibilities in which the claim is false, either it is a trivial truth that any possibility of error is ruled out or the account isn't going to apply to mathematical truths at all and hence will fail for that reason. Let's let this point pass, though, since one can resist the point by insisting that the possibilities are epistemic ones, not metaphysical or logical possibilities, and the space of epistemic possibilities includes logical and metaphysical impossibilities.

Even granting this point, the proposal will founder on problems with the notion of ruling out itself. One quite natural account of ruling out can be given in terms of knowledge itself: if p is known to be true, this fact alone is adequate for ruling out any possibility in which p is false. So if fallible knowledge is possible, I acquire the ability to rule out all possibilities of error simply by fallibly coming to know something that is incompatible with these possibilities. In order to block this response, a defender of this approach is going to have to characterize a special kind of ruling out that goes beyond that just described. What might that be? What won't help, of course, is to appeal to a special kind of ruling out that involves infallibility, so that it is not enough to be able to rule out every possibility of error, but that one must be able to *infallibly* do so. We can grant that such an account would be accurate, but at the cost of being uninformative.

So, where else to look? Perhaps the language of certainty itself will help, perhaps in terms of having an epistemic probability of one. Some of our discussion in the last chapter casts doubt on proposals resorting to the language of probability, since that language will have to be understood as something distinct from the mathematical notion of probability characterized by the Kolmogorov axioms.[1] In particular, those axioms imply that all logical truths have a probability of 1, and we certainly don't want an account of infallibility on which any knowledge of a logical truth is automatically infallible.

Moreover, the language of certainty itself is not what separates infallibilists from fallibilists, for if it did, G.E. Moore would automatically count as an infallibilist. As we saw in the last chapter, Moore holds that the many commonsense things that we know are things that we know with certainty. Yet, Moore resists skeptical demands of infallibility, using the Moorean shift to conclude that something must be wrong with their arguments for this claim, since it is obvious that we know many things with certainty. Pretty clearly, then, Moore is committed to giving an account

[1] Kolmogorov, (1950[1933]).

of certainty that won't satisfy those who demand infallibility from certainty. Perhaps, for example, Moore might propose that certainty on a matter involves the possession of information or evidence adequate to warrant closure of inquiry on the matter. One might still choose to continue the investigation, of course, but one needn't, when one is in the possession of information that legitimates stopping the inquiry. Certainty, so characterized, doesn't imply infallibility, but it fits the Moorean strategy for defending the idea that we know for certain the claim of common sense.

In response, the skeptic will need to insist that this notion of certainty isn't the right one, if hope is to be sustained for characterizing infallibility in terms of certainty. Yes, that's precisely the point. So the question is what notion of certainty is being used here, and again, it is tempting to short-circuit the hard problem by using the language of infallibility itself to characterize the kind of certainty needed. We can't resort to the language of having sufficient information to guarantee the truth of what we believe, for that is little more than a paraphrase of the language of ruling out all possibilities of error. Hence, it is hard to see how appeals to epistemic certainty are going to be useful for characterizing infallibilism unless that notion is characterized in a way that makes the proposal uninformative.

There remains the language of metaphysical certainty, derived from Descartes, and I will postpone discussion of this notion till later, since it will take us in a direction different from the ideas mentioned already as well as relatively common approaches to Cartesian certainty in terms of reasons for doubt and quality of evidence. As already noted, these approaches don't give us what we are looking for, and when put in service for characterizing metaphysical certainty, leave us absent a notion of certainty needed for clarifying the skeptical gold standard.

To see why, consider Peter Markie's characterization of metaphysical certainty for Descartes:

> p is metaphysically certain for $S =_{df.}$ (1) believing p is more reasonable for S from the standard epistemic perspective than doubting or denying p, and (2) it could never be more reasonable for S to believe some proposition q, than it is at present for S to believe p. (Markie, 1986, 39)

This account, quite Chisholmian in spirit,[2] is both too strong and too weak for characterizing the skeptic's gold standard. It is too weak because of pragmatist

---

[2] Compare his account in the second edition of *Theory of Knowledge* (Chisholm, 1977, 27):

> h is certain for S at $t =_{df.}$ (i) Accepting h is more reasonable for S at t than withholding h (i.e., not accepting h and not accepting not-h) and (ii) there is no i such that accepting i is more reasonable for S at t than accepting h.

For both Chisholm and Markie's Descartes, certainty involves the highest level of epistemic support, in the former case a *de facto* claim, and for the latter a modal claim, in terms of the language of possibility. This difference disappears so long as some of the things we are certain of in Chisholm's sense are also maximally certain across all of the relevant modal space.

90 INFALLIBILISM AND IDEALIZATIONS ABOUT KNOWLEDGE

points already noted. Central to the pragmatist attempt to undermine the significance of skepticism is the idea that the best we could possibly do, intellectually speaking, won't satisfy the skeptical gold standard: the best we could possibly do might still not be very impressive. That remains a theoretical possibility, and if it is, one could be metaphysically certain on the above account without achieving a level of epistemic standing that would meet an infallibility requirement.

It is also too strong, since nothing about the skeptical gold standard requires that there can't be better and worse ways of meeting that standard. This point applies to any attempt to define infallibility in terms of an unsurpassable epistemic status. The skeptical gold standard simply doesn't require any such flattening within the realm where the standard has been met. Moreover, that is a good thing, because as noted above, such flattening contravenes what we know about the epistemic value of (reliable) testimony. To see why, imagine you have a belief that satisfies the skeptical gold standard, whatever that is supposed to be, and then imagine (what you know to be) an all-knowing and perfectly good God telling you that you are correct in your beliefs. Being told that you are correct by an intellectual superior makes it more reasonable to believe that claim than it was without such testimony, and an all-knowing and perfectly good God is obviously an intellectual superior. It is thus possible to have two beliefs, one of which is better supported epistemically than the other, and yet both of which meet the skeptical goal standard for knowledge.

We can also resist accounts of metaphysical certainty that involve epistemic flattening even apart from examples involving testimony, for Descartes himself would chafe at the idea. Descartes thought he could explain how most of what we take ourselves to know we do in fact know, by appeal to the *cogito* and by appeal to the existence of a non-deceiving God. We can grant that the project fails, but our point is about the project itself, not whether it succeeds. He thought the project succeeded and hence that much of what we believe can be metaphysically certain for each of us. But he never hinted at the idea that such a result would wipe out any epistemic distinction between, say, our *cogito* beliefs and our beliefs about advanced scientific and mathematical ideas. Nothing about the notion of metaphysical certainty requires such flattening, and the Cartesian project allows the possibility that some of what we know is epistemically superior to other things we know. So any Chisholmian approach to certainty that implies epistemic flattening once the level of certainty has been reached should be resisted.

So if we think of Cartesian metaphysical certainty in anything like that above, employing talk of reasons or evidence, rationality or reasonability, we'll face problems like those just noted. There is a quite different approach to metaphysical certainty that we'll look at later, but for now, the language of metaphysical certainty isn't going to be helpful without a quite different approach to it. As we'll see, Descartes's ideas give us as good a way of characterizing infallibility as we will be able to find, but the approach to be identified is different enough from the above proposals that I'll table it for now.

As for the language of incorrigibility, we should relegate it to its natural home, one where elders of the community are remarking on youth in the community who keep disappointing them. Yes, they might just be incorrigible. Such talk is about what can be corrected and what can't, but that would make infallibility too dependent on psychological facts. We are all aware of dogmatic fundamentalists whose opinions are incorrigible in this sense, but certainly far from infallible. So, a special sense is needed beyond this idea of what can't be fixed or altered, and we end up back where we began, still searching for a way to characterize infallibility.

Similar problems plague accounts that focus on indubitability or indefeasibility. The former is too subjective, as revealed by the phenomenon of true believers who can't seem to doubt anything they believe, in spite of those beliefs often lacking very good epistemic credentials. The latter idea leaves open the idea of fortuitous certainty, where a beneficent deity makes sure that all potential defeaters are actually false and thus not actual defeaters.[3]

Moreover, a careful skeptic should be impatient with this focus on what we might call "static" epistemic relations anyway, for much the same reasons that led us to part company with entailment accounts of infallibilism in the last chapter. A careful skeptic will want to know about the process of coming to know, and what is involved in that process, rather than on whatever system of information is involved once knowledge is (purportedly) present. How does inquiry progress, and what assurances does it provide against error? That is the issue, according to responsible and careful skepticism, and it is a question about who is in control regarding the possibility of error and how that control arises. Not only the entailment account, but any account focusing on static elements concerning systems of information, will err by dropping talk about locus of control and focusing only on the resulting body of information and what it includes.

The point to note here is that the skeptical worry is, at its core, a concern about the dynamic elements involved in trying to find the truth and avoid error. Coming to know is, or can be, a cross-temporal process. Even if once the epistemological summit has been achieved, we have in our possession entailing evidence, as in Williamsonian epistemology, we can question whether the process of climbing that particular mountain is one riddled with luck and good fortune from a purely cognitive point of view. The skeptical worry, then, is best understood not in terms of what statically obtains once the summit is reached, but must instead be understood dynamically, in terms of the kind of control a person might have or want over the project of getting to the truth and avoiding error.

My point, then, is that we can develop a more careful and less objectionable approach to the notion of infallible knowledge by focusing our attention on the

---

[3] For discussion of this problem, and other related discussion, see Reed (2022).

issue of who or what is in control regarding the possibilities of getting to the truth and avoiding error, whether it is the individual in question or other things, with the limit case being an individual who is in full control over these possibilities.[4]

A helpful analogy on this point aligns the perspective of skeptics with that of ancient Stoics. If we consider the dichotomy of control central to Stoic thinking about how to live a good life, we find a rather stark perspective that resonates with ancient skeptics. For Stoics, the idea is that we are not in control of anything except what is directly within our power to will. All the rest is a matter of what we can influence, but over which we have no control. Our health, wealth, reputation, and accomplishments all fall outside our locus of control, even though there are ways we can affect their probability.

The skeptic might join forces with the Stoic on this idea about control. There is full and complete, total control, and then there is everything else. For everything else, there is an absence of control. And knowledge is present only in situations where this dichotomy of control is on our side, and when it isn't, we might be lucky in finding the truth but we certainly haven't acquired knowledge.

Other skeptics might be more amenable to modifying this digital idea about control, endorsing an analog conception of it instead. On the digital conception, the idea of control is a binary one, with the switch either on or off and never neither. On the analog conception, control comes in degrees, between a range where we have absolutely zero influence over an outcome to cases where the outcome is completely up to us. (Presumably, Stoicism itself could be modified in similar ways, while still insisting on the same basic point that we should focus on the arena where things are completely up to us.)

In epistemology, this Stoic idea reverberates in Descartes's claim that error arises when the will outruns the understanding, and if one also thinks that one has control over whether there is intrusion by the will into cognition, the resulting position allows that each of us has control over the tasks of getting to the truth and avoiding error. (Note that we need both possibilities here because of the by now quotidian point that if we focus on only one of the two, we do best by being gullible or by never believing anything.) In order for such control to exist, the person in question must have certain capacities or abilities involved in the faculty of understanding, so on this approach to characterizing infallibilism, we should ask about these capacities and what idealizations of them might involve. We can make progress in understanding what infallible knowledge involves by exploiting the heuristic of a perfect cognizer, one for whom there is simply no chance or possibility of succumbing to the temptation to do anything but believe in accord with what is revealed by the understanding or operations of cognition, and where such operations of cognition involve faculties, abilities, or skills at truth-detection that

---

[4] For extended discussion of this way of thinking about fallibilism, see Kvanvig (2014, especially Ch 2, section 5).

render it capable of immunity from error except for intrusions from non-cognitive dimensions of the cognizer.

Unfortunately for Cartesian epistemology, this locus of control point can become ancillary to the demand for information and arguments that make a given conclusion metaphysically certain. This approach, like the related probabilistic approaches that focus on certainty and having a probability of one, offers a static approach to the problem of characterizing infallibility, and thus gives away the perceived advantage of talking about an ability to believe in a way that isn't affected by non-cognitive interests. Supplementing this latter idea is, of course, well-motivated, since it is pretty obvious that never believing something because we want it to be true isn't going to make error impossible. It might purge one way for error to arise, but the springs that feed the stream of fallible opinion are found in lots of places, including purely cognitive limitations and defects that won't go away just because one has purged one's noetic operations of non-cognitive influences.

So the Cartesian project both disappoints and offers a positive idea at the same time. The disappointment won't surprise either skeptics or fallibilists—most have long ago concluded that the Cartesian story falls apart at least by the point at which a proof is demanded for the existence of God and the claim that God is not a deceiver. But the more telling point in our context is the disappointing replacement of a dynamic approach to understanding infallibility with a static one. For, as we have seen already, an optimist about knowledge can meet static characterizations about quality of evidence and epistemic grounds that will satisfy entailment demands, or demands in terms of probability or certainty, and yet fall short of standards for knowledge on which skeptics insist.

Even though the skeptic's dissatisfaction with static proposals can be understood in this fashion, what isn't clear is what a dynamic conception of infallibility in terms of locus of control is supposed to be. We should note immediately that there are some obviously outrageous demands that someone might place on the possibility of knowledge, requiring that knowledge can only arise for those for whom false belief is metaphysically impossible. Such a position conforms to the locus of control idea, but in a way that goes far beyond the skeptical standard for knowledge.

So if we are to pursue a dynamic account of infallibility concerning locus of control, we can't attribute to the skeptic absurd claims about such control, as when we imagine them insisting that total control over the process of getting to the truth and avoiding error, unassailable by any force or power either actual or possible. None of us have such control over our own existence, so it would be silly to demand a kind of control that one couldn't have without also having total control over the continuation of our lives.

The skeptical response will be, of course, to focus on control over the ways in which we come to hold beliefs. For the resulting beliefs to be infallible, it has to be up to us whether we find the truth or land in error. That doesn't mean we can't end up in error, but that we must have powers or abilities to keep us from error if we use them properly. Moreover, these powers or abilities or capacities have to be possible for us to have rather than some potential power that only an omnipotent being could have.

It is tempting to take a modal approach to such control, thinking about whether there are possible worlds in which one is in error in the same kinds of circumstances as those of the actual situation. Those attracted to possible worlds construals of powers and abilities are free to follow that path, but I won't do so here, since the language of powers and abilities is clear enough for present purposes. Besides, possible worlds construals suffer from problems for dispositions associated with finking and masking. Masking occurs when different dispositions interact in situations where both are triggered, and there is no reason I can see for denying that a given disposition might get masked in every possible situation by other dispositions. Finking occurs when a disposition disappears in precisely those circumstances that trigger it, and, again, there is no reason I can see for thinking that this can't happen across all of modal space.[5] These complaints about modal analyses are, at bottom, reasons for being realists about dispositions more generally, declining efforts to characterize them in conditional terms of one sort or another.

For our purposes, we don't need to settle this issue about realism, but simply note the issue while declining to take sides on it. All that is needed in our context is the idea of degree of control over whether one lands in error, with the extreme version of being in total control involving a power or ability to keep from making a mistake. Such a power or ability can be present without being exercised, so it would be a mistake to characterize total control in terms of lacking the power to believe falsely. Instead, one is in total control of an epistemic situation when the complete explanation of whether one has gotten to the truth and avoided error is given in terms of such powers or abilities and whether the person has exercised them.

Here, though, fallibilists can question whether such powers are even possible, at least for non-divine and non-omniscient beings. Moreover, even if some such powers are possible in some cases, why generalize from these instances? That is, the possibility claim that can be questioned can't be defended by simply pointing to some exalted theology in which such powers can be found, or by identifying one arena where such powers are possible, but must be defended more generally,

---

[5] The original discussion of finking was by C.B. Martin, though his work did not appear in print until the idea was already fairly commonly known. For discussion, see Martin (1994) and Armstrong et al. (1996), with Lewis (1997) offering an attempt to save conditional analyses from finks. The literature on finks has grown enormously since the publication of Martin's paper and Lewis's counterproposal, but for early rejections of Lewis's approach, see Bird (1998), Kvanvig (1999), and, most extensively, Mumford (1998).

regardless of subject matter or types of inquiry. For example, if such powers are found for mathematical inquiry, the task of characterizing the skeptical ideal isn't complete, for there are types of inquiry that are obviously different from what we find in mathematics. So, if a skeptic generalized from what we know about mathematical inquiry, claiming that knowledge can only arise *a priori*, such a skepticism would be worthy of immediate rejection. Such a position would count as a blatant form of epistemic imperialism. Failure to address the generality issue is the core of the imperialism charge, the complaint that what we say about some kinds of knowledge isn't something we have to say about all kinds of knowledge. The challenges faced in developing a significant skeptical epistemology thus involve defending the possibility claim in a way that doesn't generalize from things that might be true but only in supernatural realms, or in any other way that succumbs to the imperialism charge.

Evasive maneuvers regarding these tasks are tempting and easy to spot, and they count as evasions because the effort needed is a substantive, rather than trivial, one. For example, suppose the skeptic characterizes the powers in question in terms of the demand itself: the power to render one's investigations immune from error. Such a characterization is no help whatsoever regarding the possibility claim. We know that we don't have such generic powers. Perhaps we'll grant that such powers are possible, on the basis of the possibility of divine or supernatural beings. But we are not them, nor could we be. So we should wonder why the bare possibility of a being with such powers would translate to the sphere where ordinary human efforts at getting to the truth and avoiding error are on display. Why think, for beings such as we, that such powers are possible? To address the demand for defending the possibility claim, we will need a substantive characterization of the imagined powers, capacities, and abilities that makes clear how and why there is such a possibility.

Another evasive maneuver involves analogizing from one power to another. For example, suppose skeptics can defend the possibility claim when it comes to perceptual capacities, and then wants to generalize, doing so by saying, "The ideal for all other powers and abilities is like that." This analogical maneuver is an evasion that shouldn't be tolerated. Imagine someone defending global skepticism by noting the existence of what Keith DeRose (2018b) calls "knowledge deserts": topics and issues where knowledge cannot be found. Potential deserts of this sort concern ethics, politics, and religion (not to mention philosophy. . .).[6] So suppose the argument proceeds from the presence of knowledge deserts by analogy:

---

[6] Care must be shown here, for no such area is really an area where knowledge cannot be found. The claim would have to be more circumspect, ruling out knowledge of a positive variety while granting that negative knowledge may be found in these areas. For example, one might be wary of positive claims about the nature of God, but be fully on board with the idea that God isn't an atom. The distinction between positive and negative knowledge is a vexed one, of course, but something like it will be needed in order to explain the idea of a knowledge desert.

everything is just like those. I expect we can all agree that this is about as lame an argument for skepticism as we'll find. And just so for the needed defense of the possibility of powers of the sort needed to develop a skeptical position. Relying on an analogy with success in one area is mere hand-waving, and if that is all that can be given, dismissive attitudes toward skepticism are appropriate and to be expected.

So the skeptic will need to begin with a list of powers, capacities, or abilities that human beings are thought to have for detecting truth and avoiding error, and then characterize the notion of ideality or perfection for each of them that is being relied on to undergird the demand for total control over the possibilities of finding the truth and avoiding error. We note initially, for example, that we have sensory capacities for discerning the truth, reasoning capacities for extending our knowledge, and perhaps some sort of rational intuition for detecting necessary truths of a certain sort. Fallibilists, whether sensitive or complacent, recognize the lack of immunity from error in these capacities, powers, and abilities, but skeptics look askance at letting such a recognition allow talk of fallible knowledge. They claim that perfect, ideal uses of these abilities would yield immunity from error, and knowledge requires such ideality.

Let's hold off on the second part of this claim—the part that claims that knowledge requires ideality—in order to focus initially on the first part. What is this notion of perfection or ideality, for each of the powers of detection noted, that the skeptic thinks we need to display?

4.3 Acceptable Idealizations

On this issue, we have some historical precedent to rely on, for there is a significant body of literature concerning appropriate idealizations developed by intuitionists in the philosophy of mathematics in support of semantic anti-realism, deriving from the work of the philosophical logician Michael Dummett,[7] where the idea is to try first to understand mathematical truth in terms of provability and then to extend these ideas to the empirical realm.[8] One central focus in the literature, especially in connection with anti-realist conceptions of truth, is on the idea of an acceptable idealization, and here we find talk of finite extensions of ordinary human capacities. If one wishes to understand truth in terms of knowability, for example, it is unacceptable to talk about what is knowable to the infinite mind of God. Instead, one must theorize in terms of finite extensions

---

[7] Intuitionism is found first in Brouwer (1907). For Dummett's version of Intuitionism, see especially Dummett (1977) and Dummett (1978), and for the connection with the theory of meaning, see Dummett (1975), Dummett (1976), and Dummett (1993). For the link of these things to metaphysics, see Dummett (1991).

[8] See, for example, Tennant (1997) and Hand (1996).

of ordinary human minds, abstracting from factors such as merely medical limitations,[9] such as life span and various decays of cognitive function, as well as liabilities to boredom, various attention-deficit conditions, or the lack of resilience shown in giving up on an issue when things get hard to figure out. So we can begin to think about characterizing the skeptical ideal for knowledge by thinking about finite extensions of the human mind and the powers of detection associated with it.

As with semantic anti-realism, skepticism can begin in the amenable arena of mathematical truth and the related notion of mathematical reasoning. For semantic anti-realists, it provides the most receptive area in which truth and provability might seem to merge. In our context, it provides the skeptic a fertile field in which to plant the idea of immunity to error, since the territory involves conclusions based on reasoning that involves a guarantee of truth, given the truth of the premises. Here the relevant power, ability, or capacity is simply that of being able to master perfectly the practice of mathematical reasoning, never succumbing to inattention or weariness in a way that results in error. After all, we can write a program to tell us whether mistakes have been made, and if a computer can do it, so can we. For what computers can do falls under the rubric of what finite extensions of ordinary human abilities involve. So it is possible to display the power of immunity from error when it comes to mathematical reasoning, and the account generated doesn't result from any appeal to God-like capacities or points of view, but arises through finite extensions of ordinary human capacities, idealized by abstracting from merely medical limitations.

It doesn't take much philosophical insight to see that this idealization of ordinary human capacities isn't adequate as it stands for characterizing the high standards that must be met for mathematical knowledge, since it is dependent on the need for the premises to be true. Moreover, mere truth for the premises won't get us knowledge of the conclusions, since one could get lucky by picking the right set of premises that just happen to be true. So the skeptic needs not only to characterize and idealize the mathematical reasoning that is needed for mathematical knowledge, but also how the premises are known as well. If we follow the typical approach to such matters, everything will trace here to knowledge of the axioms of the mathematical system in question,[10] and the account of ideal knowledge of the

---

[9] Terminology borrowed from Bertrand Russell who, in Russell (1935, 143) tells us that the infinite decimal expansion of π is "medically impossible" for us to inspect, though that limitation doesn't undermine the idea of an extension of the capacity to inspect from finite cases to infinite ones. Dummett appeals to this idea in Dummett (1977, 59–60), writing of what counts as a "mere medical impossibility."

[10] At least in the ideal case for mathematical systems, where an axiomatization is available. A cautionary word, though: mathematical knowledge involving probabilities seems to have been present long before the Kolmogorov (1950 [1933]) axiomatization, and the same point can be made about simple arithmetic and the Peano axioms. To accommodate these points, we will need some distinction between the axioms themselves and an axiomatic system, regarding which we can ask about consistency and completeness and other interesting metatheoretical properties.

axioms will require appeal to some power of rational intuition, rather than some further piece of mathematical reasoning.[11]

What can the skeptic say about ordinary human cognitive powers to characterize the ideal of perfect knowledge based on rational intuition? Careful attention to the history of such discussion reveals a tendency to think of rational intuition on the model provided by ordinary perception. Even our language is that of perception: can't you just see that, for example, there is a successor for every natural number?

This perceptual model of rational intuition can only succeed if we can find an adequate finite extension of ordinary perceptual powers that leads to perfect knowledge of the sort the skeptic demands. The danger for the skeptic on this score is the appearance/reality distinction itself. For wouldn't any idealization of the sort imagined have to eliminate that distinction in epistemically ideal perceptual worlds, and if that is so, how could the idealizations legitimately claim to involve finite extensions of ordinary powers instead of imposing a God's-eye point of view on human knowledge?

This concern about the appearance/reality distinction is most pressing concerning ordinary perception, but it is worth noting that it is relevant as well in the case of mathematics and logic. Russell's paradox for Frege's attempt to reduce mathematics to logic is a case in point, and the incompleteness results of Kurt Gödel fuel this objection, too. In particular, how could some finite extension of powers of rational intuition prevent the possibility of thinking an axiom obviously true even though it is internally inconsistent or inconsistent with the other axioms of the system?

The objection isn't compelling, however, and we'll be able to say why after turning to the arena of ordinary empirical knowledge to see what appeals to finite extensions of ordinary human capacities can do in terms of providing a characterization of the kind of perfection skeptics say is needed for knowledge. In this arena, two capacities are crucial, memory and perception. When it comes to memory, we can use the same analogy with computer capacities to note that a finite extension of our ability to remember would involve never forgetting and never altering anything entered into the system. Idealizing in this way doesn't threaten the distinction between remembering and seeming to remember, since that distinction only relies on there being some memories that are only putative. What is needed, then, for modeling control over memorial mistakes is the computer analogy together with some account of control over the inputs into memory,

---

[11] I note here that the conclusion in the text resists the infinitist claim defended by Peter Klein in several places. A good introductory piece is Klein (2011), and more detail and defense can be found in Klein (2005a), Klein (2007a), and Klein (2007b). How exactly one would use such an infinitism to defend knowledge of the axioms isn't quite clear to me, though perhaps the idea would be to subsume each mathematical system into a more general one, where level of generality never ends. For criticisms of infinitism, see Borges et al. (2019), and for my own reasons for resisting the view, see Kvanvig (2012).

so that nothing is introduced into memory except material from the display of some other power or ability over which control can also be present. The obvious approach here is thus to focus on perception, hoping that once perception is modeled appropriately, we'll have the ingredients needed for the model of idealized memory.

The computer analogy will be no help, however, when it comes to perceptual abilities. The best hope for a model of the kind of perfection imagined for perception is found in fictional entities. In recent times, what comes to mind most readily is the eye of Sauron from Tolkien's *Lord of the Rings* trilogy. Note that this fiction does not resort to a God's-eye point of view, since the eye of Sauron is not all-seeing: characters in the books and in the movie renditions of the books often hide themselves from it. What the eye doesn't do, however, is misperceive: once falling within the field of vision, it doesn't mistake you for a tree or a cloud or an apparition. It is, in a word, faultless, even though it can be faulted for failing to detect some things.

If such an idealization of perception is possible, so will be a similar idealization of rational insight or intuition regarding the axioms needed for mathematical reasoning and knowledge. Perhaps, on analogy with Sauron, one can posit Spock as an having the kind of unfailing rational insight that the eye of Sauron has with respect to visible things. Well, perhaps not Spock, for his virtue is supposedly that of having cognitive powers ruled by logic and never by emotion, which seems to have something to do with reasoning powers rather than powers of insight. Yet, there remains some hope for a fictional model here, since being logical must advert at some point to initial premises from which to reason, so even if we are stretching Spock a bit to use this character for purposes of fictional modeling of intuition for logical starting points, the stretch won't break the model.

There will be questions and objections that skeptics will need to face in characterizing such fictional models, of course, but I see no reason to think that things will be worse for rational insight than for ordinary vision. In each case, the model provided gives us some idea of how development of a skeptical position for these kinds of abilities might proceed, so in spite of a desire for further details, we can at least at least grant the point that some progress can be made in developing skepticism beyond mere argument and conclusion.

A further idealization is needed to address the role of testimony in our efforts to find the truth and avoid error. Here, things are a bit more complicated, given the variety of views about the epistemology of testimony, whether it is a basic source of epistemic standing or whether derivative. The complications, however, don't appear insurmountable for a skeptical account of ideal testimony. The central element of such an idealization will be to idealize the virtue of honesty among testifiers, so that deceptive practices aren't part of worlds where ideal testimony occurs. Then, if idealizations for other powers, abilities, and capacities can be appropriately characterized, the skeptic will be in a position to characterize ideal testimony as either a basic source of epistemic standing from such idealized testifiers or one derived on the basis of epistemic assessments of one's sources of information. The former possibility will introduce no complications to accounts of the ideal that are not present already in idealizations regarding sensory capacities, but the latter will need elaboration beyond the kind of account already in place. In particular, it is one thing for one's sources of information to be utterly reliable and quite another for one to recognize that they are. The eye of Sauron may be a nice fictional idealization that is useful for ordinary perception, but it is hard to see how the difference between perfectly reliable informants and those who are not can be treated in terms of something visually detectable or detectable by some other sensory modality.

If reliability of this sort is not detectable by sensory powers, the obvious source for recognition of it is through reasoning. If so, the skeptic should table this issue and return to it after addressing the problem about knowledge of the future and other kinds of knowledge depending essentially on (defeasible) reasoning. For if this latter problem can be solved, the resources involved can be adapted to the problem of how to use our reasoning capacities to discern whom to trust as informants. If the basis for assessing trustworthiness is not (wholly) sensory in character (as they are not likely to be if the cues are supposed to be ideal), then we are in the position of having to assess trustworthiness through the same kind of reasoning by which we figure out the truth in non-observational contexts, including what will happen in the future.

It is worth reinforcing the point that the idealization needed will be one concerning reasoning, and that no perceptual model will suffice. First, the idea of *seeing* the future is sheer metaphor, an inadequate substitute for sober theory. The future can be predicted, anticipated, and even envisioned, but it isn't, and can't be, perceived. Some may be tempted in this direction by talk of the power of prescience, but we shouldn't think of any such power as a kind of vision. To do so would saddle the skeptic with an undesirable metaphysics according to which backward causation is possible, since vision is a causal process. Skepticism is better developed on metaphysically neutral assumptions, on pain of losing credibility because of special and idiosyncratic metaphysics. Moreover, even if backward causation were possible, that isn't how any of us function in aiming to ascertain what the future will be like, nor is it the basis on which commonsense epistemologists rely when claiming that we know many things, some of which are about the future. So the right approach here is to assume that the future can't be perceived any more than the past can. More carefully, we need a different model for memorial knowledge than we do for ordinary sensory knowledge, and a further different model for knowledge of the future.

One may wonder here about time travel, for if it is possible, won't there be a sense in which we can see the past? No. For what will be seen will in fact have become present to the observer in virtue of the fact that they have traveled back in time. So, even if past times can be re-visited, what one learns through perception upon so visiting would fall under the category of knowledge of our current surroundings. Under usual assumptions, it is only present times that are candidates for being current, and if time travel is possible, there is a way to make times other than the present count as current to the time traveler. So the point remains: knowledge of what is in the past, relative to whatever times are current, are to be accounted for in terms of memory or testimony or on the basis of reasoning from signs causally resulting from the past, not perception.

The metaphysics of time travel complicates things here in another way. If you travel back in time, then, relative to the time that becomes current to you, there will be future times about which you could have memories. One might then think that we could model all knowledge of the future in terms of memorial knowledge of possible time travelers. It is a strange idea, but likely not one for skeptics to rely on, since the metaphysical baggage required is, again, substantial. Such a view requires that Presentism as well as Growing Block theories of time are mistaken, since on both of these views, the future doesn't have the required reality to it to make such an account work.[12] Future times will become real as time passes, but they are not now real. So even if the possibility of time travel is granted, it cannot help with respect to knowledge of future times that have not yet occurred. It could only help with respect to knowledge of future times that have already occurred, and from which one traveled into the past, thereby making those times future times from the point of view of the time traveler.

The point remains, then, that the skeptical gold standard for knowledge of the future is something that needs to be characterized in terms of patterns of reasoning that we use in our attempts to learn what the future holds. This same point holds for idealizing our efforts to ascertain which sources of information are trustworthy and which are not, an essential component on at least some approaches to testimonial knowledge. If it turns out that no such idealization is possible, theory development of the skeptical position will be in trouble along both dimensions. But if the problem about knowledge of the future can be properly handled, we have reason to conclude that testimonial knowledge won't present an insurmountable problem either.

This disjunctive account of what to say about ideal testimonial knowledge, then, offers one straightforward idealization for testimony and a second, buck-passing possibility if testimony turns out to be a derivative source of epistemic standing. Either way, the idealization needed with respect to testimonial knowledge does not appear to be what would undermine the skeptic's development of a position from which to denigrate our intellectual achievements.

Even so, there is much in each of these idealizations that can be questioned, requiring further efforts at explaining exactly how these finite extensions of ordinary human powers get us to immunity from error. Here, though, it is worth

---

[12] In brief, Presentists hold that only the current time is real, and Growing Block theories hold that reality encompasses both past and present. For further discussion, see Emery et al. (2020, Section 6).

acknowledging a good start, for after noting the theory development that skeptics need to undertake in order to turn their position and arguments into a serious competitor among theories of knowledge, we have here a glimpse of what such theory development can look like. Even if further questions are asked about the fictional model for perfect sensory equipment, and even if there are further issues concerning the computer analogy for memory and logical reasoning, and even if there are facts about the nature of mathematics from Gödel and others that cause problems for the perceptual model for rational intuition of the truth of the axioms of mathematical systems, the models offered form a significant theoretical advance over bare appeals to skeptical arguments.

Moreover, since there is a deeper concern to pursue here, one concerning knowledge of the future, I propose to forego further reflection on the quality of each of these models and the problems involved in characterizing them. So let us grant this much to the skeptic: the fictional, perceptual, and computer models show enough promise for generating accounts of ideality for sensory awareness, mathematical reasoning, and rational intuition that we will assume success along these fronts is within reach.

One cautionary note, though, about this concession. These efforts at explaining the needed enhancements of ordinary cognitive powers through finite extensions of these capacities would be useless without something like Descartes's idea of having control over whether intrusion from outside the cognitive system is under our control. Even the most gifted in terms of extraordinarily sensitive sensory apparati and reasoning abilities will be plagued by false belief if what they want to be true intrudes into their judgments about what is in fact true. Imagine, for example, hoping (prior to 1993) to be the person who finally proved Fermat's Last Theorem, and how easy it would be for that potential honor to make one think that one has found a proof when in fact a less motivated appraisal would see quickly the fault in the proof. Human beings have a considerable capacity to see what they want to see, hear what they want to hear, and without an idealized capacity for keeping cognition separate from the affective side of our being, the enhancements described won't get us to the characterization of perfect, ideal knowledge.

So, we not only need finite extensions of human capacities for detecting truth, we also need finite extensions of the human capacity to resist non-cognitive intrusion into our cognitive systems. Here, we need some appeal to the executive function of the will, imagining it to have more effective control than is typical for mere mortals. That is, we will need to imagine people being capable of such willpower that they are able, always and everywhere, to resist the temptation to be influenced in what they take to be true by anything other than truth-apt elements. In particular, affective motivations have to be able to be eliminated entirely.

There is a problem with such an approach that I want to note, though will also pass on pursuing. For it isn't clear that cognition can be separated from the non-cognitive aspects of our being, nor that it would be good or right if it were. If we begin with the topic of the cognitive penetrability of ordinary perception, we might come to the conclusion that the informational encapsulation claim involved in Fodor's modularity thesis is mistaken.[13] If that conclusion turns out to be correct and what we believe plays a role in what we see, for example, the question is whether what we believe is itself influenced, and appropriately so, by non-cognitive features. For example, there may be non-epistemic reasons for belief, though that too is a controversial issue, and there may be further intrusion needed into the cognitive system from non-cognitive aspects of mentation in order to account for moral perception and knowledge.

I note this issue only to put it aside, though, for it is another complexity facing the task of characterizing the finite extensions of ordinary capacities in order to articulate the skeptical ideal for cognition. The problem here is a significant one, because it pushes us to find a non-Cartesian characterization of the executive function of the will, one that doesn't merely keep out non-cognitive influences but rather one that performs the gate keeping function of letting in what is needed for finding the truth and keeping out everything else. Perhaps such an account can be found, but there are hurdles to clear. The main one is that performing this executive function appears to require discernment about what needs to be let in and what needs to be blocked, but such discernment presupposes knowledge and thus could not be epistemically prior to efforts at getting to the truth and avoiding error.

Perhaps, though, this claimed need for discernment can be replaced by something less cognitive. We are familiar already with ways in which the behavior of organisms does not always get explained in terms of mentation, so perhaps we could imagine the happy coincidence of behavioral stimuli for producing the right balance for this ideal for executive control over which non-cognitive aspects to let in as epistemic influences. These issues are troubling and complicated, but since there is no obvious reason to find such an idealization of this executive function incoherent, I propose that we take the same attitude toward this non-Cartesian account as we would need to regarding the Cartesian proposal itself. For both approaches, idealized control through the executive function of the will is needed, and the possibility of such control can be characterized at least in some cursory fashion, though these characterizations require further clarification and elaboration in order to explain fully how such control can work.

In this way, idealizing the executive function of the will is in the same position as the other idealizations for particular powers and abilities, from perception to memory to the capacity to learn from testimony. So in all these cases, there is room for those attracted to complacent fallibilism to resist skeptical theory development in support of a false presupposition account of concessive attitudes and attributions. The deepest difficult for the project of skeptical theory development hasn't been addressed yet, though, so I propose to assume that these grounds for

---

[13] See Fodor (1983).

104 INFALLIBILISM AND IDEALIZATIONS ABOUT KNOWLEDGE

complacency aren't going to be sufficient for undergirding complacency, in order to focus on the more serious problem concerning knowledge of the future and other non-observational contingencies, and the charge of epistemic imperialism when it comes to what counts as a legitimate logic for proper reasoning. We turn to this issue next.

4.4 Logic and Reasoning

It may have been noticed that when characterizing the ideal for matters of reasoning, I focused on mathematical knowledge and the kind of reasoning employed in it. The logic relevant to such reasoning is typically assumed to be standard first-order logic, inspired by Frege, which is monotonic in character. Yet, the scope of logic and the ways of evaluating reasoning include not only monotonic logics but non-monotonic as well. Monotonic logics use a consequence relation that cannot be undermined by additional information added to the set of premises in question; non-monotonic logics do not have this characteristic.

Mathematical reasoning easily admits of evaluation in terms of monotonic logics, as do certain patterns of reasoning in philosophy. There are vast areas of investigation where this is not the case, and in much of this territory we find things that commonsense epistemologists say are among the many things we know. One paradigm example of such an area concerns the future and our knowledge of it. Among the many things we know, a commonsense epistemology will claim, are things about the future: on the positive side, that the sun will rise tomorrow; and a bit darker, that we are going to die. More generally, we use our predictive capacities to decide how to behave, relying on those capacities to decide which direction to go to find our car when it is time to go home, where to find a drinking fountain when thirsty, where's a good place to have lunch, and a vast array of other decisions that are part of ordinary life.

It is tempting here for the skeptic to try to squeeze such reasoning, in procrustean fashion, into the category of mathematical reasoning, and then evaluate it by the standards of monotonic logic. Such an approach, however, is the poster child for epistemic imperialism. Epistemic imperialism shows itself in a variety of contexts, where things are denied when they don't fit some preferred list of criteria. Some people maintain that they won't believe anything unless they can touch, taste, or feel it; others claim that nothing should be believed unless confirmed by science. Wry smiles at the self-referential incoherence of these ideas are expected and appropriate, but there is a different point to note as well. In our context, we are thinking of the high standards skeptics point to in terms of the locus of control, and the idea is to try to explain what these high standards are with respect to the powers, abilities, and capacities human beings have for finding the truth and avoiding error. If this task proves difficult or appears impossible in certain cases, no progress is made by pretending that such cases are different from what they in fact are. So, for example, good science of a theoretical nature shows us how to detect the unobservable, and any idealization of this capacity that models it on perception itself is pretense. It pretends that capacities for detecting what can't be observed are really a type of capacity for detecting what can be observed. That is a mistake. If knowledge of unobservables is really impossible, as skeptics claim, we should be told what the gold standard is for investigating what is unobservable in terms of finite extensions of ordinary human capacities, where the finite extensions reveal what it would be like for the locus of control over the possibilities of truth and error to reside completely within us. Put negatively, if no such ideal can be characterized, the right attitude to take is that the skeptic has made an unfounded generalization about one type of knowledge to other types of knowledge rather than having demonstrated that such things are not among the things that we know.

It is easy to lose sight of this point and to let skepticism off the hook here. It is easy to do so because we can make some progress in some areas showing how to model the locus of control idea for characterizing infallibility. We wouldn't be so sanguine, however, had the skeptic stopped after characterizing the ideal for mathematical reasoning, and then insisted that powers of perception had to fit the model for such reasoning. Instead, while it is fine to acknowledge the progress made by saying what locus of control involves in the domain of mathematical reasoning, we must also insist that a different model be proposed when it comes to sensory capacities. As we saw above, the skeptic has some options for how to model ideality with respect to these capacities, and it is not an approach that tries to shoehorn sensory capacities into the category of mathematical reasoning.

This need for specificity with respect to each kind of power or ability or capacity for finding the truth arises because of our inability to characterize the notion of locus of control without it. The account we seek is not merely one about control over the possibility of error, but also about control over finding the truth. Characterizing this positive side of the epistemic goal requires idealizing each of the ways in which we go about this task, and the path we are following here approaches such idealization in a way that relies on nothing beyond finite extensions of human capacities, rejecting the idea that it would be acceptable to substitute God-like capacities and perspectives for ours. Failure to differentiate between these latter two ways of characterizing ideality risks the criticism that skepticism results from wishing we were God. For any standard on which our possession of the great intellectual goods requires that our capacities are just like God's is a standard worthy of being ignored.

As an aside, it is worth noting that it is for precisely this reason that the best versions of semantic anti-realism don't argue for the identification of truth with some epistemic notion such as knowability or verifiability solely because God is necessarily omniscient. The point isn't that verificationists weren't theists, which of course is true, given their use of the verificationist criterion of meaning to render all theology meaningless. For one needn't be a verificationist of this sort to be a semantic anti-realist. Rather than deriving their view from any piece of theology, the view needs to connect the notion of truth with what we ordinary human beings can verify or come to know. No claims about what divine beings are like or could know is relevant to that task.

Just so with the task of characterizing the cognitive ideality skeptics claim is needed for knowledge. The needed account should involve the locus of control idea, and the idealization of our intellectual capacities should proceed in terms of finite extensions of these capacities.

These points coalesce to put pressure on skepticism precisely at the point at which non-monotonic logics are the best tools for evaluating the reasoning processes used in coming to the conclusions that we reach. Knowledge of the future is a paradigm example of such, though any knowledge of contingent reality that involves unobservables will raise similar issues, as will knowledge of the past, and statistical knowledge more generally. Here, though, we'll focus on the future, since these results will generalize quite easily to these other areas, and knowledge of the future so obviously relies on patterns of reasoning instead of sensory powers of detection. In that way, it is more like mathematical knowledge than perceptual knowledge, but it is not able to be modeled in the way mathematical knowledge was modeled above. For mathematical knowledge, modeling in terms of monotonic logics was appropriate and perhaps adequate, but not for knowledge of the future.

If we wish, we can call the attempt to model knowledge of the future with monotonic logics "Hume's mistake." Hume wanted to know how we know that the sun will rise tomorrow, and claimed that we'd have a good story to tell if the future always resembled the past. This point is of course correct, but this approach suffers from two ailments. First, the future needn't resemble the past, and second, mere truth isn't enough for the premise to generate knowledge of the conclusions that follow from it. In addition, one must know that the premises are true. And yet, inductive generalizations seem to be in precisely the same category as inductive predictions when it comes to the kind of explanation sought for how we know them to be true, so even if the future does always resemble the past, no vindication of induction will yet have been given.

What ought to strike us about this dialectic, though, is why anyone would look in this direction in the first place. After all, reasoning is how we extend our knowledge, and reasoning can be evaluated in a number of ways, some of which advert to monotonic logics and some to non-monotonic. If evaluated by the former standards, the reasoning has an implicit premise, one which is often false and knowledge of which is in need of explanation even when true. But why think that's the appropriate evaluational standard? Such an assumption presumes that all reasoning is to be evaluated as we evaluate mathematical reasoning, and that is a paradigm example of epistemic imperialism. Those who are attracted to this conclusion need to argue for the claim that appropriate standards for evaluating all reasoning are monotonic in character, rather than simply assuming it.

This charge of imperialism, first occurring in the literature in Alston (1993) (where Alston argues against refusing to count religious experiences as genuinely perceptual on grounds that doing so displays imperialism), has to be treated carefully to avoid a slippery slope. The slippery slope concerns some of the talk about ways of knowing, where no proposals can ever be rejected, perhaps for fear of cultural bigotry of one sort or another. Tarot card readings, readings of tea leaves and the entrails of dead animals come to mind, as well as consulting the oracle at Delphi and the idea that being true to yourself is the only sure path to knowledge. Once the charge of imperialism is raised, we also find this slippery slope danger that no proposal about some unusual way of knowing can ever be rejected.

There is danger here, but no necessity. It is clear that there is a difference between recognized and commendable ways of trying to uncover what the world is really like and ideas like that above that are not commendable in any way. It is an understandable desire to be able to tout some criterion for dismissing bad epistemology, but the fact is that good epistemology is complicated and controversy is to be expected. Even so, complications and controversies don't require abandoning all standards, but instead require better efforts at coping with the intricacies of the epistemological labyrinth. In the process, there is no God's-eye point of view allowing us to dictate what claims can be challenged and what can't, but it is equally a mistake to think that just because any given claim can be challenged, we must turn pessimistic and conclude that every proposal is as good as every other one.

So the charge of imperialism doesn't force open the floodgates. Instead, the concern that it does should lead us to proceed carefully when making the charge. In doing so, we consider the possibility that a given method of finding the truth really has no decent credentials at all, but we also pay attention to the fact that some of our practices are worthy of being relied on while others aren't to be relied on. So, when our practices generate positive epistemic standing, the imperialism charge must be avoided; and when a proposal like being true to yourself is suggested— one unable to produce positive epistemic standing—the charge of imperialism is without merit.

Among these obviously credible ways of inquiry are sense perception, reasoning, memory, and reliance on the testimony of others. And when we look at subcategories in each of these areas, it is equally imperialistic to dismiss credible subkinds. So if sense perception is included but only when it is visual, that's imperialism. Just so, when reasoning is included but only when assessable in terms of monotic logical systems, that too is imperialism.

Some will remain concerned here, noting the relativity of positive epistemic standing. Can't other peoples and cultures and even individuals see things differently than we do on these matters? Of course that is possible. All that implies,

108 INFALLIBILISM AND IDEALIZATIONS ABOUT KNOWLEDGE

though, is that they will avoid the slippery slope problem in ways that are different from the ways we will avoid it, and it is important to note here that it is the slippery slope issue that needs addressing. Moreover, addressing it can be done while at the same time endorsing fully general relativity about positive epistemic standing for different ways of pursuing the epistemic goal. We can honor the ubiquity of rational disagreements without having to embrace an epistemological anarchism or libertinism on which anything goes.

Imperialistic strategies are especially tempting when it looks so obvious that there is an intellectual train wreck coming, apart from denying the presupposed way of knowing involved. If you are a skeptic and think you have no way of undermining the claim that we extend our knowledge by ordinary reasoning which is neither mathematical nor scientific, one might be tempted to insist that all reasoning has to be of the same sort we find in mathematics or science. Yet, commonsense informs us, we don't need a double-blind study to find out that young children cooperate better when offered a treat, and we don't need an axiomatic system combined with deductive rules of inference to learn that we are all going to die. If the skeptic is right that we know no such things, that position needs to be developed in philosophically respectable fashion, without having to retreat to more comfortable territory for fear of failure because unable to idealize these ordinary capacities so as to satisfy the locus of control idea that is central to infallibility.

The fear of failure is most salient when we talk about knowledge of the future, for it is obvious that no such knowledge involves mathematical reasoning from axiomatic systems. The fear is that if we countenance any role for non-monotonic logics in our evaluation of human reasoning, all hope is lost. For, it might seem, there is no way to idealize with respect to such logics so as to yield the demanded control over the possibility of error that infallibility involves. Maybe it looks even worse than hopeless, maybe it looks downright contradictory, in much the same way that trying to explain how probabilistic reasoning could provide guarantees of truth of the sort we find in standard first-order logic looks contradictory.

Such a result will set complacent fallibilists to rejoicing, for that is all the ammunition they need to justify saying, "I told you so!" Put more carefully, if skepticism is to be taken seriously, theory development is a central component in being so taken, and if the best that can be done is procrustean mangling that demonstrates epistemic imperialism, the skeptical project is in a shambles. Memory needs to be modeled differently than sense perception, and what the skeptic says about vision can't be used against the idea that we acquire knowledge by using the other senses as well. So if all the skeptic can say about ordinary reasoning is that can't be modeled by the standards for mathematical reasoning, that's not proper theory development, but should instead be categorized as a failed attempt to characterize the locus of control idea for the domain in question. The conclusion to draw would then be that skepticism can't be developed properly, and so complacent fallibilism is fallibilism enough.

So, there is a task that needs completing here in order to show that a more sensitive version of fallibilism is needed. Once we reach this conclusion, however, it looks like all hope is lost. For we grasp the future by non-demonstrative reasoning, and it appears hopeless to give an account of perfect, infallible knowledge of the future that involves non-demonstrative reasoning. Non-demonstrative reasoning simply can't be truth-preserving in the way deductive reasoning is.

I will argue, though, this conclusion is mistaken. To do so, we will need to find a characterization of the ideal for such reasoning so that the locus of control point about avoiding error can be sustained.

Before turning to this task in the next chapter, however, there is one more tactic that might be used to avoid the need for such theory development. For some may find hope that we can appeal to determinism to show how putative knowledge of the future can be treated adequately in terms of demonstrative rather than non-demonstrative reasoning. The idea is that any putative knowledge of the future could only be concerning the parts of the future that depend deterministically on the past and present, and thus that the reasoning in question must be presupposing some deterministic laws or other that link the past and present to the future. Once we get this far, it might be thought, we are in a position to see that the reasoning used to come to knowledge of the future must in fact be presupposing these laws, and because of that presupposition, have an ideal form that is adequately characterized in terms of reasoning that is demonstrative rather than defeasible, monotonic instead of non-monotonic.

We will then need to show why this last attempted evasion lead to a dead end before turning to the constructive task in the next chapter. Once we see that the hope involved is illusory, we will be in a position to focus in a better direction.

4.5 Why An Appeal To Determinism Must Fail

First note a textbook characterization of determinism in terms of an entailment claim: The laws of nature plus initial conditions entail all else. Given this understanding, if one knew the laws and the initial conditions, one could predict the future with perfect accuracy, if determinism were true. For the conclusion follows deductively from this information.[14] So, even if determinism is false as a completely

---

[14] I note that we could be more careful here about the difference between an entailment claim and a deduction claim. The former is a semantic claim and the latter a proof-theoretic one. Given soundness and completeness for the correct logic, these claims would be logically equivalent. Once we articulate this point, though, it is obvious what the problems are with identifying entailments with deducibilities: soundness and completeness are nice to find, but we have no guarantees that a correct logic will embody them.

We can be more confident, though, in the inference from deduction to entailment. We might put the point this way: completeness for a logic is a very nice thing to have, but soundness is essential. So if we find that deducibility and entailment come apart in this way, it is clearly time to find a better logic. It is

110 INFALLIBILISM AND IDEALIZATIONS ABOUT KNOWLEDGE

general account of our universe, so long as there are parts of it where determinism reigns, we can rely on this demonstrative account to explain what perfect knowledge of the future would be like.

We might put the point this way. If we understand determinism as involving an entailment claim, then if knowledge of the laws and initial conditions could be gotten without reliance on non-demonstrative reasoning (say, by some combination of perception, testimony, and memory), then we could get knowledge of the future by demonstrative reasoning alone. Moreover, this result mirrors the attraction of reducibility of theory to observation in the heyday of Logical Positivism, for if reducibility is obtainable, then there is hope that non-demonstrative reasoning from theory to observation could be modeled by deductive reasoning.

For simplicity, though, let's focus on the problem of knowledge of the future, since that problem alone will undermine hope for embracing a deductive model of such. One problem for this appeal to determinism involves the "if" clause: to get the story off the ground, we need knowledge of past and present to include knowledge of the laws and initial conditions. The appeal to the all-seeing eye of Sauron, however, only yields complete knowledge of observables, and no matter how we think about laws and initial conditions, they will include information about unobservables. Our own knowledge of laws and understanding of what was involved in, say, the initial singularity is knowledge gained by the kind of non-demonstrative reasoning that underlies our purported knowledge of the future, so if we imagine a perfect cognizer relying on some entailment feature of determinism to make such knowledge rely only on demonstrative reasoning, that story is undermined if the antecedent knowledge of the laws and initial conditions is itself partly non-demonstrative.

Some will want to resist by appeal to theology, insisting that, given a deity characterizable in the language of Classical Theism, the problem disappears. The reason would be that the choice of laws and the choice of initial conditions fall within the scope of what God would select in order to create a universe. But there are (at least) two reasons to reject such an appeal.

The first is a point we've already seen: we need a story from the skeptic about knowledge of the future that generates perfection in knowledge through finite extensions of ordinary cognitive abilities, powers, and capacities. So even if God could know the future, or at least the parts of it that are determined, in the way imagined, that result is useless in our context, for it fails to honor the restriction to finite extensions from the ordinary.

There is a second reason for rejecting this appeal to philosophical theology, and it concerns the textbook characterization of determinism that we have been using. This textbook account is in tension with the possibility that any moment of time is

---

this direction of implication that is central to our discussions here, and it is for that reason that I don't complicate matters in the text to keep the proof theory and the semantic theory separate.

the last, not just for us but for the universe as a whole. One might insist that such a possibility would involve a miracle, and that may be correct, but the point to note is that miracles such as this would be possible only by some imagined change in past circumstances or laws of nature, if the entailment claim is correct. For this reason, many prefer to think of miracles in terms of violations of *ceteris paribus* clauses in laws of nature—intrusions from outside the system which the laws govern—thus allowing the possibility of a miracle without the miracle constituting a counterexample to a purported law. In this way, a miracle can occur without requiring a change in the laws or in past events.

On this conception of laws, they are *oaken*—always containing *ceteris paribus* clauses in their antecedents—rather than *iron*—containing no such clause.[15] Only iron laws entail anything about the entire mosaic of local particular fact, and so the entailment conception can only be defended if laws are iron rather than oaken. But the fact that iron laws entail the entire mosaic in question shows that the possibility of miracles involves a change in laws, since laws plus initial conditions can't entail both that some time in the future is not the last moment of time and leave open the obvious possibility that it is.

One might try to avoid this problem by insisting that there are no laws with diachronic import, but rather only synchronic laws. This idea, though, conflicts with a central theme of modern science, where conservation laws are always present, including laws about the conservation of mass/energy as well as the second law of thermodynamics, according to which entropy increases in closed systems. If laws of nature are assumed to be iron, they entail universal generalizations about the future, and would thus entail the falsity of the claim that any moment of time can be the last. As a result, an iron law of nature is both future future-infected and capable of becoming false, in order to accommodate the possibility of the universe ending.

The bottom line, then, is that whether or not one wishes to maintain the entailment construal,[16] determinism provides no way to come to know the future by demonstrative reasoning alone, without appeal to enhancements of our condition that clearly are not finite ones. On the entailment view, since you can't change the past,[17] the story must be that the laws of nature go at least as far as summarizing the entire mosaic of facts, past, present, and future. And if they do that, knowledge

---

[15] The terminology is that of Armstrong (1983), where he defends the former against the latter. See also Cartwright (1983).

[16] It is worth noting as an aside that this characterization of determinism underlies the Consequence Argument, best articulated in van Inwagen (1983) and admirably resisted in Lewis (1981), revealing that the notion of miracle at work in the argument in the text need not be a supernatural intrusion of any grand sort but may also be the ordinary miracle of being able to do otherwise.

[17] This assumption raises a further problem, which I'll note only here. Maybe the past can be changed, and if so, that creates even worse problems for any account of perfect knowledge of the future through demonstrative reasoning from premises involving the laws of nature and claims about the past, including initial conditions of the universe.

of the laws can't be in place in a way that is epistemically prior to the conclusions drawn about the future that rely on the laws being known as premises for the inference. Perhaps, for God, knowing the future could be explained in this way, since God could predict the deterministic future just by knowing which acts of will God will perform, in terms of instituting laws and establishing initial conditions. But we are not gods, and skeptical theory development can't proceed by pretending we are.

For those interested in philosophical theology, there is a side note of interest here as well, for this story of divine foreknowledge isn't as straightforward as it might seem. For on the assumption that there is a divine being capable of performing miracles, the future could be known by God from eternity only if God knows in advance what divine miracles will occur, and this knowledge would go beyond the knowledge of which laws and initial conditions are put in place at creation. To get knowledge of the future, something more will need to be added, something about the immutability of divine choices at creation, so that God couldn't initially intend one thing and then have a change of heart and mind later. Though such immutability is one aspect of Classical Theism, it isn't a part of generic theism and has been rejected by many, including process and open theologians.

The relevant point in our context, though, is that no account of determinism creates any possibility for an idealization of our ordinary capacities in order to explain how knowledge of the future could occur by something other than non-demonstrative, where the support provided to a conclusion does not guarantee the truth of the conclusion so supported. The hope that determinism seemed to provide, the hope of making some knowledge of the future possible through demonstrative reasoning alone, is illusory. So we must face the problem head-on, the problem of trying to saying how non-demonstrative reasoning could generate the kind of immunity from error that demonstrative reasoning promises. To that task we turn in the next chapter.

Chapter 5
Infallibility Through Non-Demonstrative Reasoning

5.1 Introduction

The goal of this chapter is to develop a skeptical position capable of articulating the gold standard for non-monotonic reasoning, of the sort central to our knowledge of the future. The gold standard in question involves the idea of the locus of control over getting to the truth and avoiding error that is within cognizers themselves, in such a way that infallibility can be properly characterized in terms of this idea of locus of control. We ended the last chapter insisting that the development of this idea must not proceed in terms of epistemic imperialism, rejecting both Hume's mistake and the attempt to account for our knowledge of the future by appeal to metaphysical doctrines such as determinism. It is worth noting that the appeal to determinism and Hume's mistake share this imperialist tendency, for both hope to explain non-monotonic reasoning in terms of deductive argumentation of one sort or another.

Once these parameters are in place, however, it is easy to see why a skeptic might despair. For it is of the essence of non-monotonic reasoning that the truth of the premises does not guarantee the truth of the conclusion. That is, there is no non-monotonic consequence relation that can live up to the truth-preservation features that characterize the logical consequence relation of standard first-order logic itself.

Despair, however, is premature. For one thing, we've already concluded that infallibility is not to be understood in terms of any entailment relation, but rather in terms of the idea of locus of control. This theoretical shift provides at least a glimmer of hope that the failure of a truth guarantee may not be the end of the story when it comes to the attempt to clarify a gold standard of infallibility for defeasible reasoning. Even if the glimmer is exceedingly dim, something is better than nothing here.

So the project for this chapter is to take a skeptical stance and see if it can be developed into a position that both articulates the gold standard for non-monotonic reasoning and provides motivation for commonsense epistemologists to be less dismissive of the view. As we will see, the skeptical stance can be developed along these lines, showing that from the lowly beginnings of ordinary

---

Skepticism and Fallibilism. Jonathan L. Kvanvig, Oxford University Press. © Jonathan L. Kvanvig (2025).
DOI: 10.1093/9780198924821.003.0005

114 INFALLIBILITY THROUGH NON-DEMONSTRATIVE REASONING

defeasible reasoning that is fully fallible, an account is possible of how such reasoning can lead to a position where infallibility in terms of locus of control is achievable. It is a surprising result, but it won't by itself settle the question of whether any of our purported knowledge can survive scrutiny. That will be the topic for the next chapter, but before getting to it, we first need a reason to engage in that further discussion. So, for the present, we join forces with the skeptic to see if a position can be developed having the promise just noted.

5.2 Beginning Assumptions

Our discussion will be aided by granting some assumptions to the skeptic, to help keep things a bit more focused. These assumptions will be ones that are generally attractive to a wide range of philosophical viewpoints, though of course none of them are universally endorsed. The justification for making some assumptions is this. If, before proceeding, we had to settle every question in metaphysics and philosophical logic, we'd never get to our project. Moreover, if we tried to engage the project through the lens of every competing set of initial assumptions, it would take a team of collaborators over many centuries to complete the work, for philosophy is noteworthy for the wide variety of perspectives one can take on the whole of reality. So we will allow the skeptic to make some assumptions in favor of positions that are widely held in philosophy, even if not universal.

One might wonder whether this approach will make the significance of skepticism hostage to these assumptions. That is a legitimate concern, though there is also the possibility that what we learn under these assumptions will show ways to proceed to show the significance of skepticism even when these assumptions are denied. Perhaps, though, the best attitude to take is that there is always intellectual room to adopt a set of commitments that can justify denying any given claim about any issue, and so we should lower our expectations a bit on what sort of skeptical account we are looking for. Perhaps, then, it will be enough if the assumptions are at least widely held and fairly plausible in their own right, and as we will see, the assumptions we'll grant to the skeptic are of this sort. Moreover, our goal is more modest than the skeptic's ultimate goal of showing that the skeptical position is correct. Our goal is to see if bare skeptical arguments and the conclusion derived from them can be developed into a theoretical position that deserves consideration beyond providing fodder for reflective equilibrium, as dismissive approaches to skepticism assume.

So, first, let's assume bivalence and excluded middle as well as a denial of any metaphysics that leaves us with a picture of an incomplete world, one that cannot be fully specified by the truths about it.[1] Excluded middle is the proof-theoretic

---

[1] For discussion of the latter concern, see Grim (1991), Grim and Plantinga (1993), and Williamson (2003).

claim that the disjunction of a proposition with its negation is a theorem of our (best) logic, and bivalence is the model-theoretic claim that there are exactly two truth values and every proposition has exactly one such truth value. Both assumptions have been disputed, with Intuitionists in the philosophy of logic refusing to endorse the former even while being committed to the theoremhood of its double negation, and defenders of many-valued logics obviously denying bivalence. In spite of these objectors, these assumptions remain quite popular ideas about what our best logic should look like.

Our first assumption is thus metaphysical and logical in character, while our second assumption falls within the sub-discipline of epistemology. This assumption is anti-skeptical in nature, for it would not be appropriate for the skeptic to start out insisting that everything is unknowable or that we never have good evidence or reasons for believing anything. So we can't begin with any idea in the vicinity of the claim that truth itself is impenetrable to us. Such skeptical assumptions would undermine the goal of skeptical theory construction, for the idea behind developing skepticism along the lines envisioned is for it to count as a serious competitor among standard epistemologies, worthy of consideration even by those who will find it wanting in the end. To begin with obviously partisan and parochial skeptical standpoints would undermine this goal.

So, instead, we will imagine our skeptic assuming from the outset that, to put it metaphorically, truths leave tracks. That is, we assume that once events or happenings enter the temporal dimensions of past and present, evidence (fallible though it be) of their occurrence can be found, even if they couldn't be predicted prior to their occurrence. We assume, thus, that there are no inscrutable truths among those probed by defeasible reasoning.

The strongest argument I know against this assumption comes from the knowability paradox, and it is important before proceeding further to explain why this paradox doesn't preclude making the scrutability assumption. The knowability paradox threatens epistemic conceptions of truth according to which truth should be understood in terms of epistemic notions such as verifiability or knowability. The paradox arises once it is granted that there are truths that will never be known. If there couldn't be such truths, then verificationism becomes the view that not only are all truths verifiable but they will all, in the end, be verified. As Frederic Fitch labeled that view, it is a silly verificationism indeed![2]

So suppose there are unknown truths. That claim is a conjunction of the idea that some given claim is true and yet forever unknown. Let p be the truth that is unknown. Then there is a true conjunction of p together with the claim that p is forever unknown. If all truths are knowable, then this conjunctive truth is

---

[2] The first published version of the paradox is in Fitch (1963), though there is a fascinating backstory of the paradox and this publication of it that traces to Alonzo Church. The paradox is often called "the Fitch Paradox," and perhaps it could more accurately be termed "the Church-Fitch Paradox." For details on the backstory, see Joe Salerno's introduction to Salerno (2008), and for extended discussion of the paradox and some questions concerning its paradoxicality, see Kvanvig (2006b).

knowable, so (on the standard possible worlds semantics) there is a world in which it is known. Given that knowledge distributes across conjunctions, that means that there is a world where it is known that p is true and it is known that it is forever unknown that p is true. Since the kind of knowledge in question is factive, this latter conjunct entails that it is forever unknown that p is true, but this claim contradicts the former claim that it is known that p is true. So truth can't be identified with knowability.

Note, however, that this lesson is compatible with the claim that there are worlds in which every truth is known. Perhaps the most obvious such world would be one in which Classical Theism is true, for on this conception, God knows all truths. Other such worlds are possible as well, worlds where knowledge is spread out among various cognizers so that no truth goes unrecognized by everybody. For the assumption that there are unknown truths doesn't imply that such truths weren't discernible at some point in time. The easiest case to make for unknown truths are truths about the past that weren't noticed at the time by anyone and are now forever undetectable. Such truths did leave tracks, but tracks can fade over time and be lost forever. At the same time, they can be noticed, and it doesn't take an appeal to theology to make this point.

So one way to think of the assumption being granted to the skeptic is in terms of an idealization of ordinary capacities for knowledge and finite extensions of them. For it is a finite extension of ordinary capacities to imagine truths being noticed that went unnoticed at the time they could have been detected. Idealizing in this way allows the skeptic to pursue the task of characterizing ideal non-monotonic reasoning, of the sort that is at the heart of our knowledge of the future.

Thus, we can think of our second assumption as the first idealization made by the skeptic in attempting to characterize the gold standard for knowledge of the future. The most plausible view to hold about what is actually true is that there are lots of unknown truths, at least unknown to ordinary cognizers such as we. Note as well that if we restrict the knowability paradox so that the knowledge operator is interpreted in terms of knowledge by ordinary cognizers, we can still generate the contradiction involved in the paradox, so epistemic conceptions of truth will still be threatened by the paradox even if there are worlds where the scrutability assumption is satisfied. Nonetheless, by appeal to the role of idealization in the story the skeptic is attempting to tell, we can grant this assumption to the skeptic, because idealization is already at the heart of the skeptical project. Once granted, the central question that remains is to see whether the skeptic can complete the project of explaining ideal knowledge of the future so as to give us some idea of what infallibility through locus of control might look like for non-monotonic, defeasible reasoning.

There is a different approach one might take here on behalf of the skeptic as well. Notice that the unknowable truth generated from an unknown truth relies centrally on a conjunction, and whatever rules of implication govern it. So while the existence of an unknown truth does not by itself cause any conceptual difficulty, one is created when we conjoin the truth in question with the idea that it is forever unknown. We then get a different truth to consider, one that is also unknown, but from which it (putatively) follows that it is unknowable. For this threat to the assumption we are making that truths leave tracks, one might insert a restriction for our assumption, to the effect that it applies to basic truths rather than ones that are compositional constructions from such. This point will have to be made carefully to avoid unwanted limitations of our assumption, but something like the following looks adequate. We want first to determine when the meaning of a sentence is a compositional construction out of the meanings of its component sentences. Then we apply the assumption that truths leave tracks to these compositionally more basic sentences. So, for knowability sentences, the claim that p is true is one that is detectable at some point in time, and the claim that no one ever discovers whether p is true is also one that is detectable. That leaves open the central claim that the conjunction of the two isn't detectable, but doesn't threaten this more limited assumption about the detectability of basic propositions.

Let me reiterate the role that these assumptions are playing in our discussion. Because these assumptions are not certainties but are disputed, it may be that our explanation of the importance of skepticism and its role within epistemological reflection will not be adequate. If so, skeptics will have to find a different path to follow in attempting to show why dismissive attitudes toward skepticism undersell its importance. Even so, we shouldn't be surprised by this limitation, for it is a limitation that is central to all of our cognitive endeavors. Guarantees of success are rarely if ever available, so we shouldn't expect more of a development of a skeptical position than we would ask for regarding the development of any philosophical position.

Once these assumptions are in place, we turn to theory development. For this purpose, we begin with the idea of a defeasible reasoning machine. If we want, we can think in terms of a computing machine that engages in defeasible reasoning. Its starting points are *suppositions*, and we can imagine giving the machine any set of suppositions we might wish. The fundamental idea here, of course, is to identify various sets of suppositions with potential initial conditions of the universe. How possible knowledge of these initial conditions can arise is something beyond the scope of this part of theory development, for it isn't meant to be accounted for in this skeptical attempt to explain high standards for knowledge when the reasoning in question is defeasible and non-monotonic. It is precisely for this reason that we began with idealizations of other sorts of knowledge, in order to show that the central difficulty facing skepticism isn't elsewhere, but precisely in the territory in which we find the possibility of knowledge of the future. So, granting the already discussed idealizations of other kinds of knowledge, we are in a position to grant that the skeptical account concerning defeasible reasoning will founder on the reasoning itself if it is problematic, and not on the role that suppositions play in characterizing the starting points for such reasoning, possible perfect knowledge of which will have to be explained via idealizations already explored.

So our defeasible reasoning machine begins from suppositional starting points, and the reasoning itself will proceed by relying on *epistemic conditionals*, which will be grounded in metaphysically necessary *epistemic principles*. I have explained and defended this approach to the foundations of defeasible reasoning in Kvanvig (2014), but will give a cursory summary of the view here. An epistemic conditional is an indicative conditional specifying in its antecedent a piece of information that evidentially supports or epistemically grounds its consequent. It is the sort of principle we use when taking information and calculating what it shows to be true. You wonder whether red sports cars are stopped and ticketed more frequently than other kinds of cars, so you gather some data. Once you have that data, you reason from it to a conclusion about whether your hypothesis is true. In doing so, you use an epistemic conditional that has the data in its antecedent and a conclusion about your hypothesis in its consequent.

Along similar lines, you cross paths with your supervisor while walking through your office building. Your supervisor says, "How are you? I haven't see you lately." You form two hypothesis, one problematic and the other not. The problematic hypothesis is that you must not being doing your job very well, and that you are being criticized for being a no-show. The other hypothesis is nothing of the kind, merely a factual statement that you and your supervisor haven't run into each other lately.

You reason about which of the two hypotheses is true. You think about the tone of voice and the body language of your supervisor while the remark was made. You use this information to decide whether to take offense. In reaching a conclusion, you employ epistemic conditionals, conditionals that have your evidence as antecedent and one of the two hypotheses as consequent.

So, the role of epistemic conditionals in the story of suppositional reasoning is that they are the vehicle by which we get from information we possess to conclusions that this information is (taken to be) evidence for.[3] It is important to notice that the assumption that there are such conditionals that are usable in this context doesn't fall prey to generalized skeptical stances maintaining that we never have good enough reasons for any cognitive commitment we make. As we saw in Chapter 2, such generalized skepticism has to be formulated carefully to avoid the problem of paralysis, and when it is carefully developed, it does not target any and all cognitive commitments. Moreover, our task here is about propositional support itself, not the kind of support involved in cognitive commitments. When the commitments in question are assumed to be beliefs, the latter kind of support is standardly described as doxastic support, where the latter can be understood in

---

[3] The parenthetical is there to avoid being sidetracked by the issue of to what degree epistemic support is subjective. That is an important issue in epistemology, but ancillary to present concerns.

terms of propositional support plus proper basing.[4] Hence, claims about propositional warrant don't have any immediate implications for whether any given cognitive commitment is epistemically appropriate. Finally, the generalized version of skepticism might simply be a restriction on what can be in the antecedent of an epistemic conditionals, as when the idea of "acquiescing to the appearances" is understood in terms of the idea that nothing but appearance statements give grounds for whatever cognitive commitments are involved in solving the problem of paralysis. In consequence of these points, there is no basis to be found in any generalized skepticism for rejecting the idea of epistemic conditionals and the role they will be playing in the story of defeasible reasoning. In what follows, then, I'll be using epistemic conditionals that are common in the literature, with the understanding that various forms of generalized skepticism might favor some of these over others, but noting that these differences won't affect our results any more than does, for example, the differences between Chisholmians and Bayesians about which epistemic conditionals are the right ones to use in our theory of defeasible reasoning.

Regarding such conditionals, the central epistemological question concerns when and where one has license for using the conditionals that one in fact uses. The answer to this question appeals to epistemic principles, which are related to epistemic conditionals but distinct from them.

An epistemic principle adds to the components already noted for epistemic conditionals. For epistemic conditionals, we find conferrers of positive epistemic status in the antecedent, and the target of such conferrers in the consequent. An epistemic principle includes, in addition, a strong modal operator, a grounds-for-doubt clause, and an epistemic operator on its consequent.[5] Paradigmatic principles of this sort are Chisholmian: it is necessarily true that if appeared to F-ly without grounds for doubting that something is F, it is reasonable to believe that something is F.[6] Diagramming such principles, identifying each of their components, gives a good sense of what such principles involve. Here are a couple of examples, the first in the spirit of Chisholm and the second more evidentialist in character:

-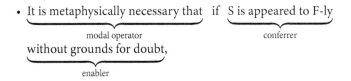

---

[4] For details on this approach, see Kvanvig (2014).

[5] In Kvanvig (2014), I argue that this list of aspects of epistemic principles is incomplete, in need of supplementation to account for the role that reflection plays in the story of rational belief. That additional element, however, won't affect our discussion here, so I ignore it in what follows.

[6] See Chisholm (1977) for more examples of such principles.

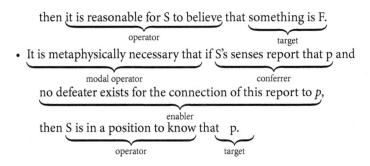

Epistemic conditionals of the sort used in ordinary reasoning differ from epistemic principles along two dimensions. First, epistemic conditionals are contingent claims, whereas epistemic principles are metaphysically necessary if true. Second, epistemic conditionals are much simpler in structure than are epistemic principles, and this simplicity is a function of the context in which the epistemic conditionals are being used. When the use of an epistemic conditional is suitable for generating inferential warrant for a claim, the context is one in which the antecedent of the conditional is true and the grounds for doubt clause satisfied. In such a case, inferential warrant at the level specified by the epistemic operator in the consequent of the epistemic principle is generated for the target proposition. Moreover, as is typical of such contexts, the warrant might involve actual reasoning involving the epistemic conditional, or only a transition or instance of reasoning from the antecedent of the conditional to its consequent, a step licensed by the conditional but where no reasoning through the conditional itself occurs.

It is worth taking a moment to appreciate the motivation for this way of thinking about fallibilist epistemology and the foundations of defeasible reasons (or justification or warrant). The initial step in understanding defeasibility might seem to be a matter of explaining what it is to be a reason or a justifier or whatever generates warrant or positive epistemic status, but any approach limited to the identification of what these items might be can't be adequate. For an account that only identifies what count as conferrers doesn't tell us what level of support is provided by any given conferrer. Conferrers have a valence, and this valence is fundamental to a proper account of what level of epistemic support arises for any given claim with respect to any support base.

Chisholm wasn't especially pellucid about what counts as a conferrer except when it came to the matter of defending foundationalism and identifying the foundations in terms of self-presenting states. These states, however, do not tell the whole story of what counts as a conferrer in Chisholm's epistemology, and it is an interesting historical question to figure out what he took to be the supervenience or explanatory base for epistemically normative properties.[7] It is clear that sense-data,

---

[7] Chisholm's central epistemological works are Chisholm (1957); Chisholm (1982) and the three editions of *Theory of Knowledge* (Chisholm (1966), Chisholm (1977), Chisholm (1989)). The remarks

conceived of adverbially, play a significant role, and so count in some sense as reasons for belief, and when it comes to *a priori* knowledge, a foundational role is filled by what is axiomatic for a person—that is, something that a person accepts that is necessarily true and is also certain for anyone who accepts it. With respect to the former (but not for the latter), they need not count as conferrers in virtue of reasoning from them to targets whose epistemic status they undergird. Sense-data are things that generally prompt belief, but not in terms of explicit reasoning. So the epistemic principles that tie sense data to a target having some particular level of epistemic support are not to be conceived of as limited to principles involve in reasoning. For the same reason, the epistemic conditionals related to these principles may be involved explicitly in reasoning, but may also function simply as a background condition that explains the adequacy of transitions from antecedent to consequent.

The second thing to note, for Chisholm, is the account of the valence for conferrers and the role that coherence among already-specified reasons for belief plays in the story of rationality. According to Chisholm, the story of intellectual rationality involves the mental states of beliefs, disbeliefs, and withholdings, and the possible support levels from various supervenience or explanatory bases for epistemic standing run from being counterbalanced (believing and disbelieving have equal status) to being probable (believing beats disbelieving), to being epistemically in the clear (withholding doesn't beat believing), to being beyond reasonable doubt (believing beats withholding), to being evident (believing is at least as justified as is withholding on the counterbalanced), to being obvious (believing is more reasonable than withholding on anything), and to being certain (nothing else is more justified than is believing the claim in question). The epistemic principles Chisholm lists employ these levels in terms of the epistemic operators on consequents, and the antecedents begin from sense-data (which he calls "self-presenting states") and beliefs about being in these states, and the ladder toward knowledge is climbed from this supervenience base by linking self-presenting states to the kinds of things that the cognizer thinks are being presented in this way. Through this link, one ascends to the level of being beyond reasonable doubt, and then if no defeaters are present (defeaters are sets of propositions that, if one's total evidence, make the denial of the claim in question probable), and the final step toward knowledge of the sort that gets outside the circle of one's own mental attitudes involves coherence among things that are at least epistemically in the clear and include at least one thing that is evident.

So the story of defeasible rationality or justification, for Chisholm, involves a supervenience base of self-presenting states and things that are axiomatic, together with coherence among these things and what they epistemically support. Specifying the supervenience base, though, is something Chisholm does by

---

in the text are primarily in reference to the third edition, though the same general ideas can be found all the way back to the initial expression of his views in the late 1940s.

developing principles that identify the epistemic valence of these items, and the role they play in moving from elements at the foundation to knowledge or fully justified belief.

I mention this Chisholmian way of thinking about the story of rationality because it contrasts with typical "X-first" approaches. In recent times, we have seen touted "knowledge-first," "reasons-first," "experience-first," and "evidence-first" epistemologies. Chisholm is not on the side of any such approach, since they do not encode in what is taken to be fundamental anything about the epistemic valence of these fundamental items. The Chisholmian standpoint is a principles-centric one, where no account of what is fundamental can be adequate if it doesn't include epistemic principles that account for the epistemic valence of whatever imparts positive epistemic status.

Could we describe this Chisholmian position as a "principles-first" epistemology? Perhaps so, but I have reservations, since the principles can't be articulated without containing within them an implicit account of the conferrers of positive epistemic status. So the theoretical approach starts with epistemic principles, but that is compatible with the fundamentality of both the principles and the implicit account of conferrers. We can maintain, however, that the Chisholmian position is principles-centric, since that encodes the idea that a theory is developed by beginning with principles and these principles are fundamental to the theory that is generated.

We can appreciate the formal aspects of this approach, involving a central and indispensable role for epistemic principles, without endorsing the particular commitments regarding levels of epistemic support that Chisholm proposes. Perhaps Chisholm is right that there are exactly 13 levels of epistemic support (six positive and six negative with respect to the counterbalanced), but the formal picture requires no such assumption. For example, if we are probabilists, we might think there are as many levels of epistemic support as there are real numbers between zero and one inclusive.

Once we adopt this principles-centric approach, we can connect this formal structure for fallibilist epistemology with the history of confirmation theory in the twentieth century, together with the lessons learned from the attempt to make the language of confirmation scientifically respectable. The tradition arising after the first world war, involving the Vienna Circle and other similar groups, held scientific inquiry to be pre-eminent and in need of careful articulation of key notions such as truth and confirmation. Concerns about the former were assuaged by Tarski (1944), and for the latter, an account was needed that made confirmation into something more than subjective and not succumbing to the difficulties that plague the language of religion, metaphysics, and morality regarding empirical significance. The idea, then, was to try to find an account of confirmational valence that could be characterized in "objective and logical" terms.[8] Exactly what

---

[8] This language is from John Maynard Keynes (1921).

logicality involves isn't always clear, but one idea is Fregean: if confirmation could be understood in terms of a mathematical probability theory, where positive epistemic relevance is defined in terms of probability enhancement, then logicality could arise in virtue of a reduction of mathematics to logic, as Frege was hoping to show.[9] Perhaps there are other aspects to the idea of logicality, such as wanting the confirmation relation to be a two-place relation just as the first-order notions of derivability and semantic entailment are two-place relations. The direction of confirmation theory in the twentieth century, though, proceeds through the connection to probability theory, so I'll focus on that idea for preserving logicality.

Objectivity could then be pursued in a number of ways, but one way would be in terms of a logical interpretation of probability itself. Doing so is the starting point for the Carnapian project, and the story of that project throughout Carnap's life is the story of diminishing hopes for this kind of objectivity in the theory, both in terms of the logical interpretation of probability, but also for the idea that the confirmation relation is, at bottom, a two-place relation.[10] If subjective Bayesians are right about where all this ends, objectivity is significantly curtailed by unbridled optionality regarding initial priors, with objectivity remaining only in place in terms of immunity from synchronic incoherence, and whatever diachronic rules for getting from one set of attitudes to another can be defended.

For diachronic possibilities, the easiest to specify is conditionalization, where one's new attitudes are a function of one's old conditional attitudes together with a full specification of what new learning has occurred, but we needn't concern ourselves with the details here. For our interest is in how all of this ties into an approach to fallibilist epistemology that centers on epistemic principles. Here the lesson is as clear as it is in the theory of justification itself. If confirmation arises from inequalities between conditional probabilities based on previous information and those based on old plus new information, we have an approach to confirmation theory that puts the notion of the valence of that which generates positive epistemic status at the heart of the theory. The elegance achieved here is a matter of being able to measure this notion of epistemic relevance in terms of probability theory, an elegance not achievable by the Chisholmian approach.

Chisholm's contribution is thus best conceived in terms of the central role of epistemic principles in the story of rational cognition, and this fundamental role for epistemic principles puts it at odds with another way of attempting to find a logical and objective notion of confirmation, suitable for defending respect for

---

[9] A question I won't pursue here: given that Frege's Logicism fails, on grounds that mathematics can only be reduced to a combination of logic and set theory, would that mean the logicality would be lost if confirmation could be understood in terms of mathematical probability theory? I suspect that would be logicality enough, but won't delve into the matter, since it is ancillary to the line of thought relevant to our project here.

[10] Key moments in this progression can be found in Carnap (1928), the English translation Carnap (1967) appearing later, Carnap (1945), Carnap (1962), Carnap (1967), Carnap (1971), and Carnap (1980).

124 INFALLIBILITY THROUGH NON-DEMONSTRATIVE REASONING

scientific inquiry. For it was clear in the early history of confirmation theory that the connection to logic was a central feature to pursue, and Chisholm's principles-centric approach rejects such explanations of the logicality of confirmation.

One can see this targeted connection to logic in both A.J. Ayer and in C.I. Lewis. Ayer struggled to identify confirmation in terms of a mirror image of entailment. The idea is that you take a hypothesis and figure out what it entails in the form of experience, and then you run your tests to see if what was entailed by the hypothesis actually occurs. If things go well, you get confirmation; if not, you get disconfirmation (and maybe outright refutation). More precisely, incremental confirmation from E to H arises when and only when there are true auxiliary assumptions which do not themselves entail E but which together with H entail E (but not $\sim E$). Ayer wrote:

> [T]he function of an empirical hypothesis is to enable us to anticipate experience. Accordingly, if an observation to which a given proposition is relevant conforms to our expectations ... that proposition is confirmed. (Ayer, 1936, 142–143)
>
> [I]t is the mark of a genuine factual proposition ... that some experiential propositions can be deduced from it in conjunction with certain premises without being deducible from those other premises alone. (Ayer, 1936, 26)

Putting the two claims together, we get the idea that the way in which an empirical hypothesis enables us to *anticipate* experience is by *entailing* it "in conjunction with certain premises."

The problem here is that the needed entailments are hard to find. Confirmation may be the mirror of theoretical prediction, but what a theory or hypothesis predicts about the course of experience is rarely a matter of entailment. That is the fundamental lesson Chisholm argues for in Chisholm (1948), where he is commenting on C.I. Lewis's specific claims in favor of the idea that objective, material object statements entail experiential ones. As Chisholm shows, the possibilities of hallucination and illusion undermine even the most carefully articulated ideas about what sense-data will arise from any particular statement that is not wholly about such data. So the idea that confirmation from experience will be quasi-logical in virtue of being the mirror image of the logical notion of entailment is chimerical. What Chisholm shows, though he doesn't put the point this way, is that although confirmation is the mirror image of prediction, prediction itself is not a logical notion but an irreducibly epistemic one, and it is this irreducibly epistemic idea that is encoded in the epistemic principles that are fundamental to any adequate epistemology. Any given hypothesis, or material object statement, reasonably leads us to expect experience to take one course rather than another, and thereby creates the opportunity to confirm or disconfirm it. But that doesn't make confirmation a logical notion, or even a quasi-logical one, for prediction itself isn't to be understood in terms of entailment. Instead, confirmation and prediction are both essentially normative in nature, and it is for this reason that epistemic principles are foundational.

Compare this approach to confirmation with the Hempelian effort to move beyond Ayer's own account of confirmation. Hempel rejected the simple account Ayer presents, but his approach to confirmation in Hempel (1945a); Hempel (1945b) still thought of any initial steps in characterizing confirmation as involving its relation to logical notions. His four initial principles—the Entailment Condition, the Special Consequence Condition, the Special Consistency Condition, the Converse Consequence Condition[11]—all involve the relationship between confirmation and logical conditions such as entailment, logical implication, and logical incompatibility. The hope seems to be that, if we have the right set of first principles linking confirmation and logic, we might still yet be able to find a confirmation theory that is both objective and logical. As is well known, these conditions generate the Raven Paradox, but what is more interesting in our context is the way in which appeals to logic distorts the connection between theory and prediction. The hypothesis "All ravens are black" entails for each raven that that particular raven is black, but it doesn't entail that there are any ravens, or that I'll ever experience a raven, or that if I do experience a raven, I'll experience it being black. It is a reasonable prediction from that hypothesis that the next time I run into a raven, I'll perceive it to be black, but that prediction is hostage to the problems of hallucination and illusion, as Chisholm stresses. Chisholm makes these points in the context of criticizing Lewis's attempt to defend a translatability thesis regarding the content of material object statements,[12] but the points made are relevant to any view that maintains an entailment relation between objective statements and the related predictions about the course of experience.

The takeaway from all of this for both the theory of warrant or justification or rationality as well as for the theory of confirmation needed for a proper understanding of and respect for science is two-fold: the hope for objectivity and logicality should be replaced with an appreciation of the irreducible normativity of these central epistemological notions, and this irreducible normativity reveals the need for a principles-centric approach to epistemology that clarifies the central notion of epistemic valence. Thus, the hope of somehow linking epistemic support with the logical notion of entailment, whether through the idea that confirmation is the mirror image of entailment or in some other way, is an idea to be abandoned. It should be abandoned in favor of viewing rationality and confirmation in terms of

---

[11] The details for each of the four are:

The Entailment Condition: if E implies H, then E confirms H

The Special Consequence Condition: if E confirms H, and H implies H', then E also confirms H'

The Special Consistency Condition: if E confirms H, and H is logically incompatible with H', then E does not confirm H'

The Converse Consequence Condition: if E confirms H, and if H is implied by H', then E also confirms H'.

[12] The account found in Book II of Lewis (1946).

a mirror image of the predictions and expectations regarding experience that are generated by our theories and hypotheses about the nature of the world, where the predictions and expectations are generated in a way infused with normative valence, just as their mirror image of rationality and confirmation is. As a result, central to the epistemological project will be principles that identify the epistemically normative valence of whatever items one claims generate positive epistemic status.

The essential normativity of the epistemological project, whether in the form of the theory of justification or in the form of the theory of confirmation, is anathema to followers of the tradition arising out of the Vienna Circle, for that tradition relegates normativity to the land of noises and scribbles that have no cognitive significance, unless translatable into other language and thus reducible to the non-normative. So it isn't surprising to see the Chisholmian approach finding little place in this tradition that aims at legitimating the demand that science be pre-eminent in ascertaining what is true. From our perspective, though, the Chisholmian tradition undergirds both the importance of a fallibilist theory of defeasible reasons and also the need for approach this theory through some collection or other of epistemic principles. I note, as I did above, that this reliance on epistemic principles is not that constraining, however——for a principles-centric approach to epistemic normativity leaves open a variety of options regarding how many levels of epistemic appraisal there are and on what ascending these levels depends. Its historical significance is a matter of identifying the need for a principled understanding of defeasibility for fallibilist epistemology, and the lesson that any full understanding of reality will have normativity spread throughout. We may hope with the Logical Empiricists that the fallibilist epistemology so characterized will not be subjective, but we won't engage in any pretense about theoretical reduction or elimination.

It is this understanding of defeasibility that the skeptic can employ in an attempt to characterize the high standards claimed to be required for knowledge, when it comes to things like knowledge of the future that depend essentially on defeasible reasoning. This understanding identifies such reasoning as relying on epistemic conditionals, whose acceptability is a contextual matter identified and characterized by the epistemic principles related to these conditionals. The initial stage of this approach begins in contexts where there are no grounds for doubt about the link between a conferrer and a target from a given set of initial suppositions, and that the level of epistemic support is sufficiently high to satisfy whatever standard a fallibilist epistemology appropriately demands for full belief. Since all information is an epistemic conferrer for something at some level of epistemic support, by imagining various suppositional starting points, we are imagining the reasoning machine being given bodies of evidence from which to reason defeasibly.

The theoretical machinery guarantees that the program moves from one state of rational (suppositional) opinion to another, but in a way that is fully fallible.

The key for development of a skeptical epistemology is how to exploit these humble beginnings to identify the high standards a skeptic wants to insist on for knowledge. As we will see, doing so involves two steps. The first is to move from defeasible reasons to indefeasible ones, and this is accomplished in virtue of the fact that the suppositional system can be *complete*: it tracks all epistemic implications of any possible original suppositional state, and so if given a complete set of initial conditions, it can generate a complete outcome. Such calculation will, in some cases, come to naught, as we will see as well. There will remain the possibility that the system halts at some point because the information suppositionally supplemented beyond the initial suppositional state will not go to completion, will not yield a system of information that specifies a complete outcome. To develop a skeptical epistemology, such a result is not needed. Instead, all that is needed is the possibility of the system going to completion, for in such cases we will be able to move from defeasibility to indefeasility, and from the latter to the high standard of infallibility that the skeptic is aiming to characterize for knowledge of the future. For if the system goes to completion, then the system in question is in place to draw another inference, one that involves reasoning in a way that displays full control over the possibility of error, in spite of the fact that every inference from initial supposition to complete outcome was susceptible to error.

Developing such an account can be done using a dynamic semantics that is quite different from the usual truth-theoretic semantics we find in first-order logic and the possible worlds semantics we use for extending our first-order language into the intensional realm. Let's turn, then, to an explanation of this approach and how it can be used for theory development on behalf of the skeptic.

5.3 Basic Elements

We can begin to see what this skeptical account of ideal defeasible reasoning looks like by working through a simple version of an update semantics. The slogan for such a dynamic semantics differs from that of a truth-conditional semantics:

> ... the slogan "You know the meaning of a sentence if you know conditions under which it is true" is replaced by this one: "You know the meaning of a sentence if you know the change it brings about in the information state of anyone who accepts the news conveyed by it". (Veltman, 1996, 221)

To generate the simple theory,[13] we begin with a language $L^{\rightarrow}$, which is the language L of propositional logic supplemented with the epistemic conditional. L is constructed from the smallest set of atomic propositions $A = \{p, q, r, \dots\}$, closed

---

[13] What follows rehearses what I first proposed in Kvanvig (2011c).

128 INFALLIBILITY THROUGH NON-DEMONSTRATIVE REASONING

under negation and conjunction. We obtain $L \to$ by closing under the binary connective $\to$ as well, assumed to be a different connective from the material conditional of standard propositional logic.

On this approach, we will understand a world in terms of a function from atoms to truth-values. That is, for a set of atomic propositions A, a world w is a function from A to $\{0, 1\}$. Letting W be the set of such worlds, we can understand an informational state s as a subset of W: $s \subseteq W$. S is the set of such subsets.

In our context, the original informational state prior to engaging in any suppositional reasoning, is just W itself, the total space of possibility. The first question facing our defeasible reasoning machine is whether it is possible to get from this initial state of information to a complete story, one involving a state of information s which is identical to some specific possible world, i.e., where $s = w$. To get from the initial state of information to any more specific state of information involves the resources of suppositional reasoning, so we imagine supplementing the original state of information with various possible sets of suppositions. The process employed by the program then updates to a new state of information, one derived from the original state of information together with each suppositional collection. The updating will need to follow specific rules, for that is the heart of our defeasible reasoning machine, so we need some account of what the update rules might look like.

The complete set of update rules for a complete theory of defeasible reasoning will be different from and more complicated than those that we can specify here, but this beginning gives us a glimpse of how update rules are specified and what they might look like. The update rules for our simple theory involve an epistemology in which all epistemic reasoning is monotonic and proceeds via epistemic conditionals of the sort described above. We can understand transitions from one state of information to a new state of information in terms of an informational state update function.[14] For any $w \in W, s \in S, p \in A$, and $\Phi, \Psi \in L \to$, $\uparrow$ is a function on S defined recursively on the following conditions:

    I. $s{\uparrow}p = \{w \in s : w(p) = 1\}$
    II. $s{\uparrow}{\sim}\Phi = s \setminus (s{\uparrow}\Phi)$
    III. $s{\uparrow}(\Phi \& \Psi) = (s{\uparrow}\Phi){\uparrow}\Psi$
    IV. $s{\uparrow}(\Phi \to \Psi) = \{w \in s : ((s{\uparrow}\Phi){\uparrow}\Psi = s{\uparrow}\Phi)\}$.

In English: updating by adding a proposition restricts the state of information to worlds where that proposition is true, and updating by adding a negation involves subtracting whatever would have survived updating by the unnegated claim; updating by adding a conjunction is just the sequential updating by each conjunct, and updating by adding a conditional occurs when the epistemic commitments of

---

[14] I here follow Gillies (2004), which in turn derives from Heim (1983).

adding both antecedent and consequent are the same as when the antecedent alone is added.

Understanding how this approach works requires giving detailed attention to the last clause, since the other clauses provide the resources needed for seeing how all truth-functional connectives will work in the theory because we can define them all in terms of negation and conjunction. This point implies, then, that the last clause, the one for our epistemic conditionals, is different from that for ordinary material conditionals, since it would otherwise be unnecessary. So let's see how and why the clause for → and the clause for ⊃ (our symbol for the material conditional) will be different and have different updating implications.

The clause for → yields two options. At an intuitive level, it reports on the epistemic significance of a state of information, for it looks to see if it makes any difference whether one updates by both the antecedent and consequent of the conditional or by the antecedent itself. It is thus a test of the epistemic structure of the state of information, and the test is run comparing two ways of updating it. The first is to update by both antecedent and consequent and the second is to update by the antecedent alone. Two possibilities are available here: either the same state of information results from both updatings, or the states of information differ. If these output states are the same, the function returns the initial state of information itself. If it doesn't include it, the conditional is inconsistent with that state of information, and returns the absurd state of information, which is the state of information corresponding to the empty set of worlds.[15]

As a test on the epistemic structure of a state of information, this clause thus tells us whether an epistemic conditional is available in a given system of information, for use in reasoning or to support reasoning involving transitions from antecedent to consequent. This point corresponds to the less formal characterization given above where the availability of an epistemic conditional depends not only on which epistemic principles are true, but also on contextual features of the actual circumstances in which one finds oneself. As formulated, then, these features allow us to say efficiently what it is for a given state of information to make reasonable or to epistemically support some claim. A given state of information contains an adequate rational basis for a given claim just in case there is some bit of information in the system and an epistemic conditional linking that bit of information with the intended target proposition, for in such a case, the antecedent of the conditional is already present as well as the epistemic conditional in question, so updating with the target claim returns the very same state of information. To repeat, then, the independent clause for epistemic conditionals

---

[15] This explanation shows why clause 4 does not involve a typographical error, even though it may seem to involve one at first glance. It has this appearance because there is no reference to w after the colon, which is atypical but grammatical. In this sense, it is like formulas such as "$\forall x(p)$," which is a wff but inclines readers to think a typographical error has occurred.

130 INFALLIBILITY THROUGH NON-DEMONSTRATIVE REASONING

allows us to assess the epistemic structure of a state of information to determine which propositions are rationally supported by that state of information and which are not.

A further virtue of this clause is non-negotiable, for it is a sacrosanct principle about any conditional that the combination of true antecedent and false consequent is intolerable. The clause above for epistemic conditionals honors this principle. If a state of information includes both p and $\sim q$, then updating first by p and then by q will result in the absurd state of information, whereas updating only by p will not (unless the state of information already included the negation of p as well, something that need not be true). So updating by the conjunction of antecedent and consequent needn't return the same state of information as updating by the antecedent alone, and hence the epistemic conditional in question will not be part of that state of information. Thus, the sacrosanct principle is preserved in this account.

Compare these features of the update rule for epistemic conditionals with a clause for the material conditional $\supset$. Suppose we begin with a state of information s, which is nothing more than proposition r, and consider updating s by $p \supset q$ (where each p, q, and r are all logically independent). We update s by finding the updated s' resulting from updating s by $p\&\sim q$, and then subtracting s' from s. The result of this subtraction is a new state of information corresponding to the union of the $r\&\sim p$-worlds with the $r\&q$-worlds. Where the logical independence assumption holds, this union is neither identical to s itself nor to the absurd state of information, which is the empty set of worlds. Thus, updating by the material conditional does not typically yield as output the same state of information as the epistemic conditional.

Even so, these clauses for $\rightarrow$ and $\supset$ guarantee that the former entails the latter, which is also a virtue of this account. This fact holds because the clause for the former honors the sacrosanct principle, that the combination of true antecedent and false consequent is not to be tolerated. Because of this fact, every $\rightarrow$ formula entails the related $\supset$ formula. Thus, our understanding of epistemic conditionals identifies them as being logically stronger than material conditionals, since a state of information can include a material conditional without also including the related epistemic conditional. As such, our toy theory satisfies one constraint on a theory of conditionals, where a proper understanding will make material conditionals the weakest conditional, and various other conditionals stronger, including epistemic conditionals.

It is also a condition of adequacy on a theory of conditionals that strict conditionals are strongest of all, so we should expect our clauses for $\rightarrow$ and $\supset$ to bear this out. Let's show why this is the case for the clauses we've already seen. Where $\Rightarrow$ is the symbol for this strict conditional, we can formulate an update clause for it as:

$$s{\uparrow}(\Phi \Rightarrow \Psi) = s \text{ if } \sim\exists s^*\exists w((w \in s^*)\&(s^* = (\Phi\& \sim\Psi))) \text{ and } \emptyset \text{ otherwise.}$$

According to this clause, updating by a true strict conditional returns the very state of information with which one began, and updating by a false strict conditional returns the empty set. Thus, this clause informs as to whether the conditional in question was already contained in the state of information, and, just as for the epistemic conditional, returns the original state of information if it was so contained and the absurd state of information if not. But the clause used to establish whether the strict conditional is in s is stronger than what is used for the epistemic conditional, since any given strict conditional is contained in every non-empty state of information or in none. That is, this clause for strict conditionals quantifiers over all possible worlds, requiring that there is no world at all in which the conjunction of true antecedent and false consequent is found. Not so for epistemic conditionals. Unless they are the corresponding version of a strict conditional, they will be included in some states of information but not all, and this feature of strict conditionals is achieved because the clause in question does not quantify over all worlds but only in those worlds that are part of the informational state s that we are testing. Hence, this clause for strict conditionals shows that there can be information states containing the strict conditional but not the corresponding epistemic conditional, revealing that strict conditionals are necessary if true and epistemic conditionals need not be necessary even if true. As a result, strict conditionals entail epistemic conditionals, but not vice versa. So, our simple theory does well on conditions of adequacy for a theory of conditionals, making strict conditionals stronger than either epistemic conditionals or material conditionals as well as making epistemic conditionals stronger than material ones.

5.4 Beyond Simple Beginnings

As mentioned this is an initial story designed to show how update rules generate changes across time to a total state of information, and the simplicity of the story, especially its assumption of monotonicity, may leave one wondering what would be different in a more sophisticated approach. The most important difference is that an adequate theory would have to be non-monotonic and non-deductive, in contrast to our basic theory. The difference that would result is that such a change would introduce the need for backtracking in the reasoning program. Since we are assuming that truths leave tracks, sometimes further information will arise that shows that a conclusion drawn earlier was mistaken or should be retracted. The program will thus have to be able to return to the original error point, change the provisional conclusion drawn at the point, and then move forward in time through re-calculation of any derivations affected by the change. Doing so will now be done on the basis of more information than was present at the initial stage, making the changed conclusion as rational as the former conclusion was at the time it was drawn.

Adding such a feature complicates the story of rationality, but it does not, by itself, make it impossible for the program to reach completion from some initial suppositions. As before, we should expect cases where the program cannot reach completion while at the same time also expecting completion to be reachable in other cases. Moving away from our monotonic toy theory to a non-monotonic one doesn't undermine this point, but only adds the idea that a reasoning program based on a dynamic semantics can involve backtracking whereas monotonic versions of such a program will not. We might put this point as follows: when the program is monotonic, learning will be modeled as cumulative over time, and when it is non-monotonic, learning will sometimes be lost in the process of updating.

One such extension of our simple theory is Bayesianism, and it is a conservative extension of our simple theory. A conservative extension preserves the theorems of the original theory, and the value of conservative extensions is that they give support to the idea that whatever virtues are found in the theory that is being extended will also be found in the extension itself. We thus find in Bayesian approaches a well-developed example of what things might look like when we move from our basic theory to a more sophisticated alternative.

It is not the only alternative in the literature, however. The best-known alternatives include the AGM model developed by Alchourrón, Gärdenfors, and Makinson, and the Pollockian Oscar Project.[16] A useful discussion of these approaches and lesser-known alternatives is Koons (2017), and given the developments in computer science, artificial intelligence, and formal machine learning, we should expect to see continued rapid growth in the development of these kinds of ideas.

The level of sophistication for non-monotonic alternatives to our basic theory should thus be expected to rise, but the key issue for epistemology more generally and our topic in particular concerns whether or not the best developments will be conservative extensions of standard first-order logic. In all likelihood, in some contexts that is precisely what we should expect, though we should grant that we have no guarantee that this will be so nor that our context is one of them.

I say this because of what we know about Bayesian epistemology already, for Bayesian epistemology (that is, some version of it) is our best formal approach to the subject to date. And yet the conservatism it embodies is a cause for concern, facing several difficulties. Among these are the problem of old evidence and its handling of the epistemology of necessities as well as the rigidity of the conditional probabilities used in updating rules.

---

[16] See Alchourrón et al. (1982). Pollock's publications related to and concerning the Oscar Project begin with Pollock (1974) (though this book relies and builds on earlier work such as Pollock (1967)) and include Pollock (1989), Pollock (1995), Pollock (2001), Pollock and Oved (2005), and Pollock (2011). For a useful comparison of this approach with others, including AGM, see Pollock and Gillies (2000).

A brief discussion of each of these points will help us appreciate what is at stake in replacing our simple theory with something more sophisticated. The old evidence problem introduces a psychological dimension to confirmation that is masked by conditional probabilities involving the totality of one's background system of information. We often extend our learning by coming to take into account information we've already known for quite some time, but if we'd been updating properly by either conditionalization or Jeffrey conditionalization,[17] we would have already taken such information into account.[18] These updating procedures, then, don't help make sense of the idea of having information the significance of which has not yet been recognized or taken into account. The basic point can be put as follows: there is both the evidence we have and what we make of it, and Bayesian epistemology limited to the update rules just mentioned takes the former into account but not the latter.

The implication here is that even the most subjective versions of Bayesianism may not be subjective enough. If so, we can see this element of the view as another vestige of the conservative tendency to look for some logical or mathematical underpinning for our essentially normative epistemic notions, and maybe something more radical—something less objective, less logical—is needed.

This same concern afflicts the third item on our list. Standard Bayesian updating proceeds via conditional probabilities that have to be held fixed across the temporal span in which updating occurs. For illustration, note how Conditionalization works. Here there are two probability functions, Pr_{old} and Pr_{new}, where the unconditional probability for any p, under Pr_{new} is just the conditional probability under Pr_{old} for p given the conjunction of all of one's certainties plus all the new learning that will occur between the two times. Such a procedure works to ensure immunity from Dutch books,[19] so long as one's conditional probabilities don't change between the time of the old probability function and the new one. Yet, if the story of learning involves both the evidence and what we make of it, these conditional probabilities have to be mutable rather than fixed, for if we come to a new appreciation of the significance of a piece of information, then how we change our views over time must be sensitive to this new appreciation. So if the story concerning changes in view is driven by conditional probabilities at some previous time, they

[17] See Jeffrey (1984) and Jeffrey (1992).

[18] On the difference between Conditionalization and Jeffrey Conditionalization: Conditionalization involves certainty for all new learning, whereas Jeffrey's alternative shows how to update when new learning is subject to some uncertainty.

[19] A Dutch book is a series of bets all of which are regarded as fair but which if taken, guarantee a loss no matter what possible outcome occurs. Immunity from Dutch books is provably equivalent to being probabilistically coherent, understood in terms of sets of credences that form a probability function, i.e., satisfy some version of the axioms of probability theory. For simplicity here, we can specify these in terms Normality, Finite Additivity, and Non-Negativity. The first tells us that every logical truth has a probability of 1, the second that an exclusive disjunction has a probability that is the sum of each of the disjuncts, and the third says that all probabilities are greater than or equal to 0.

would need to be able to change in order to accommodate our new understanding of the significance of our evidence.

Here too, then, it looks like more subjectivity is needed in order to accommodate the significance of the distinction between our evidence and what we make of it. Perhaps, that is, conservative extensions of standard first-order theory may still leave too many vestiges of the earlier hope for finding a theory of confirmation that is both objective and logical.

The final item on our list above concerns the epistemic status of necessities. In particular, all logical truths receive the same extreme probability in standard Bayesian epistemologies, since this claim is one of the basic axioms of probability theory. Yet, we know that not all logical truths are perspicuously so, and we often find ourselves perplexed about the truth of a given claim until we finally find a proof of it. To account for such learning, we need an epistemology that allows for lack of certainty concerning logical truths, as well as other necessary truths that are not logical truths.

Can Bayesianism be modified to accommodate these points? And if so modified, would the view still be a conservative extension of standard first-order logical theory? As things currently stand, I think we simply don't know, though there are indications in the literature about why things might not be hopeless. Notice, first, the coarse-grained approach to content that logic and probability theory displays, and compare it with the more fine-grained approach to content inspired by Frege.[20] On this Fregean idea, there is both the propositional content and there is also the way in which we access that content. That is, there is both the proposition and an associated mode of presentation.

Think first about the individuation conditions for propositions. We begin by thinking about propositions as bearers of truth-value, but if we individuate only in terms of how such truth-values can vary over times and worlds, we end up with just one necessary truth. In spite of being occasionally embraced,[21] that consequence is about as close to a *reductio* as one can get without explicitly contradicting oneself. So, propositional content has to be more fine-grained than truth across worlds, or if one wants to plant one's flag on this hill, there better be another dimension to the notion of content, especially mental content, to account for the differences in cognitive significance that first led Frege (1892) to posit a distinction between sense and reference. Putting more weight on modes of presentation might allow the more coarse-grained understanding of propositional content in terms of truth-at-a-world, but any such genius is in the details.

As to the details, we are still, I think, in the early stages of theoretical development. On some approaches to modes of presentation,[22] we can think of modes of presentation simply in terms of causal roles. Yet, whatever modes of presentation

---

[20] A paradigm example of the latter approach is Salmon (1989).
[21] Most unapologetically in Stalnaker (1984).
[22] Here I have in mind Perry (1979).

are, they play a central role in human reasoning, for the same reason that it is not only our evidence but what we make of it that plays a central role in our reasoning. To play this role, our understanding must advert some sort of meaning or significance detected or noticed in or by or through modes of presentation, and that sounds suspiciously like needing something that is both semantic and epistemic in our theory of modes of presentation. Any mere causal account would not help on this score, so something more and better is needed. But we await a new Frege to provide a systematic theory of such.

An alternative to Fregeanism about mental content would involve a more fine-grained account of propositional content, but it is difficult to be optimistic about such approaches. Propositions are items introduced into a semantic theory to be the bearers of truth-value, but to the extent that we are impressed with the modal problem Kripke notes for theories of reference that rely on descriptive content,[23] we'll continue to find a logical gap between speaker meaning and semantic meaning. Since human reasoning will be sensitive to the former, it will be hard to get a semantic account of propositions to be fine-grained enough content to play the needed role in an account of human reasoning. This point, of course, simply reiterates the call for a Fregean account of mental content, so perhaps my assessment is a bit biased here. Regardless of that, however, we are not yet in the position of having anything much to offer for avoiding Fregeanism and having the resources for developing an approach to confirmation that is a conservative extension of standard first-order logic.

A second point to note concerning the prospects for Bayesian epistemology concerns the variety of proposals already in the literature for addressing the problems noted. We don't have the time here to investigate the plausibility of even a small subset of these responses, nor is doing so necessary here, for the prospects for the development of a skeptical epistemology for defeasible reasoning do not require it.

Nor is it clear that it matters whether an adequate sophisticated reasoning machine to replace our simple theory has to be a conservative extension of standard first-order logic. The advantage of conservative extensions is that we could preserve all the consequences of the clauses of our initial theory, thereby already having in place a good understanding of the epistemic conditionals central to the approach outlined here. If a replacement theory isn't conservative, part of the task for such a replacement would be to characterize epistemic conditionals in a way that satisfies the conditions of adequacy on a theory of conditionals, as detailed above. If that burden can be shouldered, the failure to be a conservative extension of the simple theory may be unproblematic.

---

[23] See Kripke (1980). The modal problem arises for any normal descriptive content that one might want to identify as the semantic content of a name. To illustrate, if we want to let the semantic content of "Aristotle" be "the most famous student of Plato," the modal problem is that whereas it is false that Aristotle might not have been Aristotle, it is true that Aristotle might not have been a student of Plato.

Our uncertainty about what a replacement theory could and should look like, however, is not a debilitating weakness regarding skeptical theory development. A full defense of skepticism would require specific solutions to the issues raised, but theory development isn't subject to these same standards. What we look for is a plausible story concerning the high standards for knowledge when it comes to the arena of defeasible reasoning, and to the extent that some path toward that goal remains open, we should allow skeptics to make their case that their demand for high standards for knowledge can be articulated when it comes to knowledge of the future. So, given the way in which our basic theory illustrates a direction to take in developing a formal account of defeasible reasoning, there is no reason to maintain that the skeptical account is hopeless because we'll never get an adequate formal account of defeasible reasoning. Perhaps we won't, but if so, the skeptic can't go down this road in the attempt to characterize the needed high standards for knowledge. At the same time, though, there is no good reason to think an adequate formal account can't be given, and even if there can be such an account, the main skeptical task remains to be accomplished. For even if we had such a formal theory, that doesn't obviously imply that knowledge of the future can have the kind of immunity from error the skeptic claims is needed for any knowledge of any kind. Hence, merely granting the formalization point doesn't by itself relieve the pressure of needed theory development by the skeptic.

So the right stance to take here is to grant to the skeptic this idea of a fully formal reasoning machine, and to grant that this idea counts as a finite extension of ordinary human capacities just as much as computer architecture of the sort we are already familiar with counts. Hence, if the project of theory development for knowledge of the future fails, it doesn't fail at this step. What remains, then, is to determine where to go from this point, since even given this assumption, the idea of infallible knowledge of the future through defeasible reasoning remains a mystery.

We then turn our focus back to the imagined reasoning program itself, designed to function on given suppositional inputs and calculate changes to total states of information by updating principles of the sort used in our basic theory. Because the reasoning is defeasible, the reasoning will not always be forward-looking in time, since mistaken inferences in the past can be revealed to be so at a later time. We thus imagine a machine that moves forward along a track, but also has to move backward to an earlier point, to start moving forward again along a different potential future. We thus think in terms of branchings into the future, with the need to backtrack in pursuit of the idea of finding the thin red line that is the story of (suppositional) reality.

As we noted when no backtracking was envisioned, the program is expected to halt at some point for some sets of initial suppositions, and adding the backtracking idea won't get rid of this possibility. More to the point, however, is the other possibility where no halting occurs, and here it is important to note that nothing about backtracking precludes this option. So, as before, halting at some point is one option, but so is a process leading to completion.

Here it is important to notice what is being asked of skepticism and what is not. The idea here is about theory development, not full defense of the truth of the view. At the initial extreme, skepticism involves nothing more than bare argument for a skeptical conclusion, and at that point, is easy to view as nothing more significant than something that needs to be taken into account when aiming for reflective equilibrium. At that stage, Moorean dismissiveness is understandable, and a complacent fallibilism that explains away the apparent infallibilist tinge in knowledge in terms of a false presupposition arising because of spending too much time talking to skeptics is easy to embrace. At the other end of the spectrum is a full and complete defense of the truth of skepticism, and if such were available, we of course would have good reason to view skepticism as having a level of significance not acknowledged properly by Moorean dismissiveness or any fallibilism, complacent or otherwise. Our focus here, though, concerns the hinterlands between these extremes, and whether we can find some significance for skepticism that doesn't require showing that the view is correct. We look for reasons or grounds to take skepticism seriously, and in doing so, we ask for theory development of the sort that would identify the high standards for knowledge that skeptics say must be met, and we do so across the various capacities we have for discerning truth from error. Failure to provide such an account would leave us in a position to supplement the false presupposition idea of complacent fallibilism with an additional thought—that the infallibilist tinge some see in knowledge is just an overgeneralization. Perhaps that tinge is present in the pristine world of mathematics and logic, or maybe even within some aspects of empirical investigation. But it is not ubiquitous, and thus to be explained away.

So we imagine the skeptic shouldering the burden of theory development, and are at a point where our focus is on knowledge of the future and other ways in which our theoretical exploration of the world depends on non-monotonic reasoning. Here, if anywhere, the skeptic will be unable to explain how any tinge of infallibility can be present, and so we imagine the skeptic pursuing the idea of finite extensions of ordinary human capacities through appeal to a reasoning program that is fully non-monotonic, but for which it remains open whether or not, for given suppositional inputs, it goes to completion. At this point, we have no good argument to show decisively that it can, nor that it cannot. As such, we should grant this possibility to the skeptic, for we are not trying to refute skepticism at this point nor are we demanding a full defense of the view. We are looking for significance in skepticism, the sort that arises when theory development occurs, and if skepticism is incapable of characterizing the high standards for knowledge needed regarding knowledge of the future, we haven't seen why yet. So, we can grant the possibility at this point that the reasoning program sometimes goes to completion and sometimes does not, in order to see whether this initial idea can be turned into an explanation of an infallibilist tinge in knowledge even in the arena of defeasible reasoning.

So, we ask, what is involved in the reasoning program coming to completion in a given case? When such completion occurs, the program comes to a conclusion which involves a complete specification of a possible world. That is, for any item of inquiry, it has reasoned to the conclusion that the item in question is true or that it is false. Such a complete system of information is still to be thought of in fully fallibilist terms, for each item arises in the fully fallible way in which defeasible reasoning gives warrant to the conclusions reached. So, the completion stage reached would still be, at most, a suppositional state involving merely fallible knowledge if knowledge at all. Thus, the mere fact of completion is not, of itself, the target at which skeptical theory development aims. Instead, the real work now begins, which is somehow to turn this idea of completion into material that can be used to move from fallibility to infallibility. That is the task of the next section.

5.5 From Fallible to Infallible

The strategy for theory development of the sort that will bridge this gap has two parts. The first part takes us from defeasible completion to indefeasible completion. The second stage moves from indefeasibility to infallibility.

Let's begin with the first stage. For this stage, we need to understand what indefeasibility involves. Defeaters come in two varieties, internal and external. The distinction is a direct consequence of the Gettier problem, where information one does not possess can result in the absence of knowledge even where one's belief is true and fully justified or warranted by the information one does possess. External defeat is thus a matter to be handled by an appropriate condition for knowledge that addresses the Gettier problem. Exactly what such a condition would look like is rather a mystery, for, as is well known, the history of this problem is laced together by new proposals succumbing to the latest counterexamples.

In characterizing the nature of external defeaters, we need not take any stand on the question of whether knowledge is analyzable nor on what that analysis is if it is. Instead, the only point needed is that sometimes the proper explanation of why you don't know adverts to information you don't possess. That can happen when psychological confidence is warranted and when it is not. That is, it can happen you have no information at all and are merely guessing, and it can also happen when the information you do possess fallibly leads you to a false conclusion. And there is one more way in which it can happen: sometimes the information you possess fallibly leads you to a true conclusion, but in a way that undermines knowledge because of information you do not possess.

5.5 FROM FALLIBLE TO INFALLIBLE   139

For those attracted to the idea that knowledge is analyzable, these possibilities give rise to a defeasibility theory of knowledge.[24] Even without this analyzability assumption, however, the insight remains that a claim to knowledge can be undermined both by information one already possesses and by information one does not possess.

Suppose, then, that we are considering a case where our idealized rational agent has followed a program of defeasible reasoning to the point of completion, for a given initial supposition state of information. We then ask whether the rationality achieved in such a process could be undermined by either internal or external defeaters. With regard to the former, the answer is simple, for all internal defeaters are already taken into account by following the defeasible reasoning program. At each step taken by the program, a conclusion is defeasibly reached on the basis of all the information available at the time, so no step is taken where internal information undermines the proposed conclusion. *A fortiori*, once the program arrives at completion, there can't be any possessed information that undermines the conclusion reached, either. If defeat is possible, then, it would have to come from defeaters that are external to the system of information on which the program operates.

There are two reasons by which we can rule out this possibility, for situations in which the program reaches completion. The first is our initial assumption that truths leave tracks, which had to be granted for purposes of developed the skeptical account. The strategy behind this assumption was to give no quarter to the skeptic, asking instead that some account of ideality with respect to defeasible reasoning be given while granting the knowability assumption (or at least the knowability assumption for logically primitive claims[25]). Once this assumption is in place, the tracks created would need to be accommodated by the reasoning program, introducing the need for backtracking at least in some cases, and thus tracks that defeat would end up being subsumed in the system of information on which the program operates, thereby counting as internal defeaters.

This result brings us to the second point, which involves the completion assumption we are under. When the reasoning program encounters grounds for drawing a conclusion, where these grounds are undermined by an internal defeater, the program won't go to completion but will instead halt, at least temporarily, not proceeding until further determinative information becomes available. If such further information becomes available, the program continues toward completion, even though the possibility of further defeating information is still present and might force the program to halt once again. Moreover, these

---

[24] The history of this approach traces to Lehrer and Paxson Jr (1969), and the best version of the view, as I see things, is Klein (1981).

[25] This parenthetical remarks concerns the knowability paradox discussion earlier, and which we shelved for discussion on the basis of this qualified knowability assumption.

steps could be repeated because of the hierarchy of defeaters and defeater defeaters. So the combination of a completion assumption together with the assumption that truths leave tracks leaves no room for external defeaters after completion is achieved, since all defeating information would have become internal at some point in the path to completion. We thus can move, in these cases, from the idea that all of the commitments are defeasibly warranted to the conclusion that in these special cases, the conclusions are not only defeasibility warranted by also indefeasibly warranted, both in terms of internal defeaters and external ones. Internal defeaters can't be present, for they would have prevented the system from reaching completion, and external defeaters can't be present because everything has been internalized in the process of reaching completion. Thus, we may conclude, the system of information has elements all of which are rational and indefeasibly so.

This conclusion might be thought to be sufficient to show that the system of information counts as suppositionally known to be true as well, since the problems faced by the defeasibility theory of knowledge cast doubt on the need for indefeasibility, but not its sufficiency.[26] While it is true that the counterexamples that plague defeasibility theories focus on the question of necessity (especially on the distinction between misleading and non-misleading defeaters, the latter of which are taken to be compatible with knowledge), this literature is orthogonal to our present concerns. For this literature is founded on thoroughly fallibilist assumptions, and that isn't relevant to the present project of trying to articulate the gold standard that skeptics claim needs to be satisfied for knowledge of the future. So we shouldn't side with fans of a defeasibility theory by endorsing the idea that the argument above that gets us from defeasible to indefeasible shows that knowledge can be achieved by appeal to epistemic factors that fall short of the skeptical gold standard. That point may be true, but the discussion so far isn't the right way to argue for it. Instead, the discussion so far should be thought of simply in terms of an intermediate step, one that leaves open the possibility that knowledge can be achieved without satisfying the skeptical gold standard for warrant, but also leaving open the possibility of characterizing the gold standard in question so that a more severe threat to the possibility of knowledge can be articulated.

So the fact that we can move from defeasible justification to indefeasible justification is merely a stage in the process of theory development on behalf of skepticism. To avoid derailing the project, then, the crucial issue is to see if the skeptical gold standard can be characterized by moving from a system of indefeasibly rational information to infallibility itself.

There are two factors that we can rely on in our suppositional reasoning story moving from indefeasibility to infallibility. First, as noted multiple times already,

---

[26] See, for example, Lehrer and Paxson Jr (1969), Harman (1973), Swain (1974), and Klein (1981) for documentation of this point. Especially relevant are cases in which it is a socially available truth that is needed, not just any truth (as in Harman's assassination case and the Tom Grabit case of Lehrer and Paxson).

the system of information in question is complete: for every proposition p, either p or its negation is in the system of information in question. Moreover, this result honors the assumption that truths leave tracks, so the indefeasibility assumption, together with the bivalence assumption shows that, given the particular suppositional inputs that lead to completion, the elements in the resulting complete system of information are all suppositionally true.

Combine, then, this result with the central idea about how to understand infallibility, which concerns having control over whether or not we are correct in our judgments. The reasoning machine in question is now in a position to conclude which initial suppositional information states lead to completion and which do not, and once this information is available, one guided by such a program would be in a position to control whether one finds the truth or lands in error. Taking full control over the process of getting to the truth and avoiding error would involve limiting one's use of defeasible reasoning to contexts where an initial supposition state leads to completion. So long as one follows the program in question in such contexts, one will have the control needed.

Given this result, fallibilists will question why anyone would be attracted to the idea of never believing anything unless and until such control were present. That is an important question for skeptics to answer, and we will say more about it in the next chapter, but here the question should be resisted. For we aren't yet at the stage of deciding whether to heed the skeptic's advice about what beliefs to hold or what judgments to endorse. We are, instead, at the point of trying to determine whether the high standards the skeptic's claims must be met in order to know can in fact be characterized when it comes to purported knowledge of the future and other non-observational conclusions obtained through defeasible reasoning. As I've been arguing, the challenge addressed in this chapter is simply about meeting the requirement for skeptical theory development. The overall argument begins by noting that it is not enough for the skeptic to insist that the possibility of error be eliminated, for as we have seen, such an approach to the notion of infallibility is inadequate. In order to complete the task of this chapter, we look for an account of the gold standard in terms of full control over whether one gets to the truth, in a way that is not susceptible to the charge of epistemic imperialism. To show that no such imperialism is present, the skeptic must shoulder the burden of saying, for each of the various human capacities whose function is truth-detection, what such total control involves. Once we get to this point, the hardest cases are those involving reasoning, where the reasoning itself is best understood in terms of a non-monotonic logical consequence relation.

The results noted above, then, are not to be understood in terms of how to live one's intellectual life, but rather only in terms of whether there is a skeptical position that can be developed adequately. Skeptics will use the results of this chapter to support the idea that we should never undertake inquiry except when full control is present, but that point of view doesn't follow from the theory development

142 INFALLIBILITY THROUGH NON-DEMONSTRATIVE REASONING

undertaken in this chapter, but instead requires further discussion. The point to note here, however, is that the substance needed for such further discussion is now in place, for the conclusion we have reached is that such development of the skeptical position is possible. Total control over the possibility of error is within reach, even for defeasible reasoning. All that is needed is the list of which possible suppositional input states lead to completion and which don't, and the ability to refrain from drawing conclusions by such reasoning except in cases where the input state leads to completion. It is in this way that the skeptic can answer the charge of epistemic imperialism and characterize the high standards demanded for knowledge even in cases that essentially involve non-monotonicity.[27]

Once we keep a clear focus on what the dialectical demands of the moment are for the skeptic, one might still wonder whether the skeptic has succeeded. For the story above is only as good as its starting points, which involve suppositional states that lead to completion. Full control over the possibility of error will require full control over conclusions one might reach about which of these suppositional states are actually true, and there is nothing in the story as told above that gives full control over that matter.

This point is correct, but it is for this reason that we discussed first the idealizations the skeptic can use when it comes to other human capacities whose functions are cognitive. As noted when discussing these other capacities and abilities, skepticism might founder at these earlier points, and if so, skeptical theory development will need to begin anew. Even so, our attention here is focused, not so much on the truth or falsity of skepticism, but rather on its significance. As I've been arguing, its significance depends on theory development, and such development can be accomplished even if we, for good reasons, reject the theory later on. So we began with idealizations of various human capacities other than that of defeasible reasoning, and then moved on to this more difficult topic. If the idealizations of other capacities can succeed, so can this one concerning defeasible reasoning, for it would be in terms of other capacities that the skeptic will distinguish between which initial suppositional states involve error and which do not.

5.6 Conclusion

Hence, the task of this chapter is complete. The implications for the present chapter, then, say something about fallibilisms. We've noted the difference between sensitive and complacent fallibilisms, and the success of this chapter argues strongly in favor of a preference for the former. In particular, it calls into

---

[27] Unrelated to this current project are the implications of this approach for the problem of freedom and foreknowledge in philosophical theology. These resources can be put in service of an account that embraces both full providential control and libertarian freedom, the details of which can be found in Kvanvig (2011b).

question the idea that we need say nothing more about skepticism than to claim that the tinge of infallibility in knowledge is nothing more than a false presupposition about knowledge induced by our normative adherence to a Gricean cooperation principle in conversations with the skeptic. While it may be true that there is such a false presupposition and while it may also be true that the explanation of how we came to have such a false presupposition is as indicated, we are in no position to explain away the tinge of infallibility in such perfunctory fashion. So we have reason to develop a more sensitive version of fallibilism, a topic we'll take up in the process of considering the skeptical identification of cognitive ideality and knowledge.

We turn, then, in the next chapter to consider this skeptical position in more detail. Skepticism claims that we are now fully aware of what ideality in cognition looks like, and that none (or almost none) of our cognitive efforts look like that. Skepticism also identifies this ideality with knowledge, and the conclusion that follows is that our cognitive efforts never, or almost never, result in knowledge. Here we have developed the skeptical position to the point where the ideality identified is within view, so in the next chapter we turn to the question of the identification of this ideality with knowledge.

Chapter 6
Close Approximations

6.1 Introduction

We have seen the kind of theory development of the skeptical position that is needed to rebut the charge that skeptical arguments and conclusions are nothing more than fodder for reflective equilibrium, a charge leading to a non-skeptical outcome virtually guaranteed by the Moorean stance of never giving up the more obvious for the less obvious. After all, what could be more obvious than that of knowing what day it is (since that explains why medical personnel worried about dementia often ask such questions first) or where one lives or whether I am more than 10 years old? Not everyone knows such things, but many of us do and obviously so. So if there is some abstract philosophical principle about what can be known that conflicts with these obvious claims, we will need to revise the principle so as to find something close that can be defended in light of our total evidence, not give up these obvious claims through some beguiling reasoning that would require these abstract principles to be more intuitive and obvious than ordinary claims of common sense.

Our skeptical response to this facile dismissal shoulders the burden of theory development. We no longer have the bare claim that knowing requires ruling out all possibility of error, we have characterizations about what the high standards for knowledge might look like for each of the capacities by which we detect truth over error. In each such case, the skeptical response is contrastive: "you think that's knowledge? That's not knowledge, here's what real knowledge looks like!" Moreover, this comparative claim is not one that relies on any appeal to occult powers such as prescience, ESP, telekinesis, or prophetic insight resulting from divine inspiration, but rather on finite extensions of ordinary human capacities.

This skeptical rejoinder has probative value, and thus calls for a response. The response might yet offer a version of complacent fallibilism, but it will need to go beyond merely accommodating a bare argument and skeptical conclusion. To appreciate this point, note the path our dialectic has taken. First, we had bare argument for a skeptical thesis, prompting dismissiveness toward that thesis through a Moorean shift. In response, those granting greater significance to skepticism noted the infallibilist tinge in ordinary conceptions of knowledge, and complacent fallibilists, if taking the time to respond, resort to explaining away that tinge by appeal to the idea of false presuppositions generated by Gricean accommodation of conversational context.

Skepticism and Fallibilism. Jonathan L. Kvanvig, Oxford University Press. © Jonathan L. Kvanvig (2025).
DOI: 10.1093/9780198924821.003.0006

6.1 INTRODUCTION 145

The next step in the dialectic has two components, the first of which we completed in the last chapter, where we characterized the ideality for cognition that the skeptic wishes to exploit. That step is crucial for resisting complacency toward the infallibilist tinge, but there is more to note. For there is also the point noted about what the great intellectual goods are, which include knowledge, understanding, and theoretical wisdom.[1] Common to each of these is a factive element, and it is this factive element that generates the infelicity of concessive attitudes, attributions, and assertions. Moreover, in each case, such factive epistemic states provide additional value over the value of mere true belief, and thus incorporate some kind of cognitive ideality beyond mere factivity. It is this additional value involving ideality that puts pressure on casual dismissals of skepticism in terms of false presuppositions about knowledge. Once the skeptical standard for ideality has been developed and acknowledged, fallibilists need to locate its place in the territory of great intellectual goods. Skeptics claim the location is in knowledge, perhaps the foundational item in this list of great intellectual goods. If they are mistaken about this location, as the false presupposition viewpoint would have it, the pressing question is where else to locate it. For if we have a list of great intellectual goods, and an account of cognitive ideality, it would be a mystery beyond belief to insist that such ideality bears no connection to any of the great intellectual goods. To belabor the point, items on our list of great intellectual goods get there in virtue of contributing some intellectual value beyond that of mere true belief, and the same is true for the skeptical gold standard of cognitive ideality. So how could there be such a disconnect between the list of great goods and the skeptical gold standard?

In short, the great intellectual goods of knowledge, understanding, and theoretical wisdom have a special status in epistemology, and once we have a characterization of ideality for cognition, it would be natural to inquire which of the great goods are tied to such ideality. If the answer by a complacent Moorean is that there is no such tie, that any temptation toward thinking there is results from spending too much time with skeptics, we should resist. For, in general, when we investigate an area and a model is developed that characterizes ideality with respect to the domain in question, we should expect the central elements in that domain to be linked to ideality in the model in some way or other. For example, when we investigate surface irregularities and recognize the value of flat surfaces, we should expect some link between the physical objects we study and the geometric characterization of ideal flatness in terms of coplanarity. So when it comes to an investigation of cognition, we have both a characterization of ideality with respect to it as well as an identification of the kinds of things that count as valuable from a purely

---

[1] By way of reminder, I categorize these items as value-theoretic, to be contrasted with what in ethics is identified as deontic. Because of the link between deontology and duty, I prefer to identify the analogous territory in epistemology in terms of normativity, not wishing to pre-judge the issue of whether justification, rationality, reasonability, warrant, and positive epistemic status more generally are to be understood in terms of the language of duty.

intellectual point of view. To put it pointedly, it would be an astonishing anomaly to have our account of the great intellectual goods be completed unrelated to the gold standard for cognitive ideality. Such a result should lead one to think that the great goods in question had been misidentified, leading to a situation where complacency in one's fallibilism requires more and more radical rejections of common ground between skeptics and fallibilists. And all this from defenders of common-sense! Without the characterization of ideality, things would be quite different and complacency would be attractive. But once we have such a characterization, there is pressure on any view that pretends that the characterization in question is not to be linked at all with the great epistemic goods. That is the point of emphasizing the centrality of value enhancement over mere true belief when generating a list of the great epistemic goods. As should be obvious, but I'll say it anyway, being in full control over whether or not one lands in error—the gold in the skeptical gold standard—is clearly value-enhancing. As a result, the theory development provided in the last chapter makes endorsement of a false presupposition account of concessive attitudes, attributions, and assertions hard to defend.

In the face of such pressure, a natural response would be to question the adequacy of the theory development detailed in the last chapter. I grant that we have seen no decisive, compelling reason to think that all such challenges will fail, in part because some of the features of the account are somewhat fanciful. So, further reflection on the adequacy of this skeptical position is certainly in order, but this fact puts this position in much the same territory as when we find developed versions of foundationalism, coherentism, reliabilism, and other mature theories of knowledge. Each such developed epistemology is liable to undoing by further reflection, for it is the bane of philosophical theorizing to have difficulty surviving sustained scrutiny. Our developed account of the skeptical gold standard will be no different on this score, but for the present, I propose both to grant the need for further theory development, but also to see how to proceed once we grant significant theoretical standing to the idealizations offered. When we do so, the next step involves the link between such idealization and the great epistemic goods, and here, once again, I'll focus on knowledge, for reasons already documented in Chapter 1, focusing on the idea that even if understanding and wisdom are to be preferred to knowledge, the latter is the step we take on the path to these greater goods. The question to address, then, is the link between cognitive ideality and knowledge, and the first conclusion to draw is that cognitive ideality is present for ideal knowledge. The important question for fallibilists to address and answer, however, is whether there is such a thing as non-ideal knowledge, and of course their answer must that that there is. They will maintain, that is, that none (or very little) of our knowledge is ideal knowledge, but non-ideal knowledge is still knowledge nonetheless.

This kind of response may look suspiciously like claiming that there are two kinds of gold: the good stuff and fool's gold. That is the skeptical view of the

6.1 INTRODUCTION 147

matter, and it is receives some support from the infelicity of concessive attitudes about knowledge. So an adequate response to this concern will have to explain the infallibilist tinge in knowledge, and do so in way that makes fallible knowledge something more authentic than fool's gold.

We have seen two ways to try to explain away the infallibilist tinge. Both approaches appeal to Gricean constraints on conversational contexts, and the more complacent version appeals to the idea of false presupposition while the second, more sensitive approach, appeals to the idea that what we say often implicates information beyond the actual truth conditions for the proposition expressed. The latter treats skepticism more seriously than the former, since the former view amounts to the idea that we wasted our time talking with the skeptic, the outcome of which was being saddled with this false presupposition about knowledge. The latter view isn't dismissive in this way, and embraces the need to say why concessive attributions and attitudes about knowledge are generally inapt. They are inapt because, as Gricean principles would have it, one shouldn't raise irrelevancies in a conversational context, so if one admits there are chances of being wrong, one's interlocutors will see this as something relevant and so conclude that these chances are significant. After all, if the chances weren't significant, they would not be relevant to bring up, and so a conversational norm would be flouted by so doing.

I have identified the first approach as a more complacent fallibilism and the second as a more sensitive fallibilism. The former can be combined with Moorean dismissiveness, but the latter takes skepticism more seriously and shoulders the burden of, at the very least, explaining away the tinge of infallibilism. But such explaining away is a defensive maneuver involving accommodating the data presented on behalf of skepticism. We can ask for more, however. We might wonder whether we should have expected the data in the first place, on the assumption of fallibilism. That is, while the infallibilist position of the skeptic clearly predicts the infelicity of concessive attitudes and attributions, we might want a version of fallibilism that does so as well.

One might think that complacent fallibilism looks better on this issue than does a sensitive fallibilism that merely accommodates the data. For if the false presupposition about knowledge is widespread, we can reasonably predict that concessive attitudes and attributions will sound inapt. So, while generic fallibilism makes no such prediction, nor does the version of sensitive fallibilism relying on a Gricean relevance principle, perhaps complacent fallibilism does and is thus better in virtue of this prediction.

This conclusion is undermined by noting where the false presupposition element of this version of complacent fallibilism enters the story. Complacent fallibilism begins with the commonsense sense view of Moore that dismisses skepticism on the basis of an appeal to the methodological principle of never giving up the more obvious for the less obvious. It sees and hears what the skeptic is claiming, and notes immediately that none of it is as obvious as the claim that we know

148 CLOSE APPROXIMATIONS

many things. These features of the view do not predict the infelicity of concessions at all. Instead, the way in which the false presupposition view arises is after the appeal to infelicity is made to undermine complacency, and this aspect enters the story as an add-on to the Moorean complacency already present. So it is a feature designed to accommodate the infelicity in question, and it would be a disastrous effort at accommodation if it didn't succeed at the task! So the fact that this feature predicts the infelicity isn't something that adds credibility to a version of complacent fallibilism that includes it, for it is a mere side effect of a successful attempt at deflecting an argument against complacency.

We can make sense of this dialectic through the hierarchical structure of a theory of defeat. In that theory, we find *pro tanto* grounds for a conclusion, making these grounds subject to possible defeat. If such a defeater is found, however, the story does not end, for the combination of the initial ground plus the defeater is itself subject to possible overriding. That is, the power of the defeater to defeat is itself defeasible, so that a defeater can be present while at the same time being overridden by yet further information. By generalizing on these points, we end up with an hierarchical theory of defeat involving a requirement that the initial *pro tanto* ground be *ultimately* undefeated—that is, either no defeater exists, or any defeater that does exist is overridden by further information.

Applied to the present case, Moorean methodology is the *pro tanto* ground for rejecting skepticism, and the defeater for this complacent rejection is the infelicity claim. The response on behalf of complacent rejection—the false presupposition claim—is presented as an overrider for the defeating power of infelicity. Once understood in this manner, the idea that complacent fallibilism predicts infelicity in a way that adds credence to complacency is no longer plausible, since the overrider of a defeater is not, in general, evidence in favor of the claim whose epistemic standing the overrider restores. In the present case, the evidence for complacency is the Moorean shift, and the defeater for this evidence is the infelicity of concession. The appeal to false presupposition enters as an overrider for this defeater, and this overrider is not itself predicted by either Moorean complacency or the evidence cited in favor of it. So the role played by this overrider is that of allowing complacent fallibilism to accommodates the data of infelicity. In granting success at this task, we do not end up with a theory that predicts the infelicity of concessions in a way that adds credibility to any theory that incorporates this accommodation. A theory that involves such an accommodation predicts the infelicity in question, to be sure, but not in a way that generates additional confirmation for that theory. Restoring the standing that was present before incorporating the defeater of infelicity is not additional confirmation for the theory, but rather only a restoration of a confirming power that was threatened by the defeater.

Note as well that if a false presupposition theorist wishes to resist by insisting that the view under consideration was always, from the very beginning, a view that combined the Moorean element with the false presupposition idea, the result avoids one criticism only to fall under another. For there are virtues for theories that this mere concatenation of elements lacks. We look for theories that are simple, and when more complex, we seek to unify and integrate the elements of the theory. So if we compare a false presupposition view that merely concatenates its parts with one that integrates them, the first can predict the infelicity data but is worse for its lack of simplicity and integration. Either way, the view is a regrettable one to have to endorse and so provides grounds for trying to find a better version of fallibilism.

So we have no trouble-free version of fallibilism that predicts the data of infelicity in the desired way, but instead only versions that accommodate it or suffer from other problems. Before trying to remedy this issue, I note that it isn't a decisive argument against fallibilism. It counts as a deficiency, perhaps, but some deficiencies aren't debilitating. For nearly every account of anything will have to explain away some data that it doesn't predict, and so in this respect, fallibilism is no different.

Even so, it is also true that some data are so central to a subject matter that the inability of a theory to predict the data in question threatens the suitableness of the theory for explanatory purposes. It is here we find a key difference between complacent and sensitive fallibilism. The sensitive fallibilist treats the data of infelicity, together with the theory development put forward on behalf of skepticism, as probative, revealing important items within the epistemological landscape. A sensitive fallibilist will thus be motivated to offer a theory that explains both the possibility of fallible knowledge as well as the tinge of infallibility and the concomitant infelicity of concessive attitudes, attributions, and assertions.

So fallibilism is, at this point, in the somewhat uncomfortable theoretical position of perhaps only being able to minimize the importance of the data or only being able to accommodate it, rather than predict and explain it. So we find motivation to look for a better version of sensitive fallibilism. We turn, then, in the next section to this search.

6.2 A Positive Account

Perhaps we can make progress here by noting the following. Fallibilism is not just a view about the standards for knowledge but rather a view that combines in one perspective the implications of the fallibility of our attitudes together with our fallibility as persons. By doing so, it not only holds that knowledge need not be infallible but also prompts efforts to improve our skills at getting to the truth and avoiding error.[2] Fallibilists maintain that we can and ought to view our

---

[2] I write here under the assumption that the purely intellectual goal is that of getting to the truth and avoiding error. I'm skeptical that this is so, but it is at least one such goal, and that is all that is

150 CLOSE APPROXIMATIONS

intellectual accomplishments as sometimes enough for knowledge but always, or nearly always, capable of being improved. This duality is in principle compatible with both complacent and sensitive versions of the view, but as we will see, it provides a way for latter versions of the view to be developed so as to yield a prediction of the infelicity data rather than a mere accommodation of it.

The first step toward achieving this result is to note that a sensitive fallibilist can join forces with the skeptic in affirming the ideals that the skeptic requires of knowledge. If we use an analogy with ordinary behavior, fallibilists grant the idea of perfection that the skeptic articulates, but instead of saying that nothing short of perfection is adequate, the fallibilist insists flawed pursuits of the good are often better than nothing, and permitted and perhaps even commendable because of it. The ideals in question thus do not enjoin one to do nothing, but rather make clear how to do better.

Applying this analogy to the intellectual sphere, the ideals are treated by fallibilists, not as a reason to go without belief forever, but as a call toward improving our ways of getting to the truth and avoiding error. Consider, for example, the gap between ordinary perception and the eye of Sauron. For the latter, there is nothing in the external environment that results in mistakes, and in addition, there are no internal motivations that lead to misperceptions. Thought of in this way, we can think of our own perceptual equipment as pretty good, but in need of improvement. First, perception can be negatively affected by cognitive penetration from the affections and the will,[3] and it is obvious that nature itself has powers over the accuracy of perception. But we can also compensate for these intrusions, thereby limiting their effect, and the more we do so, the closer we approximate the ideal the skeptic has characterized.

One might resist this characterization by pointing out that those who count to a million aren't getting closer to infinity than those who count only to a thousand. That point is correct, but pursuing ideals isn't wisely guided by a pessimistic generalization on it. Computer chip manufacturers and allergy sufferers don't think of aiming for a dust-free area in such terms, but rather see the process of eliminating sources of contamination as helping to approach the goal of such a dust-free environment. Such a judgment is accurate, even though when generalized to the mathematics of infinity, it isn't.

The lesson here is that there are ways to generalize a given claim that are mistaken, and the error of the generalization is a reminder that a complete account of the matter needs to explain how to divide the cases where improvement is made by a given process and where it is not. Since it is obvious that there is such a difference, a sensitive fallibilist need not endorse a generalization of the approximation

---

needed here. I argue that this goal may not be the only epistemic goal, nor perhaps even the main one, in Kvanvig (2005), but the issues involved are ancillary to our present concerns.

[3] For this terminology and discussion of the empirical data on this score, see Siegel (2005) and Siegel (2013).

point above that is undermined by this counting counterexample. In short, while it is true that the approximation point *might* be grounded in a generalization with such an implication, there is no reason to suppose that it *must* be so grounded. Just as eliminating sources of contamination is a way of getting closer to the ideal of a dust-free enclosure, by eliminating elements involving loss of control, we approach the limit where total control is to be found, even if we don't get closer to infinity by counting.

So sensitive fallibilism endorses the skeptical project of identifying the gold standard for cognition, across the range of capacities and abilities we have for finding the truth and avoiding error. None of that would count for much, though, unless there were a way to tie an account of these gold standard ideals with knowledge itself, as the skeptic insists.

Here we encounter the central significance of epistemological axiology. We have already distinguished between the theory of epistemic value and the theory of epistemic normativity. In the theory of epistemic value, we find the epistemic goods of knowledge, understanding, and theoretical wisdom, while in the territory of epistemic normativity we find deontic requirements concerning justification, warrant, rationality, and positive epistemic status more generally.

Given this epistemological division, a tie between the ideals identified by the skeptic and knowledge itself arises from the idea that knowledge matters. We can ask whether mere belief or true belief is better from a purely theoretical point of view, and the obvious response is that true belief is preferable. We can also ask whether one would rather be correct or know that one is correct, and here again the preference for the latter is obvious.

The common attitude found in these preferences, then, is that knowledge is fundamental to what we are really after from a purely intellectual point of view. We find this centrality along several dimensions: curiosity is a desire to know, you aren't supposed to say what you don't know to be true, knowledge legitimates closure of inquiry, emotional responses rely on knowledge (so your emotional high can't be happiness about winning the lottery without you knowing that you won the lottery), not to mention the ubiquity of the use of the concept of knowledge across natural languages.

Careful attention, then, to epistemological axiology reveals a strong inclination to find in knowledge a paradigm of successful cognition from a purely intellectual point of view. It is what we are after, and our self-improvement efforts aim at and are satisfied by how they enhance our knowledge as well as our ways of acquiring it.

Given this quite common thinking about the importance of knowledge, we see a convergence between the ideality that the skeptic explains and the pinnacle of cognitive achievement found in knowledge itself. Knowledge is the gold standard for cognition, and the ideals the skeptic identifies for each of our capacities and abilities for discerning what is true and what is not also identify the gold standard for each of these aspects of cognition. So we find a convergence between the development of this skeptical position and our ordinary and intuitive assumptions about the importance of knowledge. This convergence then explains what the cognitive ideals of the skeptic have to do with knowledge. They are quite naturally identifiable with knowledge precisely because knowledge is what we are after from a purely cognitive point of view.

Even if this intuitive epistemological axiology is mistaken, it can nonetheless provide a basis for seeing why there should be an infallibilist tinge in knowledge. The tinge arises not merely in the troubled epistemological soul of the skeptic but in the hearts and minds of ordinary inquirers, where our intellectual efforts culminate in the acquisition of knowledge (as the fallibilist would have it). That is the ideal, and it is in virtue of this acknowledgment of ideality that there is something to be said on behalf of a skeptical position as developed in the preceding chapters.

So, the connection between the skeptical ideal and knowledge is defensible in a way that reinforces the infallibilist tinge we've noted repeatedly. These points put pressure on fallibilism to account for this tinge, and yields a decided discomfort with a false presupposition version of fallibilism. It might be that our attention is turned to the tinge of infallibilism as a result of conversations with the skeptic, but the story of where the tinge comes from points in a different direction for the tinge's source. That is why we need to find a more sensitive fallibilism.

Nor will the standing of the false presupposition approach be restored by rejecting the epistemological axiology described above. In this attempted resuscitation, the importance of knowledge is challenged, claiming that it doesn't have the importance assigned to it by ordinary thinking. It is valuable, but not singularly valuable in the way required for the identification of it with the account of ideal cognition the skeptical position outlines.

This way of defending complacency is difficult to sustain, though. For once we identify a replacement for knowledge in terms of pre-eminent epistemological significance, questions will need to be addressed about the relationship between this replacement and knowledge. For example, suppose the replacement is understanding, a view I have defended in Kvanvig (2003). On one standard way of thinking about understanding, it is a species of knowledge, and if it is, the tinge of infallibilism about knowledge can be explained because of this connection between knowledge and understanding. The only way to avoid the tinge would be to deny that the ideal form of whatever is of pre-eminent epistemological significance involves full control over getting to the truth and avoiding error, and merely denying the importance of knowledge is ineffective in that regard. The need to find a more sensitive fallibilism remains.

For this task, consider the relationship between self-improvement in achieving our cognitive goals and the centrality of the idea of control in identifying the gold standard for cognition. The endowments of nature give us skills, capacities, and abilities that generate some control over whether we achieve these cognitive goals, but the control we have is rarely or never more than an approximation of the ideal rather than the ideal itself.

Even so, for any human endeavor and potential goal, the question that is always legitimate to ask is what perfection amounts to and how close one has to get to it for present purposes. The purposes in question can be either practical or purely intellectual or theoretical, and we can move toward the approximationist point I'll argue for by reminding ourselves of the ways in which practical parameters can constrain the demand for ideality. Most are familiar with the common motto among carpenters—"close enough for government work"—and musicians—"close enough for jazz." Real craftspeople in both domains often show disdain for such sloppiness, revealing an opinion that such remarks are mere excuses. So claims of suitable approximation to an ideal are often correctly resisted, but there are two quite different ways of doing so. One way to do so approaches the ideal in binary terms: if you can't do it right, don't do it at all. The other approach is the more subtle approach of one who has mastered the craft: you're not close enough yet, you need to do better to pass scrutiny, and you have it in you to do so.

These two approaches can be combined as well, and that is often what we do and what we should do. Leaders of musical ensembles ask for improvement, but even if perfection guides the process, it would be unwise to tell the musicians to be perfect or go home. At some point during the process of improvement, the results survive scrutiny, while at the same time being only close enough approximations of the ideal of perfection that continues to guide the process.

Consider, then, the same ideas in the context of cognition. We have cognitive goals, and there is a gold standard of perfection that guides our activities and efforts at improvement. With respect to any particular effort on our part, we can view the scenario as close enough or not close enough to the ideal. There is a point at which the results are good, and good enough, even if still not ideal.

The skeptic will agree on this point as well, but will insist that what is good enough will inevitably fall short of knowledge. So the dispute with the skeptic isn't about whether we can achieve a level of adequacy but instead where on this continuum from hapless attempts to perfect mastery we find correct attributions of knowledge. Here the skeptical adage will appeal to the idea of absolute terms, terms for which the adage is "it's not X unless it's perfectly X." As we've seen, purported examples are being flat, being circular, being pure gold, and, of course, being known for certain.

We've already seen reasons not to endorse this line of thought, since the project of explaining this idea of absoluteness involves elaborating a model of the property in question. In general, models abstract in a way that focuses on some purported aspects of reality, but for limit terms of the kind we are discussing here, they can also involving an ideality dimension as well. In such cases, the model characterizes the kind of perfection that governs inquiry into that aspect of reality, and what we have noted about this ideality aspect of such models is that they not only abstract from reality but distort as well. Flatness and circularity get characterized in Euclidean terms, and pure gold involves an atomic number with no admixture of any sort, but no such model accommodates the vagueness and indeterminacies we find in nature. Thus to insist that none of these limit properties are ever instantiated adopts an overly idealized conception of reality, one that refuses to acknowledge the ways in which modeling can involve not only abstraction but also distortion.

Here I counsel a more judicious approach, one that notes the ideality of the model and the incumbent need to assess where and when our judgments approximate ideality in a way that is sufficiently close. To explain this idea, we begin by noting that closeness here can be of either a practical or a theoretical matter. It is really the latter that we aim at, but let's return to the practical sphere to remind ourselves how approximations function in relationship to models that both abstract and idealize, before transposing into the purely theoretical realm.

From a machinist's perspective, for example, we can make sense of approximations to idealized flatness relative to a measuring device being used. We measure flatness by identifying tolerances that can be allowed for that surface. These tolerances can grow tighter, and can approach a limit where no deviation is present, but only when the tolerances are relative to some spatial span that is assumed for purposes of measurement. As the span is reduced, we will be detecting the field in a way that mirrors what happens through increasing magnification of it. And we know that if magnification increases enough, we'll find a lack of solidity that is present at the atomic and molecular levels, since no surface in our world is a Euclidean plane. Thus, before the spatial span goes to zero, we get to a point at which a proper measurement can no longer be made. So, from a practical point of view, we get assessments of flatness relative to some measurement device, and once a tolerance level is identified, we look for surfaces that are within that tolerance level and correctly identify them as flat. If we want, we can even insist that relative to that measurement device, no deviation is tolerated, and only then attribute flatness to the surface being measured. Note, however, that this assessment still acknowledges the ideal of perfect flatness that hasn't been achieved, for a more sensitive measuring device might still detect differences. Once this point is appreciated, we see again, as argued in Chapter 2, that the ideal involving invariance between measurements at any two points, is a mathematical one, definable in terms of Euclidean geometry, and thereby leaving open the idea that approximations to the ideal might count as close enough for the attribution of flatness to be correct when it comes to surfaces that are not Euclidean planes. Regarding surfaces in our world, there is a sequence of more sensitive measurements that might be made, and this sequence approaches a limit. This limit is the ideal, and approximations to it can involve smaller and smaller tolerable deviations. At least relative to a specified set of interests and purposes, attributions of flatness can be correct while still only approaching the limit in question.

A similar point holds about pure gold. We are all familiar with the vague boundaries of any object, at the molecular, atomic, and subatomic level, but these facts are properly ignored from an assayer's perspective. The standard of no admixture of anything other than element 79, Au, is again relative to some interest or purpose that renders moot the idea that perfectly pure gold can be found in a given spatial arena only when the substance being assayed is determinately bounded. Such substances are ideal ones, given the fact that the subatomic realm is in a state of constant flux. So when we apply the assayer's standards for purity, we are adopting some way of holding fixed what is really in flux, and trying to detect impurities relative to these fixed parameters. In the process, we can identify a limit toward which various measuring techniques approach when measuring purity. For any given setup, we can find a substance to have no impurities at all, while at the same time allowing that a more sensitive setup would detect impurities. And we can also imagine a sequence of more sensitive setups, each of which detects impurities not noticed with the prior setup, and thereby identify the limit being approached by this sequence. Relative to a set of interests and purposes, some such setups are adequate for purposes of identifying which substances count as pure gold and which do not, even though we can simultaneously note the way in which the substance wouldn't pass scrutiny at the limit.

These same points can be applied to the idea that nothing is circular unless a closed plane figure with identical distances from the center at every point on the boundary of that figure. Such objects are model-theoretic ones to which actual objects can be compared. We can assess circularity by superimposing a mathematical figure over the object being assessed, and by doing so, see once again the significance of the purposes and interests relative to which we find certain approximations to a limit concept that are nonetheless adequate for our judgments about circularity to be correct.

In all these ways, qualifications arise on the basis of practical interests for resisting the idea that nothing is flat, nothing is circular, and pure gold is a fiction. In each such case, we make identifications within a set of parameters derived from our interests and purposes for the case in question, and endorse in the process the idea that that some approximations to an ideal are adequate for the purposes in question, even when the ideal is identified in terms of a limit concept for measuring setups that are increasingly sensitive.

Such judgments are hostage, of course, to the adequacy of the assumed parameters. For example, if one's tolerances for flatness amount to allowing a one-inch disparity across any one-inch spatial distance in a given plane, that's not a remotely decent tolerance level for flatness. Note, though, that the fact that we can identify indefensible tolerance standards should lead us to note as well that some standards are decent standards, and thus that some tolerance standards give us close enough approximations to an ideal for a given surface to count as flat from a practical point of view.

156 CLOSE APPROXIMATIONS

A word of caution about this appeal to practical needs, interests, and purposes before extending this idea to purely intellectual endeavors, for it is tempting to treat this appeal as a kind of relativization. Instead of maintaining that a given factory makes finely machined flat surfaces for industrial applications, some will be tempted to say that what is being claimed is that, relative to the standards relevant to the practical concerns in question, the factory makes such things. This relativization should be resisted, since it undermines a proper account of disagreement. Sometimes people disagree about whether a surface is flat and whether an object is circular, and such disagreement can result from different standards for when an acceptable approximation to the model-theoretic ideal for flatness or circularity has been found. If we place these standards in the content of what is being endorsed and denied, we lose the disagreement, and that is why relativization isn't the proper way to handle the relationship between ideality in a model and approximations in reality. So, whatever we want to endorse when it comes to characterizing accuracy under the idea of suitable approximations, we cannot endorse any account that undermines facts about disagreement.

This conclusion puts stress on our attempts to line up mind, world, and language in such a way that we can specify a function from these to propositional contents that are the bearers of eternal truth-values. We begin this project with Frege, from the standpoint of an idealized language suitable for math and science, and try to extract propositional bearers of truth-value from the logical form of sentences in such a language. When we move away from ideal languages, to try to cope with deictic and other unruly elements of natural language, including ambiguity, indeterminacy, and vagueness, as well as the difference between speaker meaning and sentence meaning and the puzzling interplay between semantics and pragmatics, we can easily find ourselves in a position where a unique propositional bearer of truth-value is hard to find.

Exactly how to sort all this out is a separate project and can't be settled here. All we can do is note that one can't succeed in this project if one undermines when and where disagreements are to be found, nor can success be found by eliminating the model-theoretic idealizations that guide proper identification of approximations that are close enough to the ideal to count as being correct for the purposes at hand. This latter idea is about as prosaic, as banal, as can be when we think of practical contexts. What matters in our discussion about the relationship between skepticism and fallibilism are purely intellectual and theoretical contexts, so what is needed is to turn to the idea of when and where an approximation to the ideal is close enough to count as correct when assessed in terms of purely intellectual and theoretical concerns.

The structure of this approach has the following aspects. First there is an ideal, and second there is a recognition that the model in question is in fact an idealization of reality rather than a mere abstraction from it. In so noting, we can explain how it is that what is, from a practical point of view, a close enough approximation to the ideal can be a correct characterization of some parts of reality and not others. When we turn to purely theoretical contexts, we get a similar result. In such contexts, we ask what would count as an adequate balancing of our intellectual goals of getting to the truth and avoiding error, and once we get a good answer to that question, we can assess whether any, and which, approximations to the ideal count as close enough to be correct for such purposes. In this way the ideal guides judgment, but without implying immediately that approximations can never be close enough to be correct. To get to that conclusion we would need a separate and independent argument.

Seen in this way, we find a way to extend the idea of defensible parameters in practical contexts to the theoretical realm. That is, once we see how judgments from a practical point of view assess adequacy in terms of background standards, we are in a position to see that the same ideas can play a role in purely theoretical contexts as well.

The key to this transposition concerns the relationship between a simple claim, such as that a given table is flat and circular in shape, and the position that such a judgment, given our purely intellectual goals, interests, needs, and purposes, is a close enough approximation to ideality for these propositions to be correct. My claim is that we should endorse the idea that when the latter judgment is warranted and correct, so is the former, and the argument for this implication arises from the relationship between the practical and the theoretical. In practical contexts, we can rightly note that something is accurate enough for practical purposes, relying on the gap that exists between such practical purposes and purely theoretical or intellectual ones. But once we move to purely intellectual concerns, to say that some judgment is accurate enough for purely intellectual concerns tells us that the judgment is correct, full stop, in the same way that saying that a given claim is correct implies that claim itself. For practical contexts, because of the gap between practical interests and purely theoretical ones, we rightly distinguish between correctness, full stop, and accuracy enough for practical purposes. No such contrast can be found once we scale the summit of needs, interests, and purposes, looking at things from a purely intellectual standpoint.

From that standpoint, two items are foremost. The first is the one just argued for, where the implication from close enough approximations to truth is endorsed. The second point, though, is crucial as well, for it is the point that underlies the need for the first point. It is the point of modeling ideality for limit properties so as to be able to distinguish between ideality and reality. If ideality in the model were simply an abstraction from reality, results would be different, but ideality for flatness, circularity, and pure gold is modeled in a way that not only abstracts from reality but replaces the substances in which these properties inhere with idealized substances that are either mathematical or not subject to the vagueness and indeterminacy that is ubiquitous in a universe such as ours. As a result, we turn to relationships between substances and properties that are found in reality, looking for ones that approximate the ideal relationship between idealized substances and properties found in our model.

When we do so, pitfalls abound. One is to insist that idealized models are never any good, and if that is so, we are left with no explicit and precise idea what flatness is, what circularity involves, or what pure gold is supposed to be. So let's not fall into this trap. Once we avoid doing so, another danger looms, one where we side with Plato and insist that the only realities are those found in idealized Platonic heaven. It is here that Russell's healthy sense of reality is useful, and if the skeptic has to join forces with an exaggerated idealism of this sort in order to sustain a skeptical viewpoint, we really don't need anything beyond a Moorean shift to explain and justify rejecting the view. One more risk remains, however, even after avoiding these, for given that we can't dismiss idealized models outright, we also can't ignore the issue of what to say about the relationship between reality and ideality. On that score, I have counseled saying one thing from the standpoint of practice and something similar, but a bit different, from the standpoint of pure theory. In both cases we get approximations and resemblances between ideality in the model and reality itself, distinguishing between cases where the approximations are close enough for practical purposes and those that are close enough for purely theoretical ones. Once we get to this point, we have the viewpoint being defended here: in some cases, for purely intellectual purposes, the approximations are close enough to count as being correct.

More details to follow, but a preview of the benefits may be useful at this point. Once this viewpoint is adopted, we will be able to agree with the skeptic that there is an identifiable limit concept which we always or typically fall short of, but we will also be able to hold that some of our current judgments are close enough approximations to that ideal to be correct. In response, the skeptic can insist that if we used more stringent setups, we'd detect inadequacies that would render these judgments incorrect, and with that point, we will agree. At the same time, though, we may insist that the correctness of a judgment arises in terms of some set of interests and purposes, and so long as these interests and purposes are both appropriate and purely theoretical, these judgments can both be correct and also be acknowledged to fall short of ideality. They are thereby close enough approximations to the ideal to be correct, while at the same time being less than what we ideally want them to be. So the skeptical standard is important in spite of not rendering every knowledge claim incorrect.

Regarding the details, we first need to resist identifying such an approximationist idea with a linguistic claim embodied in the Chisholmian distinction between the loose and popular sense of a term and its strict and philosophical sense.[4] Here,

---

[4] Chisholm distinguishes these two senses in his discussion of identity in Chisholm (1969). It is worth noting, however, that the distinction gets perplexing once we attend to details involving application to specific cases. Chisholm claims that we find the former use of a term when identity across time is essentially defeasible and conventional, as when we question whether we have the same ship in

though, the approximationist idea isn't about distinguishing between careful and sloppy language, since it isn't about language at all. Instead, it is about explicit and precise model-theoretic accounts of ideality and the ways in which reality approximates such a model. That is, instead of trying to derive philosophical conclusions from premises about language and its features, we focus on the features of reality we are attempting to understand, encountering the need for an assumed model that renders explicit and precise the ideal form for that feature. We can then investigate to see how reality stands with respect to the feature in question, and ask what approximations to the ideal count as accurate or correct.

The important point to note here about this appeal to accuracy is that it has both practical and theoretical interpretations. As we saw above, there are practical parameters relative to which sloppy intonation and careless carpentry are good enough, or so the jokes would have it. But there are also purely intellectual interests and parameters, and when these are properly used, the issue of accuracy concerns the correctness of our judgments about the matter under investigation from such a point of view. So the approximationist idea isn't simply a crude pragmatism that replaces a concern for truth with ones about usefulness, but rather an approach that refuses to collapse the distinction between the practical and the theoretical. Whether it still counts as a version of pragmatism, I don't know, nor do I think it matters. What matters is the central ground for such an approximationist idea. The first is the needed distinction between reality and any model that identifies ideality of any kind with respect to some region of reality. The second is a rejection of nihilistic conclusion that this distinction is sufficient to show that the region of reality being investigated is in fact empty: nothing is flat, nothing is circular, nothing is gold, except in the model. In place of such nihilism we note the expectation of a gap between any model and what it models, and the accompanying value of defensible parameters for generating adequate approximations to the ideals found in the model. When these parameters are practical ones, the approximations are useful for practical purposes; when the parameters are purely intellectual ones, the approximations are capable of being correct.

In each case, the crucial question to ask concerns the difference between adequate standards and inadequate ones. In practical contexts, the point of the joke about being close enough for jazz is that there is a line that is not to be crossed in terms of intonation, and the present example is perilously close to crossing it if not already there. Moreover, when it comes to practical contexts, optionality reigns supreme. Tolerances for rocket science are vastly more restrictive than those for fine woodworking. Furthermore, we are already familiar with something similar when it comes to purely theoretical contexts as well. Statistical practices in science are regimented in terms of p-value thresholds for statistical significance, and these

---

the ship of Theseus example, whereas personal identity across time is essentially indefeasible and non-conventional. So, it would appear, we have one term with two different meanings, rather than sloppier and more precise uses of a term with the same meaning.

160 CLOSE APPROXIMATIONS

values vary considerably between, say, the social sciences and theoretical physics. In the former areas, the normal significance level is at the .05 level, whereas in the latter area, the demand is often at the five-sigma level of 3×10^{-7}.

There is another dimension of optionality that I'll mention in passing only to shelve from further discussion since settling the matter won't be needed for our project. The issue concerns the extent to which different standards can be acceptable in the same contexts. In practical contexts, the answer seems to be an obvious "yes," since we are well aware of legitimate personality differences in terms of risk takers and those who are more risk averse. The same sort of optionality may be found in purely intellectual pursuits as well, and it is one path to Permissivism.[5] We can define risk-taking in the purely intellectual sphere in terms of the competing Jamesian goals of getting to the truth and avoiding error, and the only question is whether legitimate differences can be found here as well. I argue for this view in Kvanvig (2014), but we need not rely on anything like that view here. All that is needed for present purposes is to resist the radical idea that James himself ridicules in William James (1897: Section VII), remarking that "one who says, "Better go without belief forever than believe a lie!" merely shows his own preponderant private horror of becoming a dupe." That is, all we need to do is to reject the idea that no set of purely intellectual standards can be adequate unless they discount getting to the truth entirely, so that avoiding error is the only thing of intellectual value. How exactly to apportion weightings for these competing values still needs to be determined, and in the process we may find that we must also allow different intellectual personality styles to play a role in any given context. Such a result will complicate the story of determining where and when epistemic standards count as legitimate for determining when approximations are close enough to the ideal to count as correct, but complication, even if inconvenient, leaves the same basic story in place.

According to that story, the points made concerning precision from a practical point of view extend quite naturally to purely theoretical concerns about which cognitive attitudes to take. For suppose a given weighting of intellectual goals doesn't weight avoidance of error so strongly as to demand aversion to any and every cognitive attitude of belief or high credence. Any such weighting will make some approximations close enough to be correct, and rule others out. Moreover, acknowledging the approximation element involves a concurrent recognition that things could be better, epistemically speaking. So, the standards can be acceptable and the cognitive results correct, in combination with this recognition.

Moreover, this analogy is not one concerning epistemic normativity, but epistemic axiology as well. In the practical sphere, we found a notion of adequacy and

---

[5] The term originates in White (2005), and is opposed by defenders of a Uniqueness Thesis, as first articulated in Feldman (2007). The literature on the subject has grown enormously over the past nearly two decades, and a good overview of the literature and arguments can be found in Horowitz et al. (forthcoming).

accuracy of judgment related to defensible practical standards for action and judgment. In the process of applying such defensible standards, we can distinguish circles from ovals, contaminated samples of gold from uncontaminated, and flat tables from those with undulations. The idea is that the judgments are accurate relative to the defensible practical parameters that are in place, rather than being adequate somehow in spite of being inaccurate relative to those standards. Such accuracy isn't a matter of instantiating a model-theoretic ideal, but rather as a matter of approximating in reality something that is ideal, and in a way that is close enough to the ideal to be accurate, because of the adequacy of the practical parameters governing the judgment. So when we replace these practical parameters with purely intellectual ones, the transposition yields the same kinds of results, where the accuracy of a purely intellectual judgment is for it to be correct, even though this correctness involves an approximation to a model-theoretic ideal in terms of the weighting of the values of getting to the truth and avoiding error that are involved in the approximation.

This position is obviously fully fallibilistic, and what remains is to see why and how on this view one should expect concessive attitudes and attributions to be infelicitous. The key to such a prediction involves seeing the acceptability of a given weighting of epistemic goals, while at the same acknowledging the existence of a gold standard in comparison to which one's current condition only approximates. A more demanding weighting is not mandatory, but one signals a recognition of what ideality involves by admitting the possibility of error. So even when we reject the idea that all adequate standards discount entirely the value of getting to the truth, we also recognize the ideality involved in theory development on behalf of the skeptic. The position we find ourselves in is something like that of people whose levels of charitable giving are modest, and who recognize the exemplary efforts of those who give away half of their income to worthy causes. In such cases, it is natural to think both that one gave enough, but that maybe one should have given more.

Two points are noteworthy about the charity case. First, we acknowledge and respect the standards of the person who gives more, so we are not in the position of dismissing these standards as somehow inappropriate or excessive. Second, the attitude of thinking that one has done one's duty but that maybe one should have done more, prompts the same perplexity we find in concessive knowledge attributions. To hear someone voice the conjunction is jarring: if you think you maybe should give more, maybe you should give more! And, it goes without saying, if you should give more, you haven't yet done your duty.

The variability of the standards, whether epistemic or moral, that leads to the conjunctions in question thus also predicts their infelicity. In this way, it is a version of sensitive fallibilism, to be contrasted with other versions of fallibilism that aim to accommodate the infelicity data but do not predict it. Given the explanatory superiority of approaches to data that predict rather than merely

162 CLOSE APPROXIMATIONS

accommodate, this aspect of approximationism gives it an advantage over any version of complacent fallibilism.

The central question for this version of sensitive fallibilism concerns the idea that the approximations to the ideal are close enough to count as correct. Here three points are central. The first point is has already been noted, which is that the epistemic standards underlying the approximations in question are fully adequate, falling with the range of acceptable balancings of risk and reward for the goals of getting to the truth and avoiding error.

A legitimate concern about this point alone is that there may be a difference between the level of epistemic support needed to warrant full belief, and the level of epistemic support required for knowledge. That is, one might hold that there is a property of justification, rationality, or warrant that is both weaker than what is needed for knowledge, but which is also fully adequate in terms of providing grounds for belief. If so, the first point by itself will not license the claim that the approximations are close enough to count as correct when those claims are about knowledge rather than justification.

A second point provides a response to this concern, even granting that described difference between epistemically normative properties. This point involves the functional role that infallible knowledge plays, and the way in which the approximations to this ideal share this functional role. For knowledge, whether or not infallible, plays a role in norms of assertion, practical reasoning, and action, as well as in the norms that govern inquiry itself. An idealized cognizer, bearing the enhancements of ordinary capacities, is in a perfect position, epistemically speaking, to assert sincerely what is believed, to use what is believed in practical reasoning, to act on the basis of it, and legitimately to close off further inquiry on the matter. These same roles are found in approximations to ideality found in ordinary knowledge claims, legitimating closure of inquiry as well as providing adequate grounds related to norms of assertion, practical reasoning, and action. For epistemically normative properties that fall short of what is needed for knowledge, these functional roles can remain absent. So, when we find a level of support that grounds these functional roles, we have good reason to view that level of support in terms of the normativity involved in knowledge, thereby also finding good reasons for identifying the approximations in question as close enough to the ideal to count as correct.

The final point to note is a Moorean one, noting how obvious it is that we know many things while insisting that a good methodological principle is to never give up the more obvious for the less obvious. Note as well that this Moorean component of the view can be incorporated without also adopting a dismissive or complacent attitude toward skepticism. Instead, it insists on a more sensitive version of fallibilism that embraces the infallibilist tinge in knowledge, the importance of knowledge arising through the functional role it plays, and an account of the nature of knowledge developed by recognizing how obvious it is that we know many things. It recognizes the ideality involved in skeptical standards, but insists that not every adequate approach to getting to the truth and avoiding error has to discount entirely the value of getting to the truth, thereby opening up the possibility of adequate standards that render a judgment correct in spite of being only an approximation to an ideal. By combining these elements, we find an explanation for why the fallible approximations to the infallible ideal are close enough to be correct.

For those fully versed in contemporary epistemology, this view might sound familiar, for there is a position called "Assumptionalism" that has been defended in recent years. In Sherman and Harman (2011), we find an argument for the view that all of our knowledge rests on assumptions that are being made, and one might wonder whether the role that standards play in the Approximationist view defended here is just that of an assumption, making the present view a special version of Assumptionalism. Let's take up this issue in the final substantive section of this chapter, and I'll argue that the present view is not a version of Assumptionalism, and I'll also argue the ways the two views differ shows that the former is preferable to the latter.

6.3 On the Relation to Assumptionalism

Brett Sherman and Gilbert Harman summarize their Assumptionalist view as follows: "To sum up, we have argued that knowledge often rests on assumptions that you are justified in making even though you do not know those assumptions" (Sherman and Harman, 2011, 140). On this view, knowing involves and rests on things taken for granted, and the examples used often focus on cases of knowledge of the future. Perhaps you know that you will not be able to afford an African safari vacation next summer, even though you don't know, but merely take for granted, that you won't win the lottery. Or perhaps you don't know that your flight won't crash, but merely take for granted that it won't, and thus still know that your be at your arrival gate soon. Or once more, conference lovers might know they'll be in Paris next June, but don't know that they won't die before then.

Other examples they use involve typical skeptical scenarios and examples that are of concern for those attracted to closure principles in epistemology. You know that your car is parked in front of your house even though you don't know that it hasn't been stolen since you last saw it. More generally, you know things about cars, friends, trips, and schedules without knowing that you're not a brain in a vat and without knowing that you're not dreaming (in the way skeptical scenarios are developed so as to purportedly imply that no such knowledge is compatible with these skeptical hypotheses).

In light of these claims about Assumptionalism, the bulk of their discussion turns to the matter of closure principles in epistemology and to the issue of concessive knowledge attributions and attitudes. For the former, the authors argue against closure principles, and for the latter, they argue in favor of a pragmatic account of infelicity that relies on a notion of relevance, and against a semantic account of such infelicity.

Historical precedent for such a view, at least in the twentieth century, traces to the later Wittgensteinian viewpoint in Wittgenstein (1969). It is generally unproductive to try to elicit and investigate details in the thought of an avowedly anti-theory philosopher, since that is an explicitly theoretical project, so we might look for other similar views instead. One such view is Laurence BonJour's version of coherentism (BonJour (1985). As BonJour develops the view, the possibility of knowledge turns out to rest on a "presumption" that is not known to be true. This presumption is the Doxastic Presumption, according to which, in order to have any justified beliefs at all, a cognizer "must ... have an adequate grasp of his total system of beliefs" (BonJour, 1985, 102).

The difference between this view and the Sherman/Harman view is that the latter authors deny skeptical consequences for relying on assumptions not known to be true, whereas BonJour grants the skeptical implications of the fact that cognizers simply don't satisfy the Doxastic Presumption. In this respect, Assumptionalism can count as a version of fallibilism, whereas the status of BonJour's coherentism is decidedly more skeptical. My inclination is simply to count it as a version of skepticism, and thus a view to put aside in trying to determining whether a version of sensitive fallibilism can be found or whether only a complacent one is defensible.

For this task, the question of closure isn't as central as the question of concessions, so I'll ignore the closure issue in what follows. Regarding the issue of concessions, it is worth noting that the account Sherman and Harman give provides a nice way of accommodating the data of infelicity, but as to the question of predicting it, there is no reason to think their view has resources to make such a prediction. So, in this respect it lacks a feature of sensitive fallibilism that is desirable and found in Approximationism.

The central issue, though, is whether the view defended here is really a version of the view defended by Sherman and Harman, and the similarities are noteworthy. Note, for example, that the view presented here is similar to Assumptionalism in that both accounts explain the presence of knowledge at least partially in terms of things not known to be true. Even so, the dissimilarities show that Assumptionalism is a different view from the Approximationist view defended here. The central difference is that epistemic standards involving appropriate risk/reward relationships concerning the epistemic goal are not themselves to be understood in terms of doxastic states with propositional content nor of related cognitive states such as acceptances or assumptions. These standards could come to be endorsed or believed or accepted or assumed, but they need not have such a status in order to play the role assigned to them.

There is one caveat to note in this explanation of how Approximationism is different from Assumptionalism, for our account of the significance of skepticism relies on some assumptions that were used for the purpose of showing how a skeptic can characterize the high standard for defeasible reasoning. Characterizing this standard assumed that we don't need to deny bivalence to avoid the sea battle argument for Logical Fatalism and that we aren't required somehow to endorse the metaphysical incompleteness of the world. So it would be a mistake to try to distance the view presented here from Assumptionalism by claiming that assumptions play no role in our theory.

Nonetheless, the role these assumptions play doesn't risk turning Approximationism into a version of Assumptionalism. To see why, we can first remind ourselves of the part of the task to which these assumptions are relevant. That part of the task was to uncover and address a special epistemological worry about knowledge of the future and show how to resolve it in a way that doesn't allow Moorean dismissiveness of skepticism to succeed. In the process, we have relied on some semantic and metaphysical assumptions, but these assumptions play their role at a stage prior to the development of Approximationism, the role of motivating the need for such a version of sensitive fallibilism.

I note, though, that these assumptions still pose a bit of an indirect threat to our project, for if they are abandoned the motivation for Approximationism awaits development of the skeptical position along a different theoretical path. Without such development, nothing beyond complacent fallibilism would be needed, and so the central reason in favor of Approximationism over complacent versions of fallibilism would be lost. Moreover, even if the semantic and metaphysical assumptions are true, they can play their role only by falling into a category for which the skeptical ideal can be characterized as well. Here the idea is that if the assumptions are true, they are necessarily true, and we have also been assuming that characterizing the skeptical ideal with respect to necessary truths can be handled adequately. This qualm may seem less significant than it really is, for it is easy to conflate the skeptical ideal regarding necessary truths with the ideal for logical truths. The latter may pose no serious problems in virtue of some link between logical truth and deducibility, but that alone won't give us what we need for non-logical necessary truths. We have not broached this subject of necessary truths here, however, choosing to focus on the more obviously problematic issue about contingent truths the discovery of which would need to rely on defeasible reasoning. We thus focused especially on knowing the future, as compared to past and present, and in that context, we paid little attention to the problem of what perfect knowledge of necessary truth might be like. More detailed investigation of that problem would have to treat knowledge on non-logical necessary truth on the model of knowledge of axioms, where rational intuition played the central role, and as with the idealizations regarding perception, memory, and testimony, nothing presented here offers any guarantee of success for such idealizations. The explanation given here

166 CLOSE APPROXIMATIONS

of perfect knowledge of the future presumes that such a story can be given, but this assumption isn't part of the epistemology itself, but rather an assumption to be discharged at some point in order to sustain the epistemology. So in this sense, a full justification of the view articulated here, together with the story of its significance, depends on this further assumption that the skeptical ideal regarding knowledge of necessary truths can be given.

6.4 Conclusion

We thus have found a version of fallibilism that is sensitive both to the theory development proposed on behalf of skepticism and to the resulting need for an account that predicts the infelicity of concessive attitudes and attributions. It is thus fully a version of fallibilism, one that never gets to the point of dismissing skepticism entirely, but also not succumbing to it. It does not succumb to it because it also has the resources to explain why the approximations, in light of the adequacy of the epistemic risk and reward weightings, are close enough to the ideal to count as correct.

What this version of fallibilism thereby undergirds is significance for skepticism that does not depend on the truth of the view nor on the soundness of the arguments for it. Instead, it explains the value of skepticism in terms of the constant reminder it provides that our epistemic efforts are rarely if ever ideal. This aspect of the view has important ramifications for broader normative dimensions of life, a discussion of which will conclude our investigation in the final chapter.

Before turning to that discussion, however, a brief summary of the claims in the chapter will be useful, for it is easy to lose sight of the overall themes when most of the discussion is about the details of the view. At the more general level, the first point to note is that the version of fallibilism pursued here is one that takes seriously the infallibilist tinge in knowledge. The view is not simply one where we identify a range of evidential standards that can be adequate and then conclude that the skeptical standard that places enormous disvalue on leaving open whether or not one is in error. Instead, this part of the view is added to a more basic story to reveal how we get to the conclusion that some approximations are close enough to the ideal to be correct. In between this ultimate conclusion and the Gricean accommodation of the infelicity of concessive attitudes and attributions is the prediction of this infelicity in terms of the notion of approximations.

The moving parts of the theory start from a demand for theoretical development on behalf of skepticism. Once we see how such development can proceed, we acknowledge that skepticism is not mere fodder for reflective equilibrium, but a substantive epistemological position with intuitive advantages in terms of predicting and explaining the infallibilist tinge in knowledge and the related infelicity of concessive attitudes and attributions about knowledge. We thus seek a more sensitive version of fallibilism that doesn't treat this infelicity in terms of a false presupposition arising on the basis of Gricean maxims honored in conversation with skeptics.

Instead, a different Gricean approach is needed, and one is available in terms of Gricean relevance, accommodating the infelicity data by noting that pointing out the possibilities of error satisfies the relevance demand only if the possibilities of error are significant enough to be relevant. Thus develops our first version of a more sensitive fallibilism, but one with a disadvantage that would be nice to remedy. The disadvantage is that this view only accommodates but does not predict the infelicity data. A more attractive version of sensitive fallibilism would be one that has this predictive capacity.

The final step in the development of this more sensitive version of fallibilism is in terms of adequate weightings of the competing goals of getting to the truth and avoiding error, a point that leaves intact the prediction of infelicity but also introduces the possibility of approximations to an ideal that are close enough to count as correct. Central to this approximationist point is the model-theoretic resistance to the claims that if something is flat, it can have no surface variance at all, and if something is pure gold, it has no admixture of anything else. Each of these claims has some truth in it, and so does the claim that if you know, you can't be wrong. What these claims have in common is the way in which they point to an ideal that is model-theoretic in nature, and regarding which we find nearer and more distant approximations when looking at actual phenomena. It may be that this point about models and ideality holds more generally, so that scientific models in general are not to be understood in terms of mere abstractions from reality, as Catherine Elgin has argued,[6] but we need not endorse the more general claim in order to see why the ideas concerning absoluteness for the properties involved in our discussion involve ideal models. It is this ideality that underlies the central role of approximations in the present account. Claims concerning knowledge, unlike epistemically normative claims about justification, rationality, warrant, or positive epistemic status, never lose their status as approximations to an ideal. So the move from merely accommodating the infelicity data to predicting it in a way that avoids embracing skepticism is accomplishment by embracing Approximationism of a sort that also includes the idea that our knowledge is less than ideal but nonetheless close enough to the ideal for judgments and attributions of knowledge to be correct.

We turn then to a concluding chapter to address the relationship between this view and the broader picture of the normative dimensions of human life that include but are not limited to the purely intellectual concerns appealed to in developing this version of Approximationism.

---

[6] In Elgin (2017) as well as the earlier Elgin (2009).

Chapter 7
Conclusion

7.1 Introduction

We began from a standpoint quite common in twentieth-century epistemology, that of the commonsense epistemology that traces to Thomas Reid in the seventeenth century and promulgated in the twentieth century by G.E. Moore and Roderick Chisholm. Central to this tradition is the Moorean shift, which I characterize in terms of a methodological principle of never giving up the more obvious for the less obvious. One historical consequence of this principle is a dismissive attitude toward skepticism, arising from the idea that it is more obvious that we know many things than that all the premises of any argument for skepticism are true.

This tradition thus puts skepticism on a path toward being ignored because viewed as insignificant, insignificant enough to be dismissed with an offhand remark that we do, after all, know many things. In contrast with the vast majority of the history of epistemology, conversations with the skeptic and attention to skeptical arguments and doctrines became a distraction from whatever philosophical enterprises were thought worthy of attention, akin to a pastime to pursue in our downtime if at all.

Philosophy, like politics is susceptible to pendulum shifts that often look a bit like mere changes in taste, but by the 1970s, renewed attention was directed toward skepticism. This renewed attention focused both on argumentative substance on behalf of the view and also on the issue of the significance of skepticism. The key players in this revival were Peter Unger and Barry Stroud, and skepticism became more central to future discussion than it had been in earlier parts of the century.

In this revival, the key to the significance of skepticism is the power of the arguments in favor of skeptical conclusions. This approach combined with a theme arising from the later Wittgenstein about the ultimate groundlessness of belief,[1] yielding a further element in the story about why skepticism matters, one that can focus on an epistemic angst that cannot be evaded.

This historical progression is problematic in a couple respects. First, the focus on skeptical argumentation is inadequate as a response to the Moorean shift, for no matter how impressive the arguments, they won't use premises that are collectively as obvious as the claim that we know many things. Second, the focus on

---

[1] See, for example, Williams (1991) as well as the earlier Williams (1977).

Skepticism and Fallibilism. Jonathan L. Kvanvig, Oxford University Press. © Jonathan L. Kvanvig (2025).
DOI: 10.1093/9780198924821.003.0007

argumentation makes skepticism a very thin position, philosophically speaking. For comparison, imagine if foundationalism were nothing more than a collection of variations on a regress argument for the conclusion that knowledge requires a foundation. Such a conclusion might be a good place to start developing a foundationalist epistemology, and historically it played just such a role, and it is in such theory development that we should expect to find something of philosophical significance. The same is true of skepticism. Theory development is essential to philosophical significance, and the only way to avoid the implications of the Moorean shift that makes skepticism and the arguments for a skeptical conclusion little more than fodder for reflective equilibrium.

Most important here, though, is that if such theory development can be found, the significance of skepticism will not depend on the truth of skepticism, nor will the significance that is found be something that needs to prompt passional negativity of any sort. Instead, the significance of skepticism arises in the role it plays in sustaining a life of virtue. Here in this concluding chapter I want to focus on this more general point, one that we have reached through the conclusions of previous chapters, though it never took center stage in any of them. So here we focus directly on it.

7.2 Sensitive Fallibilism, Virtue Epistemology, and Living Well

We've noted that there is little motivation for a sensitive version of fallibilism in the absence of theory development in support of skeptical arguments and conclusions. For it is only in the face of such development that we find motivation for a version of fallibilism that not only accommodates but also predicts the infelicity of concessive attitudes and attributions. Once theory development occurs, the centrality of the notion of approximations to an ideal becomes a central feature of the kind of fallibilism best suited to resist skepticism.

Note, however, that the resistance also incorporates an acknowledgment about the ideality expressed by skeptical theory development. That is the point of the approximations involved in this version of fallibilism. The value of skepticism thus arises in the form of a constant reminder that even our best efforts at finding the truth and avoiding error are not ideal. It thus encourages a focus away from self-satisfaction and any accompanying inflated view of oneself and one's community when it comes to our purely intellectual abilities. Instead, it fosters a pattern of attention that never loses sight of the ways in which our search for truth rely on approximations to an ideal.

In this way, a fruitful interaction with skepticism gives rise to the intellectual virtue of humility, where such a virtue is one concerning the patterns of attention a person displays. This first aspect of the significance of skepticism, then, involves the way in which skeptical thought prompts the development of

170 CONCLUSION

a virtue epistemology that places intellectual humility at its center. It need not be a virtue epistemology that attempts to explain epistemic normativity in terms of the virtues,[2] but will involve the central claim that no understanding of the life of the mind can be complete without a virtue-theoretic component.[3]

It would go beyond current needs to present a full treatment of humility,[4] but a few brief points will help in appreciating the interplay of sensitive fallibilism with the attentional elements involved in humility within the domain of epistemology, as well as showing how such features of our epistemology extend quite readily to the broader normative context of general human welfare. Humility involves, not only awareness of one's limitations, but also, as Whitcomb et al. (2015, 12) puts it, a "proper attentiveness to, and owning of, one's intellectual limitations."

The language of attention is especially noteworthy in this context. Central to the sensitive fallibilism defended here is the way in which judgments about ordinary knowledge fall into the category of approximations of an ideal. In this way, these judgments, when properly understood, point to limitations in our discoveries, accomplishments, and abilities. This feature of sensitive fallibilism thereby fosters the attentional feature that is crucial for understanding the virtue of humility.

This attentional feature of humility differs from other cognitive possibilities such as awareness or acknowledgment. It puts humility in a class of virtues of attention, described by Nicolas Bommarito as follows:

> The virtues of attention are virtues that are rooted in how we direct our attention. These virtues are sometimes moral but not always. It is an academic virtue of attention to be able to focus one's attention on a long and technical lecture. It is an aesthetic virtue of attention for one to pay attention to the relationship between the narrative and shot composition in a film. Gratitude is a moral virtue of attention because it involves directing one's attention to the value of what someone else has done for us. (Bommarito, 2013, 100)

Bommarito's account of humility, for which he uses the term "modesty", proceeds in two steps, as follows:

> [I]t is necessary to have a good quality to be modest about. Contrary to most contemporary views, it is not necessary to underestimate the good quality nor is it necessary to have an accurate assessment. Instead, what is necessary is to direct one's conscious attention in certain ways—away from the trait or its value or toward the outside causes and conditions that played a role in developing it.

---

[2] As in, for example, Zagzebski (1996), Sosa (2007), and Greco (2010).

[3] As I argue in Kvanvig (1992) and is articulated in more detail by a large number of philosophers in the virtue-theoretic traditional, including Baehr (2011) and Morton (2012).

[4] See Kvanvig (2018) for more extensive discussion.

7.2 SENSITIVE FALLIBILISM, VIRTUE EPISTEMOLOGY, AND LIVING WELL   171

> Attending in these ways, however, is not sufficient for modesty; it must happen for the right reasons. (Bommarito, 2013, 103)

The central idea here is that humility involves putting the focus of attention elsewhere than on one's successes or abilities, and a humble person is disposed to focus in this direction. To be humble is to be disposed toward such exercises of attention, in virtue of the commitments and stances one affirms. Such an attentional focus is clearly recommended by a sensitive fallibilism that makes ordinary knowledge fall into the category of things that are less than ideal from a purely intellectual point of view.

These points generalize outside purely intellectual contexts, where we find significant human virtues that attend to our limitations, leading to a point of view that maintains that a well-lived life is best pursued by understanding appropriate limits on such a life.[5] It is to this feature of living well to which ancient skepticism enjoined us to attend, and endorsing sensitive fallibilism is one step closer to a more general change in focus involved in acknowledging our limitations in the pursuit of a good life. Ancient skeptics plumped for a different view of the distance between our capacities and the ideal, of course, but the motivation is the same.

Most every virtue has its downside, which can appear in the form of a virtue in excess, and humility is no different. So this virtue cannot be linked in isolation to living well, but must be cultivated in the process of cultivating other virtues as well. The downside of an excessive attentiveness to one's limitations is a lack of accomplishment. Here the theory development engaged in on behalf of skepticism reveals an ideal that is worthy of guiding our inquiry, even if it is an ideal that we are only able to approximate. In this respect, it fulfills the function of encouraging the balancing virtue for humility of ordinary, mundane faith, an idea I develop in Kvanvig (2018). The slogan for this understanding of faith is that it is a disposition to act in service of an ideal.

An initial way of thinking about this ideal for cognition is in terms of the epistemic goal of getting to the truth and avoiding error. This goal is worthy of attention, but a moment's reflection reveals that it isn't merely getting to the truth that we are after, but something stronger. We not only aim at latching onto the truth, but finding it, discovering it, detecting it, and uncovering it. It is not hard to see both the factive element in these terms, but also their epistemic component. We aim at not merely being correct, but also at knowledge and understanding. We want the level of surety that comes with knowing, and it is at this point that whatever epistemic goals we have become enmeshed with the skeptical account of ideality for inquiry. The theory development of a skeptical approach to knowledge reveals a level of surety that is ideal, and our interests in epistemic surety involve aiming at the best that can be achieved.

---

[5] For a recent and relevant monograph, see McPherson, (2022).

172 CONCLUSION

It is a common trope that nothing real is ideal, and it is tempting to read into such ideas a strong enough modal component to justify adopting weaker goals. Such a conclusion, however, isn't supported by endorsing that what is ideal can't be found in reality, for there are notions of impossibility that don't justify abandoning our goals. For example, some students say they just can't learn logic, and though there may be some notion of impossibility on which this is true, it's typically not one that justifies aiming for a high F rather than a passing grade. Moreover, even when the ideal is unreachable, we make sense of improvements by identifying the ideal toward which we are reaching. In the process, the ideal plays the teleological role noted, even if there is an important sense in which it is unachievable for cognizers with our kinds of limitations.

It is of the nature of ideals to have an important role that doesn't require us to settle the issue of whether the ideal can be realized. We want a society that is perfectly just, and should pursue it without waiting on some settling of the question of whether such a society is possible. Just so in intellectual matters: the ideality identified plays an important role in the aim of inquiry, and being disposed to engage in activity in pursuit of this ideal is a worthy endeavor, and a display of the kind of ordinary, mundane faith that provides a proper counterbalance to any inclination against trying that might come from excessive intellectual humility.

So, the ideal with respect to our cognitive efforts at finding the truth and avoiding error is just what the skeptical position aims to articulate, and our efforts at finding the truth aren't (or at least shouldn't be) in the form of mere guesses or likely suspicions: we want to find the truth and do it in the most effective way we can. In doing so, we can attend to skeptical pedagogy not to overestimate our capacities, but we will also keep trying, for it is ideal worthy of acting in service of.

The central significance of skepticism is thus that of a provocateur, goading us toward a proper balance of faith and humility in our intellectual lives. This result wouldn't matter much if these virtues were mere optional accoutrements to a life well lived, akin to the virtue of being witty. This topic is typically taken up when discussing the four cardinal virtues of prudence, justice, temperance, and fortitude. In some way or other, these virtues are supposed to be foundational for a well-lived life, whereby all other virtues hinge on them in some way or other. Understood in this way, the virtues of faith and humility appear to be more central to a well-lived life than other virtues such as cleanliness, joyfulness, loyalty, or friendliness.

In this respect, it is worth considering the Stoic virtue of *apatheia*. Living a life freed from perturbations from the passions sounds like a very nice idea, and an admirable trait for those who have it. In Stoic thought, it is the ideal rational capacity for a well-lived life, and as such, might be urged as a cardinal virtue together with the classic four already mentioned. Perhaps it is, but even if this status is withheld for some reason or another, it provides a good analogy for the explanation given of the importance of the balancing virtues of faith and humility. For such

7.2 SENSITIVE FALLIBILISM, VIRTUE EPISTEMOLOGY, AND LIVING WELL   173

a balance has in its favor precisely the sorts of considerations that Stoics propose for *apatheia*. So it is at an interesting idea to propose that these virtues count as foundational for a well-lived life.

Suspicions are in order here, however, for the very idea of a foundational virtue may be mistaken. We are familiar enough with the holistic nature of normativity in general to wonder whether and why the kind of normativity involved in the virtues should be any different. With respect to general normativity, it is commonplace to note that nearly anything can be given up and yet positive normative status be retained if enough alterations are made elsewhere in the relevant normative system. This consequence of the Quine/Duhem Thesis, if true and extended to the domain of the virtues themselves, would counsel against the idea that there are any cardinal virtues, though there still could be gradations of significance to be found in terms of how radical the adjustments would need to be elsewhere in the relevant system to accommodate the loss of the more important virtues.

To be fair to the tradition of looking for foundational virtues, it isn't quite clear in Quine whether rational revisability is universal. He says so directly, but other things he says conflict with the explicit avowal. First, the avowals: (i) in "Two Dogmas of Empiricism," he says, "no statement is immune to revision" (Quine, 1951, 43), and (ii) nearly two decades later, he writes, "Logic is in principle no less open to revision than quantum mechanics or the theory of relativity" (Quine, 1970, 100). Yet, these claims are in tension with Quinean points about radical translation. Quine's "save the obvious" principle about translation (Quine, 1970, 82) suggests a different position, one that he explicitly voices in claiming that the principles of classical logic are "either obvious or can be reached from obvious truths by a sequence of individually obvious steps" (Quine, 1970, 83). So, if we encounter seeming revisions of logic, we should, as good translators, translate them away. And if we turn the social context of translation toward the more personal context of Davidsonian interpretation, perhaps we should do so with our own statements and attitudes as well. Such ideas lead Susan Haack to claim that, for Quine, "apparent conflict in logic should always be accounted the result of mistranslation" (Haack, 1996, 14), implying the regrettable thesis that no substantive philosophy of logic is even possible once transposed into the Davidsonian context of radical interpretation.

There is no need to resolve this tension in Quine's thought,[6] for the only point to note here is that, just as there may be no rationally unrevisable principles of logic, there may also be no special virtues that have irreplaceable status in a well-lived life. It is for this reason that I won't spend much time trying to defend adding faith and humility to the list of cardinal virtues. For present purposes, then, I'll settle for

---

[6] For a recent and careful effort to resolve the tension in favor of universal rational revisability, see Bryant (2017).

174 CONCLUSION

noting that there is at least a *pro tanto* case for listing these virtues among the most important, even if the holistic character of normativity undermines their status as essential to living well.

7.3 Summing Up

The challenge to skepticism, and the challenge from skepticism, are thus both present in an adequate epistemology. Skeptics owe us much more than mere argument and conclusion, for if that is all that can be mustered, it can be accommodated through the usual methods aimed at reflective equilibrium and driven by the Moorean motto of never giving up the more obvious for the less obvious.

Skeptics, though, are not stuck in this impoverished condition, and development of a skeptical position can be done. The most natural starting point for such theory development is in the context of mathematical and logical proofs, for it is here that the idea of evidential premises that guarantee the truth of the conclusion is most at home. This development must be extended to other areas, of course, for the guarantee in question is never any better than whatever guarantees we can find for the truth of the evidential premises. On pain of vicious regress—shelving for the present a needed rebuttal of the recent accounts of infinitism[7] that deny said viciousness—we need some account of rational intuition that explains how the full control over the possibility of error is possible for this capacity.

Further extensions are needed for other capacities that are different in kind from rational intuition and truth-preserving reasoning. Skeptical theory development needs to address how full control over the possibility of error is possible for ordinary perception, for memory, and for testimony. As before, failure at this task robs skepticism of its importance, turning it into an impostor in the lineup of epistemologies to be taken seriously.

Yet, even if these tasks are completed—and our discussion has shown where and how to begin to do so, even if there is still more work to be done—the strongest challenge to skeptical theory development is found elsewhere. It comes from purported knowledge of the future that depend essentially of defeasible reasoning. Among our cognitive capacities is this capacity to engage in defeasible reasoning, and if skeptical theory development can't be found in this arena, there will be no hope for the needed explanation of how full control over the possibilities of error can be found across all of the skills, capacities, and abilities we possess for getting to the truth and avoiding error. The promise of a skepticism to be taken seriously would be a mere chimera, something arising from an epistemic imperialism that is easily dismissed. It would relegate skepticism to the exile it regrettably experienced through too much of twentieth-century epistemology.

---

[7] See, especially, Klein (1999), Klein (2005b), Klein (2007a), Klein (2007a), and Klein (2011).

Even worse, the argument from defeasible reasoning to the idea that chances or possibilities of error are ineliminable for such reasoning can seem compelling. I know it did for me, for most of my career, and for this reason, I tended to agree with Moore and commonsense epistemology that skepticism was obviously false and of little relevance to the work needed to develop an adequate epistemology. As we have seen, however, the idea of defeasible reasoning doesn't foreclose the possibility of having full control over whether or not one finds the truth and avoids error, and so the axiological need for skeptics to explain themselves can be addressed with respect to this capacity just as much as it can be addressed with reference to the capacities noted above.

The result of this theory development is pressure on fallibilism to move away from complacency. Complacency arises when the infallibilist tinge in knowledge is dismissed by appeal to false presuppositions arising from conversations with the skeptic, but it can also arise less egregiously when a fallibilism attempts only to explain away the infallibilist tinge. A more sensitive fallibilism will want not only to accommodate this tinge, but also to predict it, and to do all of this without abandoning fallibilism itself.

That is exactly what this defense of Approximationism claims. The infallibilist tinge is predicted because it is part of this position that our attributions and attitudes about knowledge are typically and perhaps only approximations of an unachieved ideal, that ideal that skeptics have clarified for us. Even so, fallibilism is to be retained, because approximations can also be close enough to an ideal for them to be correct. Whether they are close enough is a function of the goals, purposes, and interests behind the approximations and whether the standards that embody them are rationally adequate to the context in which inquiry and judgment occur. When the relevant standards are purely intellectual, we can let the goal of truth over error stand proxy for whatever other epistemic goals one might wish to defend, for the same points will be transposable to these other options as well.

When it comes to the goal of getting to the truth and avoiding error, variability is to be expected when it comes to various risk/reward weightings of these competing goals, just as it is when we theorize about practical reasoning and note the variety of acceptable weightings for risk over reward in the practical sphere. So even if it can be rationally permissible to weight avoiding error so highly that suspicion reigns in every domain, that weighting is not mandatory. Other weightings that acknowledge our talents and abilities for discernment will value getting to the truth as well, thereby avoiding the pessimistic result of viewing all approximations of the ideal as inadequate. Hence, once we see this rather obvious point—that there is no mandatory risk/reward attitude for all rational cognizers—we can recognize how an approximation to an ideal can be close enough to be correct, without abandoning the recognition as well that even our best efforts fall short of perfection.

176 CONCLUSION

The result is that skepticism about knowledge, whether past, present, or future, is not an idle position of little importance. Instead, there is a clear ideal to which the skeptic calls our attention, and the response we hope to provide is that our own accomplishments with respect to trying to figure out what has happened, what is happening, and what will happen are close enough approximations to the ideal to count as knowledge. Given such a defense, we will have shown that non-complacent fallibilism about knowledge is possible, one that acknowledges the tinge of infallibilism in knowledge without succumbing to skeptical despair that this important cognitive achievement is beyond our reach.

Moreover, this role for skepticism need not lead to despair, angst, or anxiety,[8] but can be affirming instead. For in not embracing the epistemic standards that maximize the value avoidance of error over that of finding the truth, we can live in service of a goal that includes a strong role for finding and discovering the truth while at the same time approaching the search while attending to the fact that our results rarely if ever rise to the gold standard level of perfection that the skeptic has explained. The results we achieve are approximations of perfection, but they can also be close enough approximations to count as correct. They have this feature when the epistemic standards used are adequate, and where the investigation or inquiry yields information sufficient to justify closure of inquiry on the subject, even if better information could still be pursued and open-mindedness remains in order about the prospect of further learning that would undermine current opinion. Thus is the story of sensitive fallibilism told, a fallibilism that embraces aspects of skepticism in a way that contributes to an intellectually virtuous approach to finding the truth, while at the same time resisting skepticism in the end.

---

[8] For expression of such a view, see Pritchard (2015).

Bibliography

Alchourrón, Carlos E., Peter Gärdenfors, and David Makinson. 1982. "On the Logic of Theory Change: Contraction Functions and Their Associated Revision Functions." *Theoria* 48 (1): 14–37. https://dx.doi.org/10.1111/j.1755-2567.1982.tb00480.x.

Alston, William P. 1993. *Perceiving God: The Epistemology of Religious Experience*. Ithaca: Cornell University Press.

Armstrong, D.M. 1983. *What is a Law of Nature?* Cambridge: Cambridge University Press.

Armstrong, D.M., C.B. Martin, and U.T. Place. 1996. *Dispositions: A Debate*. New York: Routledge.

Austin, J.L. 1946. "Symposium: Other Minds." *Aristotelian Society Supplementary Volume* 20 (1): 122–197. https://dx.doi.org/10.1093/aristoteliansupp/20.1.122.

Ayer, A.J. 1936. *Language, Truth and Logic*. London: Victor Gollancz.

Baehr, Jason. 2011. *The Inquiring Mind: On Intellectual Virtues and Virtue Epistemology*. Oxford: Oxford University Press.

Barnes, Jonathan. 1982. "The Beliefs of a Pyrrhonist." *Proceedings of the Cambridge Philological Society* N.S. 28: 1–29.

Benbaji, Hagit. 2009. "On the Pragmatic Explanation of Concessive Knowledge Attributions." *Southern Journal of Philosophy* 47 (3): 225–237.

Bird, Alexander. 1998. "Dispositions and Antidotes." *Philosophical Quarterly* 48 (191): 227–234. https://dx.doi.org/10.1111/1467-9213.00098.

Bommarito, Nicolas. 2013. "Modesty as a Virtue of Attention." *The Philosophical Review* 122 (1): 93–117.

BonJour, Laurence. 1985. *The Structure of Empirical Knowledge*. Cambridge, MA: Harvard University Press.

BonJour, Laurence. 1994. "Against Naturalized Epistemology." *Midwest Studies in Philosophy* 19 (1): 283–300. https://dx.doi.org/10.1111/j.1475-4975.1994.tb00290.x.

Borges, Rodrigo, Branden Fitelson, and Cherie Braden. 2019. *Knowledge, Scepticism, and Defeat: Themes From Klein*. New York: Springer Verlag.

Brittain, Charles. 2001. *Philo of Larissa*. Oxford: Oxford University Press.

Brouwer, L.E.J. 1907. *Over de Grondslagen der Wiskunde*. Amsterdam: Maas and van Suchtelen.

Brown, Jessica. 2018. *Fallibilism: Evidence and Knowledge*. Oxford: Oxford University Press.

Bryant, Amanda. 2017. "Resolving Quine's Confict: A Neo-Quinean View of the Rational Revisability of Logic." *Australasian Journal of Logic* 14 (1). https://dx.doi.org/10.26686/ajl.v14i1.4026.

Burnyeat, Myles. 1980. "Can the Sceptic Live His Scepticism?" In *Doubt and Dogmatism*, edited by Malcolm Schofield, Myles Burnyeat, and Jonathan Barnes. 20–53. Oxford: Clarendon Press.

Carnap, Rudolf. 1928. *Der Logische Aufbau der Welt*. Hamburg: Meiner Verlag.

Carnap, Rudolf. 1945. "The Two Concepts of Probability: The Problem of Probability." *Philosophy and Phenomenological Research* 5 (4): 513–532.

Carnap, Rudolf. 1962. *Logical Foundations of Probability*. Chicago: University of Chicago Press.

Carnap, Rudolf. 1967. *The Logical Structure of the World*. Berkeley: University of California Press.

Carnap, Rudolf. 1971. "A Basic System of Inductive Logic, Part I." In *Studies in Inductive Logic and Probability*, edited by Richard Jeffrey and Rudolf Carnap. 34–165. Berkeley: University of California Press.

Carnap, Rudolf. 1980. "A Basic System of Inductive Logic, Part II." In *Studies in Inductive Logic and Probability*, edited by Richard C. Jeffrey. 2–7. Berkeley: University of California Press.

Cartwright, Nancy. 1983. *How the Laws of Physics Lie*. Oxford: Oxford University Press.

Chisholm, Roderick. 1957. *Perceiving*. Ithaca: Cornell University Press.

Chisholm, Roderick. 1977. *Theory of Knowledge*. Englewood Cliffs: Prentice-Hall. 2nd edn.

178 BIBLIOGRAPHY

Chisholm, Roderick. 1989. *Theory of Knowledge.* Englewood Cliffs: Prentice-Hall. 3rd edn.

Chisholm, Roderick M. 1948. "The Problem of Empiricism." *Journal of Philosophy* 45 (19): 512–517. https://dx.doi.org/10.2307/2019108.

Chisholm, Roderick M. 1969. "The Loose and Popular and the Strict and Philosophical Senses of Identity." In *Perception and Personal Identity,* edited by Norman S. Care and Robert H. Grimm. 82–106. Cleveland: Press of Case Western Reserve University.

Chisholm, Roderick M. 1973. *The Problem of the Criterion.* Milwaukee: Marquette University Press.

Chisholm, Roderick M. 1982. *The Foundations of Knowing.* Minneapolis: Univ of Minnesota Press.

Chisholm, Roderick Milton. 1966. *Theory of Knowledge.* Englewood Cliffs: Prentice-Hall.

Cohen, Stewart. 1987. "Knowledge and Context." *Journal of Philosophy* 83: 574–583.

DeRose, Keith. 1991. "Epistemic Possibilities." *Philosophical Review* 100 (4): 581–605.

DeRose, Keith. 2008. *The Case for Contextualism.* Oxford: Oxford University Press.

DeRose, Keith. 2018a. *The Appearance of Ignorance.* Oxford: Oxford University Press.

DeRose, Keith. 2018b. "Delusions of Knowledge Concerning God's Existence." In *Knowledge, Belief, and God: New Insights in Religious Epistemology,* edited by Matthew A. Benton, John Hawthorne, and Dani Rabinowitz. 288–301. Oxford: Oxford University Press.

Dodd, Dylan. 2006. "The Challenge of Concessive Knowledge Attributions." *Facta Philosophica* 8 (1-2): 221–227.

Dodd, Dylan. 2010. "Confusion About Concessive Knowledge Attributions." *Synthese* 172 (3): 381–396.

Dougherty, Trent and Patrick Rysiew. 2009. "Fallibilism, Epistemic Possibility, and Concessive Knowledge Attributions." *Philosophy and Phenomenological Research* 78 (1): 123–132.

Dougherty, Trent and Patrick Rysiew. 2011. "Clarity About Concessive Knowledge Attributions: Reply to Dodd." *Synthese* 181 (3): 395–403.

Duhem, Pierre. 1914. *La Théorie Physique: Son Objet et sa Structure.* Paris: Marcel Riviera and Cie. 2nd edn.

Dummett, Michael. 1976. "What is a Theory of Meaning? (II)." In *Truth and Meaning,* edited by Gareth Evans and John McDowell. Ch. 4. Oxford: Clarendon Press.

Dummett, Michael. 1977. *Elements of Intuitionism.* Oxford: Oxford University Press.

Dummett, Michael. 1978. "The Philosophical Basis of Intuitionistic Logic." In *Truth and Other Enigmas.* 215–247. Cambridge, MA: Harvard University Press.

Dummett, Michael. 1991. *The Logical Basis of Metaphysics.* Cambridge, MA: Harvard University Press.

Dummett, Michael. 1993. *The Seas of Language.* Oxford: Oxford University Press.

Dummett, Michael A.E. 1975. "What is a Theory of Meaning? In *Mind and Language,* edited by Samuel Guttenplan. Oxford: Oxford University Press.

Dyke, Heather. 2021. *Time.* Cambridge: Cambridge University Press.

Egan, Andy and B. Weatherson. 2009. *Epistemic Modality.* Oxford: Oxford University Press.

Elgin, Catherine. 2009. "Exemplification, Idealization, and Scientific Understanding." In *Fictions in Science: Philosophical Essays on Modeling and Idealization,* edited by Mauricio Suárez. 77–90. New York: Routledge.

Elgin, Catherine Z. 2017. *True Enough.* Cambridge: MIT Press.

Emery, Nina, Ned Markosian, and Meghan Sullivan. 2020. "Time." In *The Stanford Encyclopedia of Philosophy,* edited by Edward N. Zalta. Metaphysics Research Lab, Stanford University, Winter 2020 edn.

Empiricus, Sextus. 1933. *Outlines of Pyrrhonism.* London: W. Heinmann.

Fantl, Jeremy and Matthew McGrath. 2009. *Knowledge in an Uncertain World.* Oxford: Oxford University Press.

Feldman, Richard. 2007. "Reasonable Religious Disagreements." In *Philosophers without Gods: Meditations on Atheism and the Secular Life,* edited by Louise Antony. 194–214. Oxford: Oxford University Press.

Fetzer, James H. 1974. "On 'Epistemic Possibility.'" *Philosophia* 4 (2-3): 327–335.

BIBLIOGRAPHY 179

Fine, Gail. 2000. "Skeptical *Dogmata: Outlines of Pyrrhonism* I 13." *Methexis* 12: 81–105.

Fitch, Frederic. 1963. "A Logical Analysis of Some Value Concepts." *The Journal of Symbolic Logic* 28: 135–142.

Fodor, Jerry. 1983. *The Modularity of Mind.* Cambridge, MA: MIT Press.

Foley, Richard. 1991. "Evidence and Reasons for Belief." *Analysis* 51 (2): 98–102.

Foley, Richard. 1994. "Quine and Naturalized Epistemology." *Midwest Studies in Philosophy* 19 (1): 243–260. https://dx.doi.org/10.1111/j.1475-4975.1994.tb00288.x.

Frede, Michael. 1987. *Essays in Ancient Philosophy.* Oxford: Oxford University Press.

Frege, Gottlob. 1892. "Über Sinn Und Bedeutung." *Zeitschrift für Philosophie Und Philosophische Kritik* 100 (1): 25–50.

Fumerton, Richard. 1994. "Skepticism and Naturalistic Epistemology." *Midwest Studies in Philosophy* 19 (1): 321–340. https://dx.doi.org/10.1111/j.1475-4975.1994.tb00292.x.

Geach, Peter. 1977. *Providence and Evil.* Cambridge: Cambridge University Press.

Gillies, Anthony S. 2004. "Epistemic Conditionals and Conditional Epistemics." *Noûs* 38 (4): 585–616.

Goldman, Alvin. 1986. *Epistemology and Cognition.* Cambridge, MA: Harvard University Press.

Greco, Daniel. 2015a. "Iteration Principles in Epistemology I: Arguments For." *Philosophy Compass* 10 (11): 754–764. https://dx.doi.org/10.1111/phc3.12267.

Greco, Daniel. 2015b. "Iteration Principles in Epistemology II: Arguments Against." *Philosophy Compass* 10 (11): 765–771. https://dx.doi.org/10.1111/phc3.12264.

Greco, John. 2010. *Achieving Knowledge: A Virtue-Theoretic Account of Epistemic Normativity.* Cambridge: Cambridge University Press.

Grice, Paul. 1968. "Logic and Conversation." In *Studies in the Way of Words.* Cambridge: Cambridge University Press.

Grim, Patrick. 1991. *The Incomplete Universe.* Cambridge, MA: MIT Press.

Grim, Patrick and Alvin Plantinga. 1993. "Truth, Omniscience and Cantorian Arguments: An Exchange." *Philosophical Studies* 71: 267–306.

Haack, Susan. 1996. *Deviant Logic, Fuzzy Logic: Beyond the Formalism.* Chicago and London: University of Chicago Press.

Hand, Michael. 1996. "Radical AntiRealism and Neutral States of Information." *Philosophical Topics* 24: 35–51.

Harman, Gilbert H. 1970. "Knowledge, Reasons, and Causes." *The Journal of Philosophy* 67: 841–55.

Harman, Gilbert H. 1973. *Thought.* Princeton, NJ: Princeton University Press.

Harman, Gilbert H. 1980. "Reasoning and Evidence One Does Not Possess." *Midwest Studies in Philosophy* V: 163–183.

Hawthorne, John. 2004. *Knowledge and Lotteries.* Oxford: Oxford University Press.

Hazlett, Allan. 2010. "The Myth of Factive Verbs." *Philosophy and Phenomenological Research* 80 (3): 497–522.

Heim, Irene. 1983. "On the Projection Problem for Presuppositions." *In Second Annual West Coast Conference on Formal Linguistics,* edited by D. F. M. Barlow and M. Westcoat. 114–126. Stanford, CA: Stanford University Press.

Hemp, David. 2006. "KK (Knowing That One Knows) Principle." In *Internet Encyclopedia of Philosophy,* https://iep.utm.edu/kk-princ/#:~:text=The%20KK%20(Knowing%20that%20One,knows%20that%20one%20knows%20it.

Hempel, Carl G." 1945a. "Studies in the Logic of Confirmation (I.)." *Mind* 54 (213): 1–26.

Hempel, Carl G." 1945b. "Studies in the Logic of Confirmation (II.)." *Mind* 54 (214): 97–121.

Hetherington, Stephen. 2013. "Concessive Knowledge-Attributions: Fallibilism and Gradualism." *Synthese* 190 (14): 2835–2851.

Hetherington, Stephen Cade. 2001. *Good Knowledge, Bad Knowledge: On Two Dogmas of Epistemology.* Oxford: Oxford University Press.

Hintikka, Jaakko. 1962. *Knowledge and Belief.* Ithaca: Cornell University Press.

Hintikka, Jaakko. 1970. "'Knowing That One Knows' Reviewed." *Synthese* 21 (2): 141–162. https://dx.doi.org/10.1007/BF00413543.

180 BIBLIOGRAPHY

Horowitz, Sophie, Sinan Dogramaci, and Miriam Schoenfield. Forthcoming. "Are You Now or Have You Ever Been an Impermissivist? A Conversation Among Friends and Enemies of Epistemic Freedom." In *Contemporary Debates in Epistemology, Third Edition*, edited by Matthias Steup, John Turri, and Ernest Sosa. Malden, MA: Wiley-Blackwell.

Howard, Don. 1990. "Einstein and Duhem." *Synthese* 83 (3): 363–384. https://dx.doi.org/10.1007/BF00413422.

Huemer, Michael. 2007. "Epistemic Possibility." *Synthese* 156 (1): 119–142.

James, William. 1897. "The Will to Believe." In *The Will to Believe and Other Essays in Popular Philosophy*. 1–15. New York: Longmans, Green, and Co.

Jeffrey, Richard. 1984. "Bayesianism with a Human Face." In *Testing Scientific Theories*, edited by John Earman. Vol. 10 of *Minnesota Studies in the Philosophy of Science*, 133–156. Minneapolis: University of Minnesota Press.

Jeffrey, Richard. 1992. *Probability and the Art of Judgment*. New York: Cambridge University Press.

Kaplan, Mark. 1985. "It's Not What You Know That Counts." *Journal of Philosophy* 82 (7): 350–363. jphil198582748.

Keynes, John. 1921. *A Treatise on Probability*. London: MacMillan.

Kim, Jaegwon. 1988. "What is 'Naturalized Epistemology?'" *Philosophical Perspectives* 2: 381–405. https://dx.doi.org/10.2307/2214082.

Kitcher, Philip. 1992. "The Naturalists Return." *Philosophical Review* 101 (1): 53–114. https://dx.doi.org/10.2307/2185044.

Klein, Peter. 1981. *Certainty: A Refutation of Skepticism*. Minneapolis: University of Minnesota Press.

Klein, Peter. 1999. "Human Knowledge and the Infinite Regress of Reasons." *Philosophical Perpectives* 13: 297–325.

Klein, Peter. 2005a. "Infinitism's Take on Justification, Knowledge, Certainty and Skepticism." *Veritas* 50 (4): 153–172.

Klein, Peter. 2005b. "Reply to Ginet." In *Contemporary Debates in Epistemology*, edited by Matthias Steup and Ernest Sosa. 149–152. Malden, MA: Blackwell.

Klein, Peter. 2011. "Infinitism." In *The Routledge Companion to Epistemology*, edited by Sven Bernecker and Duncan Pritchard. 245–256. New York: Routledge.

Klein, Peter D. 2007a. "How to be an Infinitist about Doxastic Justification." *Philosophical Studies* 134 (1): 25–29.

Klein, Peter D. 2007b. "Human Knowledge and the Infinite Progress of Reasoning." *Philosophical Studies* 134 (1): 1–17.

Knobe, Joshua and Seth Yalcin. 2014. "Epistemic Modals and Context: Experimental Data." *Semantics and Pragmatics* 7 (10): 1–21.

Kolmogorov, A.N. 1950 [1933]. *Foundations of Probability*. New York: Chelsea Publishing.

Koons, Robert. 2017. "Defeasible Reasoning." In *The Stanford Encyclopedia of Philosophy*, edited by Edward N. Zalta. Metaphysics Research Lab, Stanford University, winter 2017 edn.

Kornblith, H., ed. 1994. *Naturalizing Epistemology*. Cambridge, MA: MIT Press.

Kripke, Saul. 1980. *Naming and Necessity*. Cambridge, MA: Harvard University Press.

Kripke, Saul. 1982. *Wittgenstein on Rules and Private Language: An Elementary Exposition*. Cambrridge, MA: Harvard University Press.

Kvanvig, Jonathan L. 1984. "Subjective Justification." *Mind* 93: 71–84.

Kvanvig, Jonathan L. 1992. *The Intellectual Virtues and the Life of the Mind: On the Place of the Virtues in Contemporary Epistemology*. Savage, MD: Rowman and Littlefield.

Kvanvig, Jonathan L. 1999. "Lewis on Finkish Dispositions." *Philosophy and Phenomenological Research* 59: 703–710.

Kvanvig, Jonathan L. 2003. *The Value of Knowledge and the Pursuit of Understanding*. Cambridge: Cambridge University Press.

Kvanvig, Jonathan L. 2005. "Truth and the Epistemic Goal." In *Contemporary Debates in Epistemology*, edited by Matthias Steup and Ernest Sosa. 285–295. Malden, MA: Blackwell.

Kvanvig, Jonathan L. 2006a. "Epistemic Closure Principles." *Philosophy Compass* 1 (3): 256–267.

Kvanvig, Jonathan L. 2006b. *The Knowability Paradox.* Oxford: Oxford University Press.

Kvanvig, Jonathan L. 2008. "Pointless Truth." *Midwest Studies in Philosophy* 32: 199–212.

Kvanvig, Jonathan L. 2009a. "Responses to Critics." In *Epistemic Value*, edited by Duncan Pritchard, Adrian Haddock, and Alan Millar. 339–353. Oxford: Oxford University Press.

Kvanvig, Jonathan L. 2009b. "The Value of Understanding." In *Epistemic Value*, edited by Duncan Pritchard, Adrian Haddock, and Alan Millar. 95–112. Oxford: Oxford University Press.

Kvanvig, Jonathan L. 2011a. "Against Pragmatic Encroachment." *Logos and Episteme* 2 (1): 77–85.

Kvanvig, Jonathan L. 2011b. *Destiny and Decision: Essays in Philosophical Theology. Ch. 8, An Epistemic Theory of Creation*, 140–178. Oxford: Oxford University Press.

Kvanvig, Jonathan L. 2011c. *Destiny and Decision: Essays in Philosophical Theology.* Oxford: Oxford University Press.

Kvanvig, Jonathan L. 2012. "Infinitism, Holism, and the Regress Argument." In *Infinitism*, edited by Peter Klein and John Turri. Oxford: Oxford University Press.

Kvanvig, Jonathan L. 2013. "Curiosity and a Response-Dependent Account of the Value of Understanding." In *Knowledge, Virtue, and Action*, edited by Timothy Henning and David Schweikard. 151–175. London: Routledge.

Kvanvig, Jonathan L. 2014. *Rationality and Reflection.* Oxford: Oxford University Press.

Kvanvig, Jonathan L. 2018. *Faith and Humility.* Oxford: Oxford University Press.

Lakoff, George. 1993. "The Contemporary Theory of Metaphor." In *Metaphor and Thought*, edited by Andrew Ortony. 2–202. Cambridge: Cambridge University Press.

Leddington, Jason. 2018. "Fallibility for Infallibilists." In *In the Light of Experience: Essays on Reasons and Perception*, edited by Johan Gersel, Rasmus Thybo Jensen, Søren Overgaard, and Morten S. Thaning. 161–185. Oxford: Oxford University Press.

Lehrer, Keith. 1974. *Knowledge.* New York: Oxford University Press.

Lehrer, Keith. 2000. *Theory of Knowledge.* Boulder: Westview Press. 2nd edn.

Lehrer, Keith and Thomas D. Paxson Jr. 1969. "Knowledge: Undefeated Justified True Belief." *The Journal of Philosophy* 66 (8): 225–237.

Lewis, CI. 1946. *An Analysis of Knowledge and Valuation.* LaSalle: Open Court.

Lewis, David. 1981. "Are We Free to Break the Laws? *Theoria* 47 (3): 113–21.

Lewis, David. 1996. "Elusive Knowledge." *Australasian Journal of Philosophy* 74 (4): 549–567.

Lewis, David. 1997. "Finkish Dispositions." *The Philosophical Quarterly* 47 (187): 143–148.

Littlejohn, Clayton. 2011. "Concessive Knowledge Attributions and Fallibilism." *Philosophy and Phenomenological Research* 83 (3): 603–619.

Lycan, William G. 1996. "Plantinga and Coherentisms." In *Warrant in Contemporary Epistemology*, edited by Jonathan L Kvanvig. 1–25. Savage, MD: Rowman and Littlefield.

Markie, Peter J. 1986. *Descartes's Gambit.* Ithaca, NY: Cornell University Press.

Martin, Charles Burton. 1994. "Dispositions and Conditionals." *The Philosophical Quarterly* 44: 1–8.

McDaniel, Kris. 2013. "Degrees of Being." *Philosophers' Imprint* 13.

McDaniel, Kris. 2017. *The Fragmentation of Being.* Oxford: Oxford University Press.

McDowell, John. 1994. *Mind and World.* Cambridge, MA: Harvard University Press.

McNamara, Paul. 2010. "Deontic Logic." In *Stanford Encyclopedia of Philosophy*, edited by Ed Zalta.

McPherson, David. 2022. *The Virtues of Limits.* Oxford, UK: Oxford University Press.

Mellor, D.H. 1998. *Real Time II.* Boston: Routledge.

Miller, Kristie. 2013. "Presentism, Eternalism, and the Growing Block." In *A Companion to the Philosophy of Time*, edited by Heather Dyke and Adrian Bardon. 345–364. Abingdon: Wiley-Blackwell.

Mitova, Veli. 2018. *The Factive Turn in Epistemology.* Cambridge: Cambridge University Press.

Moore, George Edward. 1925. "A Defence of Common Sense." In *Contemporary British Philosophy*, edited by J.H. Muirhead. 193–223. London: Allen and Unwin.

Moore, George Edward. 1939. "Proof of an External World." *Proceedings of the British Academy* 25: 273–300.

182 BIBLIOGRAPHY

Morton, Adam. 2012. *Bounded Thinking: Intellectual Virtues for Limited Agents*. Oxford, England: Oxford University Press.

Mumford, Stephen. 1998. *Dispositions*. Oxford: Clarendon Press.

Neurath, O. 1983. *Philosophical Papers 1913–46*. Boston: D. Reidel.

Nozick, Robert. 1981. *Philosophical Explanations*. Cambridge, MA: Harvard University Press.

Peirce, C.S. 1877. "The Fixation of Belief." *Popular Science Monthly* 12 (1): 1–15.

Peirce, C.S. 1878. "How to Make Our Ideas Clear." *Popular Science Monthly* 12 (Jan.): 286–302.

Peirce, C.S. 1905. "What Pragmatism Is." *The Monist* 15 (2): 161–181.

Peirce, C.S. 1906. "Prolegomena to an Apology for Pragmaticism." *The Monist* 16 (4): 492–546.

Perin, Casey. 2010. "Scepticism and Belief." In *The Cambridge Companion to Ancient Scepticism*, edited by Richard Bett. 145–164. Cambridge: Cambridge University Press.

Perry, John. 1979. "The Problem of the Essential Idexical." *Noûs* 13: 3–21.

Pettigrew, Richard. 2016. *Accuracy and the Laws of Credence*. New York: Oxford University Press.

Plantinga, Alvin. 1967. *God and Other Minds*. Ithaca: Cornell University Press.

Plantinga, Alvin. 1974. *The Nature of Necessity*. Oxford: Clarendon Press.

Pollock, John. 1974. *Knowledge and Justification*. Ithaca: Cornell University Press.

Pollock, John and Anthony Gillies. 2000. "Belief Revision and Epistemology." *Synthese* 122: 69–92.

Pollock, John L. 1967. "Criteria and Our Knowledge of the Material World." *Philosophical Review* 76 (1): 28–60. https://dx.doi.org/10.2307/2182964.

Pollock, John L. 1989. *How to Build a Person: A Prolegomenon*. Cambridge, MA: MIT Press.

Pollock, John L. 1995. *Cognitive Carpentry*. Cambridge, MA: MIT Press.

Pollock, John L. 2001. "Defeasible Reasoning with Variable Degrees of Justification." *Artificial Intelligence* 133: 233–282.

Pollock, John L. 2011. "Reasoning Defeasibly About Probabilities." *Synthese* 181 (2): 317–352.

Pollock, John L. and Iris Oved. 2005. "Vision, Knowledge, and the Mystery Link." *Noûs* 39 (1): 309–351.

Pritchard, Duncan. 2009. "Knowledge, Understanding, and Epistemic Value." *Royal Institute of Philosophy Supplement* 84: 19–43.

Pritchard, Duncan. 2010. "Knowledge and Understanding." In *The Nature and Value of Knowledge: Three Investigations*, edited by Adrian Haddock, Alan Millar, and Duncan Pritchard. 3–90. Oxford: Oxford University Press.

Pritchard, Duncan. 2012. *Epistemological Disjunctivism*. Oxford: Oxford University Press.

Pritchard, Duncan. 2015. *Epistemic Angst: Radical Skepticism and the Groundlessness of Our Believing*. Princeton, NJ: Princeton University Press.

Pritchard, Duncan H. 2005. *Epistemic Luck*. Oxford: Oxford University Press.

Putnam, Hilary. 1985. "Why Reason Can't Be Naturalized." In *Synthese*. 3–24. Cambridge: Cambridge University Press.

Quine, W.V. 1969. "Epistemology Naturalized." In *Ontological Relativity and Other Essays*. New York: Columbia University Press.

Quine, W.V. 1970. *Philosophy of Logic*. Cambridge, MA: Harvard University Press.

Quine, W.V. 1990. "Norms and Aims." In *The Pursuit of Truth*. Cambridge, MA: Harvard University Press.

Quine, W.V.O. 1960. *Word and Object*. Cambridge, MA: MIT Press.

Quine, Willard V.O. 1951. "Two Dogmas of Empiricism." *Philosophical Review* 60 (1): 20–43.

Quine, W.V.O. 1986. "Reply to White." In *The Philosophy of W.V.O. Quine*, edited by L.E. Hahn and P.A. Schilpp. 663–665. LaSalle, IL: Open Court.

Rawls, John. 1971. *A Theory of Justice*. Cambridge, MA: Harvard University Press.

Rea, Michael C. 2003. "Four-Dimensionalism." In *The Oxford Handbook of Metaphysics*, edited by Michael J. Loux and Dean W. Zimmerman. 1–59. Oxford: Oxford University Press.

Reed, Baron. 2007. "The Long Road to Skepticism." *Journal of Philosophy* 104 (5): 236–262. https://dx.doi.org/10.5840/jphil2007104524.

Reed, Baron. 2012. "Fallibilism." *Philosophy Compass* 7 (9): 585–596.

BIBLIOGRAPHY 183

Reed, Baron. 2013. "Fallibilism, Epistemic Possibility, and Epistemic Agency." *Philosophical Issues* 23 (1): 40–69.

Reed, Baron. 2022. "Certainty." In *The Stanford Encyclopedia of Philosophy*, edited by Edward N. Zalta. *Metaphysics Research Lab*, Stanford University, Spring 2022 edn.

Russell, Bertrand. 1905. "On Denoting." *Mind* 14 (56): 479–493.

Russell, Bertrand. 1935. *Religion and Science*. Oxford: Oxford University Press (The Home University Library).

Rysiew, Patrick. 2009. "Fallibilism, Epistemic Possibility, and Concessive Knowledge Attributions." *Philosophy and Phenomenological Research* 78 (1): 123–132.

Sainsbury, Richard Mark. 1988. *Paradoxes*. Cambridge: Cambridge University Press.

Salerno, Joe. 2008. *New Essays on the Knowability Paradox*. Oxford: Oxford University Press.

Salmon, Nathan. 1989. *Frege's Puzzle*. Oxford: Oxford University Press.

Sellars, Wilfrid. 1956. "Empiricism and the Philosophy of Mind." In *Minnesota Studies in the Philosophy of Science*, edited by H. Feigl and M. Scriven. Vol. 1, 253–239. Minneapolis: University of Minnesota Press.

Sherman, Brett and Gilbert Harman. 2011. "Knowledge and Assumptions." *Philosophical Studies* 156 (1): 131–140.

Sider, Theodore. 2001. *Four Dimensionalism: An Ontology of Persistence and Time*. Oxford: Oxford University Press.

Siegel, Susanna. 2005. "The Contents of Perception." In *The Stanford Encyclopedia of Philosophy*, edited by Edward N. Zalta. *Metaphysics Research Lab*, Stanford University, Spring 2005 edn.

Siegel, Susanna. 2013. "The Epistemic Impact of the Etiology of Experience." *Philosophical Studies* 162 (3): 697–722.

Simpson, James. 2022. "More Clarity About Concessive Knowledge Attributions." *Southwest Philosophy Review* 38 (1): 59–69. https://dx.doi.org/10.5840/swphilreview20223817.

Smith, Nicholas J.J. 2008. *Vagueness and Degrees of Truth*. Oxford: Oxford University Press.

Sorensen, Roy. 2009. "Meta-Agnosticism: Higher Order Epistemic Possibility." *Mind* 118 (471): 777–784.

Sosa, Ernest. 1999. "How to Defeat Opposition to Moore." *Philosophical Perspectives* 13: 141–152.

Sosa, Ernest. 2007. *A Virtue Epistemology*. Oxford: Oxford University Press.

Stalnaker, Robert. 1984. *Inquiry*. Cambridge, MA: MIT Press.

Stanley, Jason. 2005a. "Fallibilism and Concessive Knowledge Attributions." *Analysis* 65 (2): 126–131.

Stanley, Jason. 2005b. *Knowledge and Practical Interests*. Oxford: Oxford University Press.

Stoutenburg, Gregory. Forthcoming. "Concessive Knowledge Attributions Cannot Be Explained Pragmatically." *International Journal for the Study of Skepticism* 1–12. https://dx.doi.org/10.1163/22105700-bja10024.

Stroud, Barry. 1984a. *The Significance of Philosophical Skepticism*. Oxford: Oxford University Press.

Stroud, Barry. 1984b. "Skepticism and the Possibility of Knowledge." *The Journal of Philosophy* 81 (10): 545–551.

Sturgeon, Scott. 1993. "The Gettier Problem." *Analysis* 53: 156–164.

Sturgeon, Scott. 2008. "Reason and the Grain of Belief." *Noûs* 42 (1): 139–165.

Swain, Marshall. 1974. "Epistemic Defeasibility." *American Philosophical Quarterly* 11 (1): 15–25.

Tarski, Alfred. 1944. "The Semantic Conception of Truth: And the Foundations of Semantics." *Philosophy and Phenomenological Research* 4 (3): 341–376.

Taylor, Richard. 1955. "Spatial and Temporal Analogies and the Concept of Identity." *Journal of Philosophy* 52 (22): 599–612. https://dx.doi.org/10.2307/2022168.

Teller, Paul. 1972. "Epistemic Possibility." *Philosophia* 2 (4): 303–320.

Teller, Paul. 1974. "Professor Fetzer on Epistemic Possibility." *Philosophia* 4 (2-3): 337–338.

Tennant, Neil. 1997. *The Taming of the True*. Oxford: Oxford University Press.

Tomberlin, James E., ed. 1988. *Philosophical Perspectives 2, Epistemology*. Atascadero, CA: Ridgeview Publishing.

184 BIBLIOGRAPHY

Unger, Peter. 1975. *Ignorance: A Case for Skepticism.* Oxford: Oxford University Press.

van Inwagen, Peter. 1983. *An Essay on Free Will.* Oxford: Clarendon Press.

van Inwagen, Peter. 1988. "The Place of Chance in a World Sustained by God." In *God, Knowledge, and Mystery.* 42–65. Cornell UP.

Veltman, Frank. 1996. "Defaults in Update Semantics." *Journal of Philosophical Logic* 25: 221–261.

Watson, Gary. 1984. "Virtues in Excess." *Philosophical Studies* 46 (1): 57–74. https://dx.doi.org/10.1007/BF00353491.

Whitcomb, Dennis, Heather Battaly, Jason Baehr, and Daniel Howard-Snyder. 2015. "Intellectual Humility: Owning Our Limitations." *Philosophy and Phenomenological Research* 91 (1): 1–31.

White, Roger. 2005. "Epistemic Permissiveness." *Philosophical Perspectives* 19: 445–459.

Williams, Michael. 1977. *Groundless Belief: An Essay on the Possibility of Epistemology.* New Haven: Yale University Press.

Williams, Michael. 1991. *Unnatural Doubts: Epistemological Realism and the Basis of Scepticism.* Oxford: Basil Blackwell.

Williamson, Timothy. 1996. "Knowing and Asserting." *The Philosophical Review* 105: 489–523.

Williamson, Timothy. 2000. *Knowledge and Its Limits.* Oxford: Oxford University Press.

Williamson, Timothy. 2003. "Everything." *Philosophical Perspectives* 17 (1): 415–465.

Williamson, Timothy. Forthcoming. "Theorizing About Evidence." *Philosophical Studies* 1–9. 10.1007/s11098-022-01787-5.

Wittgenstein, Ludwig. 1969. *On Certainty.* Oxford: Oxford University Press.

Yalcin, Seth. 2007. "Epistemic Modals." *Mind* 116 (464): 983–1026.

Yalcin, Seth. 2009. "More on Epistemic Modals." *Mind* 118 (471): 785–793.

Zagzebski, Linda. 1994. "The Inescapability of the Gettier Problem." *Philosophical Quarterly* 44: 65–73.

Zagzebski, Linda. 1996. *Virtues of the Mind: An Inquiry into the Nature of Virtue and the Ethical Foundations of Knowledge.* Cambridge: Cambridge University Press.

Zimmerman, Dean. 2011. "Presentism and the Space-Time Manifold." In *The Oxford Handbook of Philosophy of Time*, edited by Craig Callender. 163–246. Oxford: Oxford University Press.

Index

a priori knowledge 95, 121
Absolute terms 36–40, 79
AGM model 132
Alchourron, Carlos E. 132, 177
Alston, William 81, 107, 177
Antony, Louise 178
apatheia 172–3
Appearance states 14–18
Appearance/reality distinction 98
Approximation to an ideal 79, 84, 153, 156, 157, 161, 163, 175
Approximationism 9, 162–7, 175
Armstrong, David 94, 111, 177
Assumptionalism 163–6
Austin, J. L. 23, 44, 47, 177
Ayer, A.J. 124, 177

Backtracking 131, 132, 136–7, 139
Baehr, Jason 170, 177, 184
Bardon, Adrian 181
Barlow, D.F.M. 179
Barnes, Jonathan 15, 177
Battaly, Heather 184
Bayesianism 19–21, 123, 132, 134, 135
Begging the question 24–5
Benbaji, Hagit 49, 177
Benton, Matthew 178
Bernecker, Sven 180
Bett, Richard 182
Bird, Alexander 94, 177
Bivalence 114
Bommarito, Nicolas 170–1, 177
BonJour, Laurence 13, 16, 164, 177
Borges, Rodrigo 98, 177
Braden, Cherie 177
Brittain, Charles 47, 177
Brookes, Frances 36
Brower, L.E.J. 96, 177
Brown, Jessica 44, 70, 177
Bryant, Amanda 173, 177
Burnyeat, Myles 15, 177

Callender, Craig 184
Cardinal virtues 172
Care, Norman S. 178
Carnap, Rudolf 123, 177

Cartwright, Nancy 111, 177
Certainty, Cartesian 22, 89
Certainty, metaphysical 22, 45, 89–91
Cheap Infallibilism 63–5
Chisholm, Roderick 6, 10, 24–6, 89, 119, 120–6, 158, 168, 177–8
Church, Alonzo 115
Church-Fitch paradox 115
Classical theism 112
Close approximations 79–80
Closure of inquiry 11, 89, 151, 162, 176
Closure principle 30–35, 163–4
Cognitive penetration 150
Cohen, Stewart 48, 84, 178
Coherence 3, 45, 82, 121, 123
Coherence, probabilistic 19
Coherentism 21, 24, 26–7, 67, 146, 164
Common sense epistemology 2, 7
Completeness 109
Concessive assertions 47–52
Concessive attitudes 47–52
Concessive attributions 47–52
Conditionalization 19, 123, 133
Conferrers 119–20, 126
Confirmation, Converse Consequence Condition 125
Confirmation, Entailment Condition 125
Confirmation, Special Consequence Condition 125
Confirmation, Special Consistency Condition 125
Consequence argument 111
Contextualism 47–8, 56–7, 84
Correct premises for practical reasoning 11
Credences 18–20, 133

Death of epistemology 16
Decision theory 16, 18, 19, 28
Deduction Theorem 64, 66
Defeasibility 52, 91, 120, 126, 127, 138–41
Defeasibility theory of knowledge 139–40
Defeasible reasoning 9, 81, 100, 113–9, 141–2, 165, 174–5
Defeaters, internal and external 138–40
Defeaters, misleading 62
Degrees of belief 16, 20

186 INDEX

Demon hypothesis 45, 87
Deontic logics 60-1
DeRose, Keith 30, 47, 48, 58, 84, 95, 178
Descartes, Rene 65, 87, 89–92
Determinism 109–13
Disquotation Schema 47
Dodd, Dylan 49, 70, 178
Dogmatism 14, 35
Dogmatism paradox 35
Dogramaci, Sinan 180
Dougherty, Trent 49, 70, 178
Doxastic presumption 164
Dreaming hypothesis 29–35, 45, 163
Dual rules 58, 60–2, 72
Duhem, Pierre 52, 178
Dummett, Michael 96, 97, 178
Dutch books 133
Dyke, Heather 81, 178, 181
Dynamic semantics 127–31

Earman, John 180
Egan, Andy 58, 178
Elgin, Catherine 167, 178
Emery, Nina 101, 178
Enablers 119–20
Epistemic angst 4, 176
Epistemic appraisal 14–17, 126
Epistemic conditionals 118–20, 126–31, 135
Epistemic goal 13, 28, 105, 108, 150, 161, 164,
    171, 175
epistemic imperialism 81–2, 95, 104, 107, 108,
    113, 141–2, 174
Epistemic logic 33, 55, 60, 64, 72, 76
Epistemic possibility 55–76
Epistemic principles 33, 118–26, 129
Epistemic status of necessities 134
Epistemological axiology 6, 7, 151, 152, 160
ESP 144
Evaluative part of axiology 6
Evans, Gareth 178
Evidence-first epistemology 122
Excluded middle 114
Experience-first epistemology 122

Faith 5, 171–3
Fallibilism, complacent 3, 45, 53, 108, 136, 147
Fallibilism, false presupposition 54–5, 77–86,
    103, 137, 143, 144–9, 152, 167, 175
Fallibilism, sensitive 3, 9, 45, 47, 51, 60, 82, 84,
    86, 147, 152, 169–74
Fantl, Jeremy 49, 70, 84, 178
Feigl, Herbert 183
Feldman, Richard 160, 178
Fetzer, James 58, 178

Fine, Gail 15, 179
Fitch paradox 115
Fitch, Frederic 115, 179
Fitelson, Branden 177
Fodor, Jerry 103, 179
Foley, Richard 10, 13, 20, 179
Formal machine learning 132
Foundationalism 3, 9, 16, 17, 21, 24, 26–7, 120,
    146, 169
Frede, Michael 15, 179
Frege, Gottlob 98, 104, 123, 134, 179
Fumerton, Richard 13, 179

Gardenfors, Peter 132, 177
Geach, Peter 80, 179
Gersel, Johan 181
Gettier problem 67–9, 75, 138
Gillies, Anthony 128, 132, 179, 182
Goal of inquiry 7
Godel, Kurt 98
Goldman, Alvin 179
Great intellectual goods 6, 21–2, 105,
    145–6
Greco, Daniel 33, 179
Greco, John 170, 179
Grice, Paul 70, 75, 77, 82, 179
Gricean maxim 70–2, 144, 147, 167
Grim, Patrick 114, 179
Grimm, Robert H. 178
Groundlessness of belief 4
Grounds for doubt 119, 120, 126
Growing block theory of time 101
Guttenplan, Samuel 178

Haack, Susan 179
Haddock, Adrian 181, 182
Hahn, L.E. 182
Hand, Michael 96, 179
Harman, Gilbert 68, 140, 163, 179, 183
Hawthorne, John 84, 178, 179
Hazlett, Alan 48, 179
Heim, Irene 128, 179
Hemp, David 33, 179
Hempel, Carl 125, 179
Henning, Timothy 181
Hetherington, Stephen 49, 79, 179
Hintikka, Jaakko 33, 55, 58, 73, 179
Holism 52
Horowitz, Sophie 160, 180
Howard, Don 52, 180
Howard-Snyder, Daniel 184
Huemer, Michael 58, 180
Hume, David 81
Hume's mistake 106, 113

INDEX   187

Humility 169, 170–3
Humility, Intellectual 4–7, 41, 170

Idealizations 92, 96–104, 117–8, 142, 146, 156, 165
Incorrigibility 3, 87, 91
Indefeasibility 91, 138, 140–1
Indubitability 91
Infallibilism, certainty account 87–9
Infallibilism, entailment account 87, 91
Infallibility 3, 8–9, 53–4, 63, 68, 77, 81, 83, 85, 86–93, 105, 108, 113–4, 116, 127, 137–42
Infallibility, static *vs.* dynamic accounts 92–3
Infinitism 26–7, 174
Intellectualism 4, 84
Intensional logics 60, 72
Intuitionism 96, 115
Iron laws of nature 111

James, William 17, 160, 180
Jeffrey conditionalization 133
Jeffrey, Richard 20, 27, 133, 177, 180
Jensen, Rasmus Thybo 181

Kaplan, Mark 27, 80
Keynes, John Maynard 122, 180
Kim, Jaegwon 180
Kitcher, Philip 180
KK principle 32–3
Klein, Peter 62, 98, 139, 174, 180, 181
Knobe, Joshua 58, 180
Knowability 96, 105, 115, 117
Knowability paradox 115, 139
Knowing the future 3, 112, 165
Knowledge deserts 30, 44, 95
Knowledge norm of assertion 51
Knowledge, factivity of 48–9
Knowledge-first epistemology 122
Kolmogorov, A.N. 19, 97, 180
Koons, Robert 132
Kripke, Saul 36, 135, 180

Lakoff, George 36, 181
Laws of nature, diachronic *vs.* synchronic 111
Leddington, Jason 44, 181
Lehrer, Keith 10, 63, 67, 140, 181
Lewis, C.I. 124, 125, 181
Lewis, David 46–7, 56, 59, 83, 94, 111, 181
Littlejohn, Clayton 49, 70, 72, 181
Locke, John 20
Locus of control 92–3
Logical Empiricism 126
Lord of the Rings 99
Loux, Michael J. 182

Lycan, William 24, 181

Makinson, David 132, 177
Many-valued logics 115
Markie, Peter 10, 89, 181
Markosian, Ned 178
Martin, C.B. 94, 177, 181
Material conditionals 130
McDaniel, Kris 79, 181
McDowell, John 44, 178, 181
McGrath, Matthew 49, 70, 84, 178
McNamara, Paul 61, 181
McPherson, David 171, 181
Mellor, D.H. 81, 181
Methodism 24, 26
Millar, Alan 181, 182
Miller, Kristie 81, 181
Mitova, Veli 71, 181
Modal logic 60
Modal operators 119–20
Modes of presentation 134–5
Modesty 170
Monotonic logic 81, 104, 106
Moore, G.E. 1, 2, 10, 22, 23, 35, 40, 44, 46, 168, 182
Moorean shift 23–30, 88, 144, 148, 158, 168–9
Morton, Adam 170, 182
Mother Teresa 50
Muirhead, J.H. 182
Mumford, Stephen 94, 182

Narrow scope 53–5
Naturalized epistemology 13
Neurath, Otto 52, 182
Nihilism 1
Non-monotonic logic 81, 106
Non-monotonic reasoning 113, 116, 137
Non-monotonicity 117, 142
Norm of assertion 11
Normativity, epistemic 4, 14–21, 50, 126, 151, 160, 170
Nozick, Robert 67, 182

Oaken laws of nature 111
Old evidence problem 132–3
Open theology 112
Openmindedness 7
Oracle at Delphi 107
Ordinary language philosophy 37
Ortony, Andrew 181
Oscar Project 132
Overgaard, Soren 181

188 INDEX

Particularism 2, 9, 24–6
Paxson Jr, Thomas 140, 181
Peano axioms 97
Peirce, C. S. 11, 182
Perin, Casey 15, 182
Perry, John 134, 182
Pettigrew, Richard 20, 182
Philo of Larissa 47
Philosophical theology 110, 112, 142
Place, U.T. 177
Plantinga, Alvin 69, 114, 179, 182
Pollock, John 10, 132, 182
Positive epistemic status 12, 17, 45, 46, 119, 122, 123, 126, 145, 151, 167
Practical rationality 16–7
Pragmatic implication 75
Pragmatics 36
Pragmatism 12–15, 17, 21, 90
Preferences 16, 18
Prescience 100, 144
Presentism 80, 101
Pritchard, Duncan 28, 44, 67, 176, 180, 181, 182
pro tanto 148, 174
Probabilism 47
Problem of paralysis 14, 17, 18, 21
Problem of the criterion 2, 24–5
Process theology 112
Proper functionalism 21
Purism 4
Putnam, Hilary 182
Pyrrhonian skepticism 14

Quantification, restricted 36, 56–8
Quine, W.V.O. 11, 12, 13, 52, 173, 182
Quine/Duhem thesis 173

Rabinowitz, Dani 178
Rational action 16, 18
Raven paradox 125
Rawls, John 2, 26, 182
Rea, Michael 81, 182
Reasons-first epistemology 122
Reed, Baron 58, 63, 66–7, 70, 75, 91, 183
Reflective equilibrium 2, 9, 26, 27, 35, 41, 43, 78, 85, 114, 137, 174
Regress argument 3, 9, 16, 26–7, 169
Reid, Thomas 1, 22, 168
Reliabilism 21
Ruling out 87–8
Russell, Bertrand 53, 97, 158, 183
Russell's paradox 98
Rysiew, Patrick 49, 70, 178, 183

Safety theory of knowledge 21, 67

Sainsbury, Mark 79, 183
Salerno, Joe 115, 183
Salmon, Nathan 134, 183
Sauron, eye of 99–100
Schilpp, P.A. 182
Schoenfield, Miriam 180
Schofield, Malcolm 177
Schweikard, David 181
Scope ambiguity 53
Scriven, Michael 183
Self-presenting states 121
Sellars, Wilfrid 16, 183
Semantic anti-realism 97, 105–6
Semantic implication 75
Semantics 37
Sensitivity theory of knowledge 21, 67
Sextus Empiricus 14
Sextus Empiricus 15–6, 178
Sherman, Brett 163, 183
Sider, Theodore 81, 183
Siegel, Susanna 150, 183
Significance of skepticism 3, 7, 18, 29–35
Simpson, James 49, 183
Smith, Nicholas 79, 183
Sorensen, Roy 58, 183
Sosa, Ernest 47, 67, 180, 181, 183
Soundness 109
Spock 99
Stalnaker, Robert 134, 183
Stanley, Jason 49, 84, 183
Steup, Matthias 180, 181
Stoicism 172
Stoics 92
Stoutenburg, Gregory 49, 183
Strict conditionals 130–1
Stroud, Barry 26, 28–35, 168, 183
Stump, Eleonore 50
Sturgeon, Scott 20, 68, 183
Subject-sensitive invariantism 84
Sullivan, Meghan 178
summum bonum, epistemic 11, 13, 19, 20, 21
Supervaluationism 38
Suppositional reasoning 118, 128, 140
Suppositions 117, 126, 128, 132, 136
Swain, Marshall 140, 183

Targets 120, 126
Tarot cards 107
Tarski, Alfred 122, 183
Taylor, Richard 81, 183
Tea leaves 107
Telekinesis 144
Teller, Paul 58, 183
Tennant, Neil 96, 184

Testimony 99
Thaning, Morten S. 181
Time travel 100–1
Tolkien, J.R.R. 99
Tomberlin, James 47, 184
Truth, epistemic conceptions of 116
Truth-conditional semantics 127
Turri, John 180, 181

Understanding 6, 50, 145, 152
Unger, Peter 26, 27, 35–40, 168, 184
Update semantics 127–31

van Inwagen, Peter 73, 111, 180, 184
Veltman, Frank 127, 184
Verifiability 105, 115
Verificationism 105–6, 115
Verificationist criterion of meaning 106
Vienna Circle 122, 126
Virtue epistemology 21, 169–74

Virtues in excess 5, 171

Warrant 11, 46
Watson, Gary 5, 184
Weatherson, Brian 58, 178
Weighting of cognitive goals 160–1
Westcoat, M. 179
Whitcomb, Dennis 170, 184
White, Roger 160, 184
Wide scope 53–5
Williams, Michael 168, 184
Williamson, Timothy 44, 51, 57, 64, 65, 66, 114,
184
Wisdom, theoretical 6, 50, 145
Wittgenstein, Ludwig 8, 164, 184

Yalcin, Seth 58, 180, 184
Zagzebski, Linda 68, 170, 184

Zalta, Edward 178, 181, 183
Zimmerman, Dean 81, 182, 184